MW01599109

CHOOSING
Eden

ADRIENNE LANGMAN started her working life as a nurse and then changed careers, becoming an executive recruiter and trainer. She ran her own companies and was a consultant to many others during a highly successful thirty-year corporate career. Adrienne is the author of *On Your Own – Money Management for the Single Parent*, and raised three children as a single parent before marrying Larry in the early 1990s. Adrienne and Larry had never contemplated country life before their major move in their middle age from the eastern suburbs of Sydney, Australia to a small rural property. She and Larry now live on a farm in Nana Glen, New South Wales, where they have dedicated themselves to learning about and creating self-sustainability.

the real dir on the coming energy crisis

CHOOSING
Eden

Adrienne
LANGMAN

RANDOM HOUSE AUSTRALIA

Random House Australia Pty Ltd
Level 3, 100 Pacific Highway, North Sydney, NSW 2060
www.randomhouse.com.au

Sydney   New York   Toronto
London   Auckland   Johannesburg

First published by Random House Australia 2007

Copyright © Adrienne Langman 2007

All rights reserved. No part of this publication may be reproduced, stored in a
retrieval system, or transmitted in any form or by any means, electronic, mechanical,
photocopying, recording or otherwise, without the prior written permission
of the publisher.

National Library of Australia Cataloguing-in-Publication Entry.

Langman, Adrienne.
Choosing Eden.
Bibliography.
ISBN 978 1 74166 549 9 (pbk.).
1. Permaculture – New South Wales.
2. Sustainable agriculture – New South Wales.
I. Title.
631.5809944

Cover illustration by Photolibrary
Cover and internal design by Greendot Design
Typeset in 12.5/16 pt Baskerville by Midland Typesetters, Australia
Printed and bound by Griffin Press, South Australia

10 9 8 7 6 5 4 3 2 1

To Larry

My husband and life partner, my fellow farmer, my best friend!

You believed in me enough to hold my hand tight as we jumped together into a new and totally unknown world. Without your belief in me, your encouragement, your wisdom and your unlimited patience this book would never have been written.

To Rick Embleton

I know you prefer to be called Richard these days but hey, this is *my* book! (And thanks for the line.)

Larry and I both owe you forever because you gave us the most precious gifts a friend can give:

You gave us time – enough time to prepare.

You gave us information – enough for us to make our own informed decisions.

You gave us courage – until we could develop our own.

My goodness, I have made you sound like a cross between the Great Almighty and the Wizard of Oz!

To Alan Gold

Your faith in me and continuing encouragement at times astounded me and humbled me. Your enthusiasm was highly infectious. Your generosity with your time was a compelling reason to keep going. When I grow up I want to be like you!

Acknowledgements

I would like to thank four talented and wonderful people for their invaluable assistance and for their wisdom and guidance. Elizabeth Cowell and Anna Crago, my editors, who made the process so effortless and painless. Your intelligent and honest critiques and suggestions were handled with great sensitivity and, thankfully, a genuine understanding of this important topic. Jeanne Ryckmans, for offering to wash my windows. (Curiously, not something one's publisher offers to do, generally speaking!) And finally, the wonderful Tara Wynne, whose calm, skilled and professional expertise made me feel at all times that I was in the best of hands.

Introduction

To the casual observer we were a middle-aged couple making a 'sea change', or, to be more precise, a 'tree change'. To people who knew us it may have appeared that we had both taken leave of our senses. Larry and I had traded Florsheim wing-tips and Manolo Blahnik sandals for muddy steel-capped work boots. We had given up brioche and cappuccino in fashionable Double Bay in favour of homemade bread and jam. In our fifties, instead of sitting happily in God's waiting room, we had taken on the heavy manual labour of farming that would have better suited us in our twenties, and our plan was to become as self-sufficient as possible. Driving in our truck to the nearest town, we still occasionally steal sideways glances at each other with some measure of disbelief at what we have actually done.

Maybe it looked to others as if we had run away. We left our children and grandchildren, an executive salary and a comfortable home and set ourselves up on a farm in rural

New South Wales many kilometres from a shopping centre, a doctor and an espresso machine. Our decision was not about whimsically chasing a dream, nor was it a backflip to the 'turn on, tune in, drop out' culture of the 1960s and 1970s. This move wasn't in pursuit of an idyllic retirement in a lush subtropical paradise ... because we have never worked so hard in our lives! No: there was another, more sobering reason behind our decision to abandon everything we knew, everything we had planned for and everything we cherished.

What motivated us to leave the security, familiarity and convenience of the city is something that in the next few years we believe will be the catalyst that will motivate many more people, of all ages and in all countries, to either make major and unexpected changes in their lives of their own volition, or else be forced to do so by the changing circumstances of the world in which we live.

Our story is not unique. What we have done here in Australia, others are doing all over the world. Young singles, young families, people in middle age like us and some older ... all have seen what we have seen, and have chosen to act now while there is still time to make an informed choice.

In the years prior to this move, like so many couples our age, we had taken on the care of elderly parents at the same time as maintaining corporate careers. I eventually decided to retire, while Larry kept working. We sold our large six-bedroom home overlooking Sydney Harbour and downsized to a cute little semi-detached cottage in a quiet suburban neighbourhood. I spent a year carefully renovating it because this was going to be our home for the rest of our lives. So certain were we that this cottage would see us out, we even installed grab rails in the bathroom in advance of the time when we got too old and doddery to take a shower without tripping over.

To allow me to indulge my passion for roses, we transformed the yard into a tiny enclosed and private picture book rose garden. I had what I'd always wanted – a beautiful, elegant home with a truly magnificent English cottage garden featuring fifty painstakingly selected fragrant rose bushes. Everything was easy-care, secure and well ordered, just as our lives were.

We have five children from previous marriages. Two of them live in Melbourne, one in Canberra and two in Sydney. Our eldest daughter and her husband lived in our street and one of our sons and his expectant wife lived a few streets away. We had our friends, our community and our favourite restaurants. We had routines and the comfort of familiarity. Local store owners knew our names and we knew theirs. We were part of the scene and that gave us not only pleasure, but a feeling of belonging, a sense of 'place' in the community. We were there for the long haul. Larry loved his job in the IT division of a major food company and I had my roses, my pretty cottage and our kids nearby. Retirement was looking very cosy. Within a few short months, though, everything would change forever.

I wish that our decision to abandon our known world and plunge ourselves into growing the ingredients for a caesar salad rather than just ordering it from a menu was as simple as having a hankering for the good life, but it wasn't.

Our decision was precipitated by a very old friendship. I had met a Canadian guy called Rick Embleton in the late 1970s when he and his wife Gwyneth were living in Sydney for a while. My first husband and I subsequently went to live in Canada and Rick and Gwyn became my best friends. Rick had spent most of his career as an international computer systems consultant in the oil and petrochemical industry.

Rick and Gwyn and I shared a deep love of Canada and its magnificent changing seasons. We would regularly go for walks, enjoying the spectacular changing colours of the autumn leaves or the snow falling in the hushed stillness of a cedar forest. We also spent countless hours locked in bitter battle over a Scrabble board where I would constantly try to defend my use of obscure Yiddish words and Oz-speak and Rick would incessantly try to slip in French words. Our friendship endured my subsequent divorce, the intervening three decades, and the thousands of kilometres of separation after I returned to Australia. Each northern winter they email me to let me know when the first snows begin to fall.

I had grown to trust Rick and to value his incredible intellect. He is a lifetime member of Mensa and he is a quietly spoken, gentle, well-read, humble and sensitive man. It was from Rick that Larry and I learned about the phenomenon known as 'Peak Oil', or the peaking of the planet's oil production. As oil production enters into a decline and prices rise, many experts see a future of severe consequences for the global economic outlook.

This story covers the period from January 2005 to January 2007. In that time Peak Oil has moved from being of interest to a small internet community to now entering mainstream news, and is becoming of concern to most governments around the world.

Chapter One

Like many city-born people brought up on a steady diet of sensationalised news, Larry and I weren't overly moved by stories about droughts, or climate change, or the price of beef or wool or petrol. Whatever we needed was always in the supermarket or the shopping mall. As globalisation and consumerism shaped our world so absolutely, we were totally shielded from the vagaries of seasons or the tyranny of distance when it came to our wants or needs. If we wanted a fresh pineapple in the middle of winter, or something that would only grow in some tropical area far from home, it was there for us to buy. Or maybe what we wanted was an item that was only manufactured in Nepal or China or Peru – no problem – I could still just go out and buy it. If the price of something went up I might look for specials, or I just might pay the higher price if I really wanted it.

Our lives were so cocooned, as long as it wasn't *our* house that was blown away in a hurricane blasting in from the

Caribbean or *my* roses being carried off by plagues of locusts raging across Nigeria or *our* neighbourhood being blown up by a stray missile in Iraq, life just went on. Sure, I could sympathise with, even lament over, the catastrophes happening in some other part of the world. They were presented to me daily like a ghoulish soap opera on the TV news. But when the report was over, and the washing-up needed doing or one of the kids phoned with a problem, or there was a new computer game to be downloaded, my mind could switch off from these horrors as efficiently as switching off the TV itself. I guess that ability is just symptomatic of the society we live in. We are as accustomed to disconnectedly flicking past any disturbing thoughts as we are channel-surfing the offerings on TV.

I always read the news on the internet each morning while having my first coffee, and together Larry and I would watch Fox or CNN or BBC news at night. You could probably have called us cable news junkies: we'd set out chips and drinks and put our feet up to watch footage of September 11 or of the 2003 invasion of Iraq or reports about the latest natural disasters with the same zeal and enthusiasm that we watched the Olympics or the Mardi Gras or *Everybody Loves Raymond*.

We grew to be so desensitised to the harsh realities of what the news channels presented to us that during the overthrow of Saddam Hussein, we even took to sending tongue-in-cheek emails to US General Tommy Franks advising him what we felt he should do next! Maybe it was just our way of coping with the dispassionate way that unspeakable horrors are presented to us complete with commercial breaks. Some people don't watch the news at all – either because they genuinely don't care or because they care so much it is just often too upsetting. I guess that although we did watch the news, we did so with a certain amount of remove.

We were certainly well informed enough about world events to hold our own in conversations with our friends, but world events didn't dominate our conversation or our thoughts. We were by no means politically active. We were the most ordinary of couples, and far from being the types who would take a radical 180-degree turn in the course of our lives.

My husband Larry was passionately involved with his IT work. He happily got out of bed around five or earlier every morning, and drove for more than an hour to his office. He had worked in IT for thirty years, for the last sixteen years with the same large company. He revelled in the complexity of his job. He enjoyed the company of his peers and the intellectual stimulation that systems work gave him. Because he worked for such a big company, he had daily challenges to tackle and interesting people around him. He would come home at around seven in the evening, and most nights he arrived with a pile of paperwork under his arm to continue after dinner. His commitment to his 'corporate family' was as total as his commitment to our family. Many nights he wouldn't come to bed before midnight or later.

On weekends, Larry was just as passionate about the community we lived in and would devote a good deal of his time to local community activities. His life was full and rewarding and to a large extent, like many men, his work and his community interests defined him and gave him good reasons to get up each day.

Larry is the kind of man who takes enormous pride in his family and in being a good provider. He is also an animal of habit, gaining a sense of comfort from the familiar. Much of his routine became automatic and it was not always easy for him to step out of that pattern. And for good reason – the routines in his life worked well for him.

Neither of us had any way of knowing how drastically, and how soon, these routines we took for granted would change.

I had been running my own recruitment agency but had chosen to close it down and retire several years ago so that I could care for my elderly, ailing parents. Having the freedom to do this had given me a great deal of pleasure. After my parents' deaths and the sudden deaths of my brother and uncle, all in a relatively short period, I had taken time to find my feet as a carefree retiree. I took up pottery as an outlet for my latent creativity and I had my garden and my family and friends. I was looking forward to becoming a grandmother, gathering a collection of children's books and putting away little things for when the first new addition to our family would be placed in my arms.

I was immensely proud of my garden, especially my roses. The first task of the day was to check each bush thoroughly and squash any aphids I found on the new growth. I had planted the roses in blocks of colour so that one end of the garden housed all the white blooms, then yellow, then orange, red, mauve, and finally pink. All were fragrant and thriving and I was proud of the comments that people made when they walked by. Having a bowl of fresh, sweet-smelling roses in the house gave me constant pleasure.

My garden walks were generally repeated a few times each day. My life was one of leisure, quiet and ease. I doted on my two little dogs, Maurice and Rebecca, and I would play with them during the day, watch TV, read, or sometimes paint or involve myself in some craft. For a while I worked for an aged-care organisation and quite enjoyed the contact with my elderly clients. Friends would occasionally drop in for coffee but mainly I led a very relaxed life where my time was my own to use or waste as I chose. After a thirty-year corporate career in the tough, high-pressure recruitment industry, managing large national agencies and then my own, this new simplicity was both a novelty and a retreat.

Our primary focus and greatest interest, though, was always our children. The kids who lived in Sydney came for dinner once a week, or would drop in, or we would go and visit them. We generally spoke to each other once a day. It had always been that way. We were close and it was a relatively uncomplicated family relationship spiced by lots of laughter. The kids are all high achievers and passionate about their careers. Our dinner conversations on Friday nights were always lively, as the kids recounted their week's highlights. Our elder daughter Katie is a primary school teacher and she always had stories about the funny things her young students had said or done. Our psychologist daughter, Missy, would have side-splitting tales about the situations she got herself into. She'd paint us pictures of the group houses she worked in, with patients whose wildly differing psychological or developmental issues caused scenes that would have better suited a TV sitcom. Our Sydney-based son Josh, who works in marketing, is just plain funny all the time, as quick and witty as a comedian like Robin Williams or Billy Connolly. Ben plays guitar in a Melbourne-based heavy metal rock band and we would see him when he was on his way to interstate gigs. And Mitchell is a martial arts instructor in his spare time. The widely differing lives they all lead have always given us endless interest and enjoyment and pride. That isn't to say we are not without our disagreements, but battles have never led to estrangement or feuds. Perhaps we were just lucky, but our kids, as they grew to adulthood, became our best friends and we remained very close.

Larry and I used to talk about the time when the grandchildren would come and stay, and once toyed with the idea of looking for a place where we could all have an annual holiday together. It was a way of creating a sort of tradition that would be something that our kids and grandkids would remember long after we were gone. We both cherished this kind of close family involvement. We took a lot of pleasure from sharing the children's successes with them, or being there for them when they needed us. Two of the five are now married and their partners have enriched the dynamics tremendously. As time went by, the evolution of the family was a source of real pleasure for me.

My contact with my Canadian friends Rick and Gwyneth via the internet in the evenings was another regular little pleasure. I would tell Gwyn my kids' latest news and she would share news of their daughter, who was about the same age as our oldest son. I was chatting with Rick on the internet one evening when he asked me if I had been keeping an eye on Peak Oil.

'Is that a new soapie?' I replied, racking my brain.

He wrote back: 'Look it up on the internet.' He suggested a site for me to check out.

He hadn't really piqued my interest, but just to be on the same page as my old friend, I did look up the website. The banner headline screamed 'Life after the oil crash: deal with reality or reality will deal with you', and the opening paragraph read:

> *Civilization as we know it is coming to an end soon. This is not the wacky proclamation of a doomsday cult, apocalypse bible prophecy sect, or conspiracy theory society. Rather, it is the scientific conclusion of the best paid, most widely-respected geologists, physicists, and investment bankers in the world. These are rational, professional, conservative individuals who are absolutely terrified by a phenomenon known as global 'Peak Oil.'*

I thought 'Oh poor Rick – what has he got himself into?' I didn't read any further, nor did I think on it any more. I wasn't interested in being assured by a doomsday cult that they were not a doomsday cult. I was more concerned with anticipating the arrival of my first grandchild. I was interested in growing my roses, I was thinking about financial plans to structure our golden years. If the 'end of the world was nigh' because of oil prices or scarcity or whatever, let the scientists and politicians sort it out – I had things to do, a family to care about, washing, cooking, gardening. Let the end of the world happen somewhere else!

Although we had been aware that petrol prices were rising, at this point the real issues surrounding the price hike didn't much concern us on any deep level. After all, Larry's car was a fully maintained company car, and he hadn't looked at the price of fuel for sixteen years. I had a little car, although I didn't use it much. Actually I had originally bought the car for our youngest daughter, who magnanimously 'sold it back to me' to fund her trip overseas! Our cottage was walking distance from just about everything we needed. I could walk to my doctor, dentist, pharmacist and hearing aid specialist. I could have even walked to the supermarket if I had a mind to, but who did that – unless they had to! I would simply zip in to the shopping mall car park, load up all the groceries I needed and then drive five minutes back home. I couldn't see how a rise in oil prices could substantially change our lives.

Soon after Rick's advice to read about Peak Oil, a couple of things happened that made us really sit up and take notice of oil prices. Firstly the price of petrol went over $1 to $1.20 a litre and following so closely on from reading the 'Life after the oil crash' website it did resonate a bit. Secondly Larry and I had begun to think seriously about our finances. When Larry realised that in a few short years he would have to give back his company car when he retired, the full implications of the fuel price rises started to show up on his radar. While we were debt-free and seemed to be in a reasonably good situation, the level of our retirement savings was not going to be high enough to keep us financially comfortable according to the recommended figures. When we began to notice that a tank full of petrol for the car seemed to be getting expensive we did worry a bit. Overall, though, we were in a situation that nobody would have considered dire and, provided life continued in the way it always had, we thought we were not too badly off.

Our interest in our future retirement and the funding of it was a multi-layered discussion involving not only how we would manage on a fixed income when Larry retired in four years, but also the financial needs and security of our kids. We had always taken pleasure in helping them financially whenever we could. Three of the kids were yet to marry so we knew we had to make allowances for contributions to future weddings. We would have liked to have been able to help with the money for deposits on houses for them, but we were becoming aware that the level of our retirement savings wasn't going to allow us to do a lot of things we wanted to do. We realised that unless we took some sort of action, our retirement savings were not going to provide us with solid security in our old age.

Alongside these questions of retirement and finance, the idea of Peak Oil kept niggling at the back of my mind. I talked to Rick a little more about it, and realised quickly how seriously he was taking the idea. He moderated a Yahoo group on Peak Oil and he was trying desperately to convince Gwyn to retire and leave Toronto. This made me think more seriously about it myself, and I began gradually to do a little research on the internet about the situation. The more I thought about it, the more I realised that the possible effects of increasing oil prices could have a major impact on our lives.

Oil is extracted from a field which has a finite capacity. At first the oil is under pressure and comes up easily. Once around half of the oil has been removed from the field (when the field has 'peaked'), it becomes much more difficult to extract oil. The field goes into decline, often very rapidly, and eventually it reaches a point when the volume of oil being extracted is not worth the cost of extraction.

There is no question that this will not happen on a global level – many of the world's oil fields have already peaked. And when Peak Oil hits, that is, when *all* the world's oil fields have peaked, supplies of oil will shrink so quickly that the world may not have had time to prepare alternative sources of fuel.

Rick explained that it wasn't just about fuel prices – in fact, he told me, oil is used to make over 300,000 products that are integral parts of our everyday lives. I realised that oil is used for *everything*. On his website he explains:

> Oil ... is the raw material for all of the plastics in our homes and offices ...
> the synthetic fibers with which we clothe ourselves, the chemicals on which
> agriculture has become dependent for growing the food that sustains us, the drugs
> and pharmaceuticals responsible for our health and our lives, the additives and
> preservatives in our processed foods, the cleaning products under the sink, the
> asphalt on our roads. It is not just the source of the fuel in your car, it is the raw
> material from which most of your car is built.

Although I found that hard to get my head around, it did really make me sit up and think. Larry and I realised that we needed to be concerned about how we would structure our finances to cope with the rising prices that would result from the end of cheap oil. It was one thing to discuss the future when it is in the context of an economy being on a continual growth path, but it is another thing entirely when the future may well mean an economy on the decline in a world lacking in cheap oil.

That sort of economic climate was one we didn't yet understand. We had both raised families during the time that interest rates had soared to 18 per cent and economically life was tough, but those times were temporary and over the previous ten years things had been relatively prosperous. We were soon to learn that some serious economic ramifications would result because of the end of an abundance of cheap oil – and these ramifications were going to be permanent.

We were enjoying the process of considering what we would do after Larry's retirement. As we discussed our future and how life could be, we had to look at the figures and work out what we would and would not be able to afford. We agreed it was a good time to consult a financial planner. A few years ago our retirement plan had involved moving from a large house into our cottage, and at that point downsizing had seemed like enough. But now, a few years later, we were beginning to realise that we might have to do something a little more drastic in order to be able to afford the kind of retirement we wanted to share. The idea that the world might be about to become vastly more expensive, if there was some kind of oil crisis, really hit home with us.

Another factor that we were beginning to consider was whether or not Larry should retire earlier than planned. He'd recently found out that his company was about to relocate further from our home, which would increase his daily commute by about an hour each way. The inevitability of the ever-increasing work pressure for Larry was a worry. His work hours per day were long and looking to get longer.

Things might have been more secure for us financially had we been together longer but we had only been married for twelve years. Divorce tends to decimate one's finances and ours were no exception so we knew we needed professional financial guidance.

Originally we had been teenage sweethearts of eighteen and seventeen and we say now that had we stayed together then, we would have had a dozen kids and been totally contented. But instead, back then, Larry had been spooked about being married so young and so we drifted apart and eventually married other people. Although we lived in the same city for most of the next twenty-five years, we never happened to run into each other. After Larry's two previous marriages and my one, we accidentally met in a gas station one Saturday afternoon. We laugh now about how prophetic a place that was to reconnect with each other. The meeting was electric. A few weeks later we had dinner together and we talked for hours as though the preceding twenty-five lost years had never happened. The fire and passion were there, that skin-tingling, blood-rushing excitement of new love was there just as it had been all those years ago, and we just knew that it was right. I invited him to dinner on the Friday of that same week to meet my kids and when he came that evening he just never left. Seventeen months later we were married.

The discussions about our retirement income developed into a nightly event. At the same time, I had begun to get a bit obsessed with Peak Oil and was now regularly reading up on it on the internet. I could see that it might have a very serious impact on the economy and subsequently on our finances. I was also spending quite a lot of time emailing Rick, who, as it turned out, was writing a book about Peak Oil. I offered to critique it for him, thinking that it would be an interesting exercise for me – and a good way to learn more.

He sent me his early chapters and what I read started to alarm me. Unlike some of the material I was reading on the internet, Rick's writing was sensible and down to earth, and it was clear how serious he thought the issue was.

I would show Larry the chapters as I read them and we found ourselves becoming increasingly disturbed about this Peak Oil 'thing', although it was bemusing that there was never anything in the daily news and no mention of it in political discussions. If this was such a terrible situation, why weren't there news stories in the mainstream media? Why weren't our politicians educating us about it? Was it possible that Rick had the wrong end of the stick, even though what he and thousands of others on the internet believed sounded so plausible?

Eventually I found one website that quoted Queensland Labor backbencher Andrew McNamara, who had addressed the Queensland parliament early in 2005 in support of the Petroleum and Other Legislation Amendment Bill. In his speech McNamara clearly stated the issues of Peak Oil and what it will mean in the coming years. He said:

> Peak Oil represents the most serious and immediate challenge to our prosperity and security. It will impact on our lives more certainly than terrorism, global warming, nuclear war or bird flu. While it may not be a term with which members are familiar now, I predict it will come to dominate debate in this place over the next ten years … The advent of world Peak Oil will change our way of life forever. The concept of Peak Oil is now universally accepted by geologists and mining engineers … But make no mistake: there is no silver bullet to defeat the most serious impacts of Peak Oil.

Interestingly, McNamara's comments were quoted around the world, but were not widely reported in the Australian media. I downloaded the whole parliamentary speech, which we both read. Having finally found an Australian politician referring to the subject somehow crystallised things in our minds and made it real to us. Up until then some part of me had felt that I was buying into some kind of doomsday scenario: even though experts across the world were worried, the fact that my own government seemed not to have noticed the problem made me feel as though I was being a wowser. But McNamara's speech to parliament was the final piece in the jigsaw for me.

At this point we set up our computer to receive Google Alerts for Peak Oil. This meant we would receive emails each day about any mention of Peak Oil on the internet or in any news media. At that time, most of the Google Alerts were internet news items from the United States or Europe. One article, called 'Peak Oil: The Twilight Zone' by a petroleum geologist and member of the British government's Renewables Advisory Board, Dr Jeremy Leggett, had some chilling content. Dr Leggett explained that:

> ... oil is depleting fast, and the age of cheap oil will soon be over. Economies can't function without cheap oil. We have no time to develop energy alternatives. Economic depression akin to that of the 1930s lurks around the corner.

The Depression of the 1930s was before our time, but we knew it had been incredibly tough. Dr Leggett's words, though, highlighted one major difference between then and now. The Great Depression had eventually been followed by growth and prosperity. It had, in the context of history, been a finite period of hardship. We were coming to understand that with the unavailability of cheap oil, the economic depression he was talking about could be a permanent thing.

With the situation put in these sobering tones, we felt compelled to find out more. We could see that if what he said was true then the end of cheap oil would have ramifications on everything that we held dear. More specifically, we could see that the decisions we wanted to make about our future finances, and those of our children, would be affected in ways we could not have imagined. Everything we had believed up until that point and all our hopes for our future were going to be compromised in some way, or shattered completely.

I thought back to the time when I was a young single mum with three little children. For some years we had to live without regular child support payments from my ex-husband. All we had coming in was a meagre fortnightly pension, and we lived from pension cheque to pension cheque each two weeks. Our first week was the 'week of plenty' when we had enough food and were a bit indulgent. The second week was the tough one, as things began to run out. We managed, but only just, and often I would take the kids to my parents for dinner in that second week so that they had regular healthy meals.

The thought of living that sort of life again was looming as a possibility in our old age, but this time there would be no parents' house to go to as a supplemental food source. Thinking about people on fixed incomes who are unable to change their situations is a serious and troubling thought for the years ahead.

Dr Leggett's article highlighted information that we were finding on other sites – that the major issue is that while experts all over the world do agree that abundant, unlimited supplies of oil are running out, they absolutely cannot agree on when this will actually happen. In hindsight, this was a turning point for us. We were not only sitting up and taking notice; we were now actively engaged in the whole issue of learning about Peak Oil and how it would affect our lives. It was something that simply wouldn't go away. Like anything one learns, it can't be 'unlearned', and this Peak Oil thing most certainly seemed to take on a life of its own in our thinking. Leggett's words kept repeating in my mind: 'Economies can't function without cheap oil. We have no time to develop energy alternatives.'

So, the big question was 'when would Peak Oil occur?' We found that there were actually three conflicting opinions. It seemed that no one could accurately estimate the point at which recoverable oil would reach the halfway mark.

The first opinion was from those who believe that Peak Oil is upon us – that oil fields around the world have now reached, or will reach peak production within the next four or five years and then start to decline. The second opinion put the peak somewhere around 2030. The third opinion was that Peak Oil is not an issue at all.

If the first opinion was correct, then our lives were going to be affected very soon. If the second one was right, then the lives of our children and grandchildren would be affected in the future, although by 2030 Larry and I would be wearing bibs at mealtimes and complaining that we couldn't find our teeth. The third opinion we could not accept. It doesn't take a genius to understand that oil is a finite resource and must at some point run out. It just isn't renewable.

There is a theory originating from Russia that oil is 'abiotic', meaning that oil does not and never did contain or support living matter but is generated in the earth's mantle (as opposed to a biotic substance which is generated from the remains of plants and animals over millions of years). In the abiotic theory, oil wells will perpetually refill. This is a theory that is generally rejected by experts within and outside the oil industry.

Others who disagree that Peak Oil is an issue believe that there are many possible alternative sources of energy generation, such as tar sands, oil shale, deep sea oil, methane, CTL (coal to liquid), GTL (gas to liquid) or hydrogen fuel cells, and that these sources will be turned to in time to prevent any kind of collapse of civilisation as we know it. These people also believe that these supplementary energy-forms wouldn't run out for hundreds of years – therefore solving the problem in the medium term.

With the amount of reading and research we were both doing, we felt sure that these alternatives were not the panacea for Peak Oil – no matter how optimistic the articles were. Perhaps the use of a combination of these alternatives would go some way to mitigating the depletion of oil, but it was very clear that for them to become viable, a tremendous global commitment would need to be made *right now*, along with trillions of dollars of investment.

At the same time, the Organisation of Petroleum Exporting Countries (OPEC) was suggesting that trillions would have to be invested in oil exploration and development *alone* just to continue to be able to meet global oil demand. For huge investments in alternatives to happen, governments would have to admit that there was an issue and that admission wasn't happening, most particularly not in Australia.

Even more confusing and worrying was discovering just how global oil reserves are actually estimated or calculated. Industry specialists stated that OPEC had been exaggerating their reserves for many years ever since they agreed to a quota system for production based on size of national reserves. A former energy adviser to the Bush administration and author of *Twilight in the Desert: The Coming Saudi Oil Shock and the World Economy*, investment banker Matt Simmons, believes that 'The Saudis – the nation with the largest reserves in the world – are already past their topping point.'

Again and again we consulted Rick via the internet. We bombarded him with questions and, in his gentle, unassuming way, he guided us through the hills and mountains of information we were gathering. One evening, I asked him to tell me honestly, in his estimation, when all this chaos from oil depletion is going to happen.

He answered my question with one of his own: 'Let me ask you this: knowing that the shit is going to hit the fan at some point, what would you rather do – prepare for it to happen in five years and find out it happens in fifty, or prepare for it to happen in fifty years and find out it happens in five?'

Larry and I both stopped talking at this point. We looked at each other. It is a moment frozen in my memory. The question hung in the air between us like a test question on a blackboard. I felt as if we would be let out of school early if we got the answer right, but if we didn't get it right we would be kept in after the last bell forever.

'Hold on a second,' said Larry. 'Let's look at this thing another way. Let's pretend for a moment Rick is talking about something we can visualise instead of a world without oil which *no one* can visualise. Let's say he is warning us about a monstrous tsunami heading our way or a force-10 hurricane, or an unbroken wall of wildfire. We can picture those things because they are in our sphere of understanding.'

'I choose the tsunami. I can relate to that.'

'Okay. Let's pretend that the San Andreas Fault rips open and the entire west coast of America falls into the Pacific and causes the biggest tsunami in recorded history. It's heading for the east coast of Australia and we are living on that coast. The news broadcasts tell us it will take fifty-six hours to reach us – what would we do?'

'We'd get the kids,' I said, '… and our friends and the dogs and the photos and clothes and food and water and head west – as far and as fast and as high as we could go.'

'Okay,' Larry responded, 'yeah, but what if the news warning didn't say fifty-six hours? What if we were surfing the net and found a document from a world-renowned geologist who presented his findings – that according to this and this and this, the west coast of America is going to fall into the sea and cause a tsunami within the next ten years. What would we do then?'

'That makes it much harder,' I said, 'because my first reaction would probably be – *yeah, yeah*, is this crackpot for real? Actually I would probably ignore it because it is too hard to think about, or too scary, and anyway ten years in the future is a long way off. Anything could happen in that time.

'But my next thought is "what if he's right?" And what if everyone else on the east coast of Australia sees this report? What will that do to the price of real estate here and in the mountains where we would be safe? What will it do to the stock market, to our savings? How could we get our money out of the bank if all the banks are under 100 metres of water?'

Larry was nodding as I continued. 'But what if we rush off to the mountains now and the geologist's calculations are wrong and it doesn't happen for ten years? We will have walked away from everything we have here for nothing! But then, what if he's right – we would lose the lot anyway. Could we live with that knowledge?'

We fell silent for a long time and in my mind I had this picture of us sitting on a mountain for the next ten years wearing sandwich-boards that read 'Beware the great tsunami!' and everyone laughing at us. I felt lonely in that picture. Lonely and stupid.

My mind went back to 'Y2K' just ten years earlier. I remembered the lead-up to the year 2000 – the big 'year 2000' scare, where nobody was entirely sure whether all the world's computer systems would come crashing down, along with everything they ran. It does sound far-fetched, but it was a real issue back then. I was running a successful business at that time and tossing up whether Y2K was real. A lot of people thought Y2K was just a media beat-up, or some kind of computer-industry conspiracy aimed at fleecing big business out of lots of money.

I had to think then about whether the financial investment in getting all my computers looked at was worth it. I had to weigh up whether or not I was prepared to be wrong. Could I afford to ignore Y2K when every bit of my business was in those computers? Begrudgingly I paid the money for my computing systems to be updated and Y2K came and went without a hitch. It was easier for Larry. He was an IT professional and his company had committed around $10 million and 200 people to ensure that their systems were okay nationally. He had spent three years on that project. He knew that if they hadn't done that, their systems would have ground to a halt.

And here we were facing the same sort of dilemma – do we really believe this thing or not? We could see an almost unbelievable situation looming in the future, where the world as we knew it might change irrevocably. Our current lifestyle – one where we drove everywhere, relied on the supermarket for food, and produced nothing ourselves – might just be completely unsustainable. What if we couldn't buy food to eat, or if there was no energy to power the lights or the oven, if our water supply dried up? If we remained in the city in that kind of scenario we just wouldn't be able to survive. Would we have to head for the hills, move to a farm?

Larry and I drifted in and out of the tsunami analogy and what we should do about the threat of Peak Oil for many days and many long nights. We had sat horrified watching news of the 2004 Boxing Day tsunami that tore through the Indian Ocean killing more that 200,000 people in eleven countries. We had feared for friends we knew were on holiday in Thailand and Indonesia. Millions were rendered homeless. Yet with the spectre of Peak Oil, there were so many unknown things it would do to our way of life, the tsunami hypothesis wasn't enough.

Just like with Y2K, although the situation looked as if it could conceivably be dire, we knew there was considerable uncertainty to do with the whole oil reserve issue. Would it happen; when would it happen; how would it happen? In the face of this uncertainty, the idea of 'heading for the hills' was anathema to us. We 'had it all' right where we were and I guess it was just not possible for us to even contemplate leaving it all behind and starting over somewhere else. And it was just ridiculous to be contemplating doing so on information that seemed so outrageous, so preposterous as to be almost unbelievable! As well, if our kids weren't with us, we couldn't imagine what life would be like.

Every time we found an item refuting the Peak Oil theory (and we found many – mostly either on sites specialising in conspiracy theories or in chat rooms or groups), or proposing alternative energy possibilities we would send it to Rick in an email. We fervently hoped his reaction would be 'Wow – good going guys – this looks encouraging!' But it didn't happen.

As we searched the internet constantly for more information, we were being fuelled by the realisation that Peak Oil is not a problem that anyone can learn about and then just walk away from. The more you learn about it, the more you know you don't know. So, in endeavouring to learn as much as we could, we were seeing the true ramifications that Peak Oil would have on society in general – and it was scary.

As we understood it, with the gap between supply and demand for cheap oil growing wider with each year, our entire way of life would have to change. Farmers would not be able to afford to continue the intensive mechanised practices of broadacre farming (that is, vast tracts of land planted with one crop like wheat or corn or sugarcane which then has to be harvested by machines and watered by mechanically driven irrigation systems). That type of agriculture involves the use of pesticides and herbicides made from petrochemicals and fertilisers (which are made from natural gas, stocks of which are also reported to be on the decline). Nor would they be able to afford the transport costs to get their produce into the major cities, or to ship in natural gas from overseas.

For city-bred people like us, the thought of all of this was almost impossible to imagine. Walking into a supermarket or a shopping mall to get anything at all, but particularly food, is just a way of life. You want food, you go to the supermarket. How does the food get there? Who cares!

Without abundant cheap oil, vast numbers of products dependent on petrochemicals would simply not be able to be manufactured because of lack of raw material or what's called 'feedstock'. This would put thousands and thousands of people out of work. Large multinational companies whose investments were centred on any aspect of oil, oil production or products associated with oil, would crash. Entire economies would crumble.

All this sounded to us like some sort of far-fetched science fiction movie. What confounded us was that all the reports we were reading concurred with these outcomes. The populations of the world can't move about or travel without oil, whether they want to move by car, plane or train. The synthetic clothes we wear are the products of oil and almost everything we eat is affected by oil, whether from fuel used for farm machinery during the growing process, or pesticides and herbicides sprayed on crops, or fertilisers, or transport to market. Then there is the processing of food and the preservation of it and the packaging of it. Oil plays a major role in all of these, whether directly or indirectly, by powering the machinery used in these processes. As Jeremy Leggett wrote:

We have allowed oil to become vital to virtually everything we do. Ninety per cent of
all our transportation, whether by land, air or sea, is fuelled by oil. Ninety-five per
cent of all goods in shops involve the use of oil. Ninety-five per cent of all our food
products require oil use. Just to farm a single cow and deliver it to market requires
six barrels of oil, enough to drive a car from New York to Los Angeles.

The global economy has been built on moving the production of almost anything to the cheapest labour market and then cheaply shipping the product all over the world. That formula would not work any more with the likelihood of rapidly increasing transport costs and soon to be diminishing marine diesel. Manufacturing and food production would have to be scaled down to smaller localised centres. The glorious dream of a globalised market would go down the toilet.

Smaller localised intensive agricultural systems that grow lots of different things in smaller quantities (polyculture) would have to replace the current broadacre-farmed monoculture crops. The growing of food would have to be moved from distant rural properties that require trucking of goods into the city to areas closer to where large numbers of people were living – either that, or large numbers of people were going to have to move to where the food could be produced and, ideally, start producing food for themselves.

We wanted to deny it – we desperately wanted to reject this possibility out of hand. We wanted to find proof that we could reject it or deny it. The frustration came from not being able to find good logical reasons for rejecting the concept of Peak Oil and all that went along with it. It was becoming clear to us that the big banks and the oil companies themselves were growing concerned about the future viability of the industry.

My overriding feelings were: 'This can't be real. It can't be going to happen!' I felt like a little doll in a doll house that has suddenly been up-ended and shaken.

I felt angry, depressed, terrified, dumbfounded, and anxious. I became laconic, tearful. It must have been hard on Larry, whose handle on his emotions is rock solid. Each evening, when he walked through the door he would find me in tears with the bedcovers over my head, or focused on the computer research-ing whatever I could find, or sitting with a pen and notepad in our pergola making lists of things to do and skills to acquire. I would be fired with enthusiasm like a pioneer woman of the 1800s – bonnet and apron on, stepping up into the covered wagon saying 'Come on Pa, our destiny awaits out yonder!'

Putting a positive spin on bad times was something I had learned through necessity many years earlier when my kids were little and I was newly divorced. We were extremely poor then, but I was determined that the children would not know about our dire circumstances. We often didn't have much in the way of nourishing food, so, to mask the scarcity, I would make a pot of soup and let the kids eat it in the lounge by the fire. While they ate the soup I would read Italo Calvino short stories to them, snapping the book shut at a crucial point in the story and saying 'Okay, that's all till the next bowl of soup!' That way they were always happily looking forward to the meagre bowl of soup the next night and they sailed through those hard times only remembering the wonderful stories and the warmth of the fire before bed.

During those early days of learning about Peak Oil, I found it extremely difficult to find the creative flair to put any kind of positive spin on it because it was a situation out of my control. Short stories by Italo Calvino were not going to work. This is something that would affect all of our lives.

I thought about how life would be with needy little kids, having to pay for out-of-control fuel prices. I thought about the times when I was paying a mortgage and raising the kids, by this stage off the pension and working again. I used to count out exactly what we could spend. I knew where every cent went and I knew how much everything cost. As the cost of everyday things rises with the cost of fuel, how are average families going to cope? What will they have to give up just to make ends meet?

When Larry or I would call on Rick to clarify something for us, invariably he would be able to provide the answer with very little trouble. He had been studying the oil situation since the 1970s oil embargo, when the price of oil quadrupled and US and European economies took a beating. His knowledge base was vast and he could draw on and capably analyse a huge amount of technical information. He had read all the reports we were now blindly stumbling over and he painstakingly explained why they were not the Holy Grail we were so anxious to find.

When I told him that my emotions were up and down like a yo-yo, he assured me that my response was very typical and he had encountered it many times over. The most common responses to the Peak Oil issue are to ignore it or deny it. To accept it would mean that it has to be dealt with, and to deal with it means that one's whole world is going to have to be turned upside down. Rick told me when people actually 'get it' and begin to understand what ultimately is to come as a result of Peak Oil, they do in fact go through the same emotional stages that one can experience in the grief process. I must have been a textbook case because I certainly went through them all, individually, in clusters, several times each – denial, anger, bargaining, and depression – and I didn't know at that stage if I would ever reach the final stage of grieving, the stage of acceptance.

Rick said that Larry and I were an unusual couple because we were both simultaneously working through the Peak Oil situation. From his experience often it is only one partner of a pair who fully appreciates what the situation is. Even in his own family he had issues with getting Gwyn to take notice. He had identified a little place in the Ontario countryside where he wanted to relocate to, but Gwyn, being a lifetime city girl, steadfastly refused to even consider it. On the chat groups he was moderating, there were many cases where either a husband or a wife was plugged into Peak Oil and fully aware of the coming problems while their partner had the blinkers firmly on.

As days went on and more and more of our reading confirmed that Peak Oil was indeed, as Jeremy Leggett described it, a really serious 'civilisation-changing energy crisis', we were being forced to change our thinking completely. We would talk long into the night about it. It would have been so easy to just sit back and say that the government or scientists will solve this unbelievable global problem so that we can go on aging and getting tubby and contented. After all, we had lived our lives, we had succeeded in our careers, paid our taxes and our children were off our hands. It was time for us to take it easy and slide down the other side of young with smiles on our faces and hair dye on our greying heads just as our parents had done. That was our life script. I didn't want that to change. Not now, not ever.

We had followed along the path that most of our peers had taken. We had put money away for our retirement. It wasn't much but we had squirrelled away as much as we could. Many of our friends had done the 'right thing' financially and had invested in property or share portfolios, all in the name of retirement protection with a view to having a comfortable old age. Peak Oil threatened all that. When pensions run out and the real estate bubble bursts and when stock markets collapse and unemployment skyrockets all these well-laid plans of thousands upon thousands of people will be dashed.

But this situation would not just affect the older people in the community. The end of cheap oil would mean that young families with heavy mortgages and huge debt levels will be facing financial ruin, with no escape. It outraged us that no responsible government, no socially conscious media group was warning, suggesting, even hinting that these things could happen and would happen as the price of oil crept up and up until it was too expensive and too scarce to continue life as it was.

I had focused so heavily on giving the children a stable and happy home and a bright future that my whole purpose in living was geared to their welfare and their future. This Peak Oil thing was threatening to tear down that future, not just for us and our children but for their children too! Even though I was drowning in research material about the end of the age of cheap oil, a large part of my mind simply refused to believe that life was going to change. Trying to actually get my mind around the idea of economic chaos and real social devastation was a huge stretch for me. Those sorts of things only happened in movies or in other places or in other times. There was a part of me that felt the whole thing was just preposterous. It was like being told that the sky was going to change colour and in future it would be red instead of blue. These things just didn't happen in my hometown and in my suburb. But the more I learned, the more I could see that they were going to, and within my lifetime.

Something Rick wrote really put it in perspective for me:

Even if we could get every last drop of oil there is out of the ground, at the current rate of consumption (the rate of demand actually increases by 2–3 per cent per year, but has run closer to 5 per cent these past two years), the estimated trillion barrels of oil remaining [in the world] would last less than thirty-three years.

Every which way we turned this befuddling, complex puzzle, we would come to the conclusion that there were two things we needed to do in order to move forward. The first one was the acquisition of information – hard, irrefutable information, and as much as we could find. The second was to endeavour to construct some sort of framework in which we could place that information, process it rationally and move forward in some way. A sort of 'if this happens, then we should do that' scenario.

In retrospect, I guess by the time we had got to that stage, there must have been some sort of tacit acknowledgement that leaving the city was a possibility we may have to consider, but it wasn't yet a part of the open discussion. Acknowledging it verbally at that point would have made too much of it, and at that time neither of us was prepared to do that. The one thing we had learned and which we could see very clearly was that city life is totally dependent on cheap oil, and the era of cheap oil sooner or later was coming to an end.

Chapter Two

The effort we put into investigating Peak Oil was unremitting and it was hard in those early days to go on in our normal way as if nothing was happening. I found it terribly hard to maintain the semblance of my regular daily routine when it felt like my life was going to hit a brick wall at 100 kilometres per hour. Harder still was the feeling that we were so alone with this. No one we knew was talking about it and nothing was ever in the mainstream media about it.

Whenever we broached the subject with our friends, we were met with blank faces and when we tried to explain about Peak Oil and how the end of the age of cheap oil would affect us all, there was the 'tsk tsk' response of those who feel they are being told tall tales. The responses we got were generally statements like 'someone will come up with something' or 'it isn't our problem – it's our kids who will have to worry about it' or 'it doesn't matter'. A common attitude seemed to be that life will just go on as it always had and there was nothing that needed to be done. At times we felt as if it was just that we couldn't articulate all that we had found out sufficiently well to make people understand what we were learning, but at other times we felt like we were the only two soldiers in the parade marching in time to the music. Nonetheless, we just pressed on with our research and our concerns and fears for the future mounted.

During our internet searches we read about a DVD called *End of Suburbia*. It was a Canadian-made documentary which has won many awards, and I asked Rick about it. As it happened, the film's producer was a participant on Rick's Peak Oil Yahoo group, and Rick had reviewed the documentary's script for his book *Oilephant Down*. Since World War II, the website explained, North Americans had invested heavily in life in suburbia where a family could enjoy an affordable, comfortable life with a nice house and a yard some distance from cities where employment was centred. This urban sprawl created a new and heavy dependence on cars and fuel use and the subsequent development of super-highways to cater for them.

The description could fit any country in the world where housing sprawl has spread far from the city centres, I realised, thinking about the outer suburbs of Sydney or Melbourne or Brisbane. The blurb went on to describe how the demand for fossil fuel globally is outstripping supply and the consequences of inaction are enormous and frightening. Food won't be available in cities, clothing and everyday commodities will just disappear from the shelves of retailers, and the economic stability of countries globally will shatter.

I sent away for the DVD and when it arrived in the mail I sat and watched it to the end and just went cold. This documentary contained interviews with scientists, policy makers, oil industry experts – people whose credentials and whose life work centred on the oil production industry. They were talking about a world depleted of cheap oil. It was a world I couldn't conceive of. It was like watching science fiction – only this wasn't fiction. This was fact. This was happening in my lifetime. It is happening now. The depletion of the material that goes into making all the everyday things we take for granted was for real.

I suppose I could have dismissed it as something 'that could only happen in America' but the problem of spiralling oil prices is something that affects all countries. Suburban sprawl, broadacre farming, manufacturing and processing, importing and the use of cars and trucks have become the way of life for us all.

The narrator of the documentary and the oil industry experts interviewed had compelling and chilling details about what Peak Oil meant and what the future held for the global population. The narrator was talking to me, about my suburb, my life.

I felt that maybe this DVD would help our kids understand what we had been researching and what we were so distressed about. We had spoken to them about Peak Oil and their reactions were mixed. At that time, I guess, it was just too hard for them to consider life any other way from how it was and how they perceived it to be. Each was so busy and so focused carving out a career in the city that for them to deviate from that focus was just impossible. I understood that. I was having enough trouble with it myself, and my life was half over. Theirs, however, was just beginning. I didn't know how to give them the information that I was gathering, the information that pointed to a collapse of the global economy. The concept of such a collapse and how it would translate just in our own little family was too immense a thought, and, just like contemplating falling though space, there seemed to be no end to it. The plans and hopes and dreams that my kids had for their future were based on the known model of a global economy which continually grows. Peak Oil would crush that model and they would have to create a new one with nothing from the past to guide them. I could understand all that, but at the same time their total lack of identification with the ramifications of Peak Oil distressed me. I didn't know how to really get through to them, and it worried me.

When Larry got home, I sat with him while he watched the DVD. With each viewing I found that I picked up more from it. Larry identified with what the narrator was explaining. He could see immediate parallels between the American urban sprawl and the Sydney sprawl. He remembered that Sydney had once had trams but they had been phased out as the city expanded, and expressways and highways had been built. The car was now an essential for anyone not living close to their work.

He told me about the weekend trips he and his family took when he was a child. They would drive out to the edge of Sydney, to farmland, and they would buy fresh eggs and vegetables and fruit. They weren't terribly long drives and they were pleasant family outings. Today all that farmland has been swallowed up by suburban development. The farms are gone. The fresh produce is no longer grown at the edge of the city. After watching the DVD Larry immediately understood the necessity to be 'living close to our food' – or we just wouldn't have any.

That DVD had a tremendous impact on us both. Its explanation and presentation of the facts were so graphic and so simply explained that it brought Peak Oil into razor sharp perspective. We could, for the first time, see where the whole oil age phenomenon had come from and where it was going, and it all made sense.

I had lived through the oil crisis of 1973 (I was busy with my first baby) and the supply crisis of 1981 (I was busy getting divorced). They had so little impact on my life in my little world; I have to say that they are not even in my conscious memory. Maybe there are a lot of people who feel that way. Earthquakes, oil sanctions, famine, horrific events come and go around the world and unless it is happening right in your front yard they don't actually leave an impact. They don't make you change your day-to-day existence. They certainly don't make you pack up your entire life and relocate to another place to live an entirely different way of life.

When some event does have an effect in your own front yard, like one's country's troops being committed to a far-off war, or a threatened epidemic, or some sabre-rattling from another country over trade or drugs for example, you tend to 'feel it' more personally, but again, it isn't life-changing. I used to have faith in the government of my country to sort out such things. After all, I am just one small inconsequential person and the government was the all-knowing, all-seeing leading light.

But here was a problem which was wholly geological and it was outside the realms of clever politics, clever science or clever anything. The amount of easily recoverable oil is finite globally, and we are using it all up. And, as Rick explained, the Peak Oil crisis won't be anything like the 1973 and 1981 oil supply shortages. Both were temporary shortages, caused by external, political factors.

Rick wrote:

Why is Peak Oil a Problem? It is a widely held and unfortunate perception that the problem with oil depletion comes when we have run out. The extension of that logic says that we don't have to worry and can wait to begin our preparations for a post-oil world until we know when the oil will be all gone. Both display a dangerous misunderstanding of the depth of our global dependence on oil and impact on our global society and economy when there isn't enough oil to satisfy all the needs competing for it (there are over 300,000 products made from oil).

That figure again: 300,000 products made from oil. I looked around my pretty home with its custom-made curtains and its beautiful furnishings. I had so carefully designed my beautiful kitchen with a place for everything and all the most up to date equipment. Three hundred thousand products made from oil? As I wandered about, I could see what he meant. So much was made from plastic or some derivative of oil or imported from far away. If I took those things away, there would be practically nothing left.

I couldn't help going again to the computer and pulling up lists of things either made directly from oil or which require oil in their manufacture.

My initial list was only 128 items but they were enough to highlight for me how dependent we are on oil. Just this small number of items covered a vast range of products and uses. Cleaning products such as detergents and dishwashing liquids, personal items such as deodorant and face creams, necessary medical items from anaesthetics to bandages, denture adhesive and artificial limbs; roofing materials; movie film; telephones; toilet seats; heart valves. And the list goes on.

This partial list of products which would fall victim to the oil nightmare didn't come near to the actual number and variety of affected products that make up our current world. We are so dependent on plastic and so dependent on importing goods from faraway places, it is really hard and frightening to contemplate what life would be like without the convenience of them. From the perspective of someone running a home, just the loss of clingfilm to cover leftover food is a prospect which weakens the knees.

I am deaf and eventually when I need new hearing aids, which are made from plastic, it may be that I won't be able to have them made any more. Larry and I both have sleep apnoea and use Constant Pressure Air Pump (CPAP) machines, also made from plastic parts, to ensure we don't stop breathing when we sleep. When our CPAPs wear out, we might not be able to get replacements – and we mightn't be able to afford the power used to run them. Without our CPAPs, we could actually both be in danger.

I kept looking around the house and realised that every centimetre of electrical wiring in my home was covered with plastic, and even the light switches were plastic. Under my kitchen sink, all the cleaning products were lined up neatly in their plastic bottles with their terribly clever childproof plastic screw tops. Not only would those bottles be gone, the cleaning products in them wouldn't be available either.

I thought back to the late 1960s when I was a junior nurse. Those were the days before disposable single-use plastic equipment. I remembered the sterilising rooms full of stainless steel equipment that junior nurses like me would sweat away over for hours, scrubbing, rinsing and then sterilising tray after tray of surgical instruments and other items – syringes and needles, kidney dishes, bowls, sputum mugs, tweezers, clamps – day after day.

Plastic had eliminated all that hard work, revolutionising the process so that something could be used once and then discarded. Then I thought of all the medications that we dispensed and doctors prescribed on a daily basis. I had never considered the degree to which modern medications, even those that are not made from oil, are so heavily dependent for their manufacture on the high-density energy derived from oil. Nor had I considered the future impact on all of those people who are dependent on medication and medical care.

I thought of toys for my grandchildren, combs, brushes and clips for my hair, our toothbrushes – all plastic and all imported. And yet we were talking about a world without imports, without planes. I'd read that there was no known alternative to aviation fuel. That thought alone was just too overwhelming to contemplate. My cousin's daughter lives in London, as do the kids of friends. Would the cost of flying home eventually spiral out of their reach? The family of Tomoko, my daughter-in-law, lives in Japan. Would the day come when they could never visit us? If Tomoko had children, would she be able to take them back to see her family?

It's possible to make lots of the things on my list from different materials, like the new plastics which are being produced from plants. But in order to make these products in different ways, with materials that aren't derived from oil or petrochemicals, first the new materials have to be found, or grown or researched, and then factories would need to be retooled or changed in some way. Goods would have to be redesigned and tested. How long would all that take and what would we do in the meantime?

Well over half the oil used in the world so far up till now has been used in creating the current global infrastructure. That means that most of the remaining oil would have to be used for creating the new infrastructure and I couldn't see how that was going to happen! As no one was talking about and planning for Peak Oil, I wondered when the penny would drop. And if it dropped too late in the game, what would be the result of that for society?

I thought of something Queensland Labor MP Andrew McNamara had said in a *Sydney Morning Herald* article:

> *The challenges we face after Peak Oil will require localised food production and industry in a way not seen for 100 years. Local rail lines and fishing fleets will be*

vital to regional communities. Self-contained communities living close to work, farms, services and schools will not be merely desirable; they will be essential ...

And in McNamara's original speech to parliament, he'd said:

As fuel prices double and then double again in the years after the peak, we will be faced with some very hard choices in the fields of agriculture, food distribution and transport generally.

Food distribution? I went to my pantry and stood for some while reading the labels. I had food from all over the world. The impact of that had never occurred to me before. Why should it? It was just a part of life. A tin of asparagus from some far-off place – when had I ever cared where things came from? In fact it was rather exotic, I thought, to sit down to eat dried figs that had come all the way from Turkey, or chocolates from Switzerland, cheese from France, oranges from Israel, avocados from New Zealand, salmon from America. How nice!

It would be quite usual and very easy for me to whip up a veritable feast for my family and not use one molecule of food or even utensils that were Australian made or grown. If I was living in New York or Toronto or London the situation would be the same.

Globalisation had changed not only the way we think and buy things, but the very way in which we nourish ourselves and our families. I had been told by friends that the trend in the UK is towards highly processed packaged meals. I had seen TV chef Jamie Oliver present a cooking program which highlighted the fact that British children were so conditioned to eating highly processed packaged food that many did not even know what a fresh vegetable looked like, never mind what it tasted like or where it came from. These little children are the next generation, the ones whose lives will be directly affected by the outcomes of oil depletion. They are growing up not knowing that the fried chips they love so much originate from a dirty-looking brown thing you dig up out of the ground. How would their generation cope if pre-packaged foods disappeared?

More immediately, though, I had to think of my own family. My children had no problem recognising a potato in its natural form, but the much more serious issue wouldn't go away: would our food and utensils and other things be unavailable if oil prices skyrocketed? Where would I get food for my table? All I had growing in my garden were roses and pretty flowers! I couldn't serve them with the Friday night roast for the family.

Farmers use petrochemical pesticides, herbicides, and fertilisers while their crops are growing, and then use huge gas-guzzling pieces of machinery to plough and plant and harvest and then truck the food to the cities. If fuel costs were so high that they couldn't afford to do these primary things, where would even the most basic food for city dwellers come from? It angered me that there was nothing in the mainstream media about these things. Doing something about it would take time. Where was the plan from the government to tide us over for the next ten or twenty years? In his book *Oilephant Down* Rick wrote:

> *Those areas and industries and businesses and, indeed, countries that will no longer receive the oil they need must be able to plan ahead, either to wind down their operations or switch to alternatives. Many nations are even now formally or informally considering rationing in the oil–lean years ahead.*

It continued to worry me that I didn't see anything about any of this in mainstream Australian media, even though I found in my research that countries such as Denmark and the Netherlands were making great strides in using alternative energy sources such as wind power and solar energy.

Former CIA analyst and US energy commentator Thomas Whipple wrote:

> *It has to come sooner or later. As oil becomes scarcer and scarcer and price rises higher and higher, pressures will grow for a formal allocation system. Rationing will come, if only to calm the havoc at the gas lines and the social upheavals that are bound to occur as long as rationing is only by price.*

Rationing of oil would not only mean you could only drive your car on a certain day, or that you could only obtain a certain amount of oil. Rationing would affect everything else too. Going to the local store to buy whatever you want may well mean walking to the store to see if they have anything to sell you!

Rick explained to us that all transportation around the world is dependent on oil, if not directly for fuel then indirectly in the form of oil-derived energy used in manufacturing the transportation technology. The fundamental and most important issue is that our society as we know it simply can't function without oil. We have structured our basic way of life around the availability of cheap abundant oil and as that becomes more and more scarce or more and more expensive, there is nothing to replace it. I guess this is where my kids just didn't 'get it'. To their minds, if this oil thing was for real, we could simply switch to something else.

We lived in Sydney, a city with four million people, but we didn't appreciate just how much fuel played a part in the incredibly complex and enormous process that must be maintained in order to supply the basic needs of everyone living in a city each and every day. Tonnes and tonnes of food are trucked into and around the city each and every day and then mountains of garbage have to be removed. Imported goods are brought in and unloaded and trucked from the docks. Cars and trucks and buses have to be fuelled and used to move people all over the city, water has to be pumped in and sewerage has to be processed and pumped out. Electricity has to be generated sufficient for heating and cooling the massive office towers and millions of homes, providing energy for cooking and lighting and entertainment and manufacturing. We were living in a teeming metropolis of activity, all fuelled by oil.

The problem of switching to another source of energy other than oil, however, is the amount of time it takes. It has taken 150 years to create the infrastructure we live with today and it will take quite a few years – decades in fact – to make the changes necessary. So what do we do in the meantime? There are just no signs that we are doing anything, here in Australia at least.

Rick wrote: 'Peak Oil is a global problem, to be sure, but all of the solutions are going to have to be local …'

A local solution? What did he mean by that? I bought my bread from the supermarket and bread is made from wheat. Where does wheat grow in the centre of Sydney or London or New York? To a city woman, the words 'local solution to food production' meant 'everybody bring a plate of something nice!' Primary food production happened 'out there' somewhere, with the work done by farmers living on huge properties, people who wore checked flannel shirts and funny floppy hats – people who lived a life I could not imagine living, far from the noise and convenience and immediacy of an important major city. After all, city life was the life – the only life. Well … isn't it?

Neither Larry nor I knew anything about food production other than 'open the packet or tin, pour contents in to saucepan, heat and eat'. Likewise, when we wanted light or power, we simply switched it on. Where it came from never entered our heads. Water came from the tap. We had no need for pumps and when we wanted to go anywhere we drove, fuelled by petrol that came from petrol pumps at the petrol station. How it got there was not within our sphere of consideration. Not even an idle thought. And that was just the way the world worked. Press it, click it, turn it, zap it, send for it, phone for it. Whatever we needed was just 'there'.

With all my new, unwanted knowledge, I felt like I was living inside some hideous surrealist nightmare. I didn't know how to snap out of it. I wanted to get on with important things like putting cow poop under my rose bushes. Of course it didn't occur to me that the very cow poop I was so happy to fling about was another commodity that was trucked in to the city from far away. And it wasn't even brought straight from the cow's nether regions to me, but taken to a factory somewhere and made into something neat and 'acceptable' then bagged up in plastic and then trucked in to be sold in a supermarket or a nursery. Even my precious cow poop wasn't immune to the Peak Oil problem.

There are lots of conspiracy theories on the internet about Peak Oil. People referred to it as a scam to bump up oil prices; government reports denigrate the facts as proposed by the Peak Oil theorists and instead beat the drum of a viable growth economy. I found sites which criticised the findings of the oil industry experts, and I read articles which emphatically stated that there is no problem with oil production for many years to come. What made us both very sceptical was finding out the way these supposed experts were explaining how oil reserves are estimated. The estimates are calculated on data which in itself is very well documented to be flawed. In fact, with the amount of misinformation on the internet, there must clearly be some very powerful reasons for such heated debate and such discrepancies in opinion.

Rick explained to us why the various theories didn't make sense. He was one source of information we felt we could trust. He backed up his statements with facts from other reliable, scientific sources and his explanations were always clear and logical.

Rick suggested a compelling reason behind all this nay-saying: big business. And what he said did make sense.

> *The economy, whether the local community economy, the national economy, or the global economy, is based on one commodity, and that commodity is not oil. It is confidence ... A sudden loss of confidence has been the reality check that has brought on every economic downturn in history, from a small, hardly-noticed and quickly-forgotten double-digit decline on the stock market to a catastrophic global market collapse such as happened in 1929. If the basis for that confidence is not ... quickly restored, which it was not in 1929 ..., then a comparatively rapid economic implosion ensues.*

From the perspective of a housewife-nobody like me, trying to understand the politics of economics was all new territory. From being in business for many years I did know how corporations stimulate their markets, how consumers are led to purchase things through carefully orchestrated, psycho-logically manipulative marketing campaigns and I also knew that for the right amount of money, people will do anything. It wasn't hard to understand that the potential collapse of the economy brought about by having a nation of people really understand what Peak Oil would lead to would be unthinkable. Profits would be compromised – and profits ran the world. You and I and our consumer children had to be kept ignorant as long as possible to ensure maximum commercial viability.

On 15 June 2004, Prime Minister John Howard presented a white paper entitled 'Securing Australia's Energy Future'. Howard delivered 3450 words expounding on our glowing and energy-rich future. The only acknowledgement of any possible cloud on our horizon in that speech was a sentence of just seventeen words: He said: 'Our known oil reserves are significant, but are projected to decline in the absence of new discoveries.' No reference was made to the global decline in oil, nor was there any mention of the fact that Australian oil fields had peaked in the year 2000. There was no mention of a 'Plan B' if no new oil discoveries were made in Australia.

Larry spent hours and hours searching the internet for government papers and projections or statements which might clarify our confusion. What he found continually suggested that the government believed current price hikes in oil were a temporary thing and that oil would fall back to its usual price of $30 to $40 a barrel; but many, *many* of the experts seemed to disagree. Who was right – the scientists, geologists and oil experts, or the government?

But there were some signs that the Peak Oil story was getting out there. A website belonging to the oil giant Chevron stated:

Energy will be one of the defining issues of this century. One thing is clear: the era of easy oil is over. What we do next will determine how well we meet the energy needs of the entire world in this century and beyond.

Here was a major international oil company coming right out and saying 'the era of easy oil is over'! Why wasn't my government telling me that? Why wasn't my government telling me that they were meeting a future challenge head on, right now, and my interests and those of future generations were the most important item on the agenda?

Instead of addressing what Chevron was saying to the world, the Australian government put out a paper dismissing Peak Oil. In February 2005 the Australian Department of Transport and Regional Services put out a working paper entitled 'Is the World Running Out of Oil? A Review of the Debate'. What we read in that paper just confounded us and made us angry. It states:

> There are two very distinct schools of thought on the question of whether we are running out of oil. The 'peak theorists'/depletionists argue that half the world's oil supplies have been used and oil production has peaked or is about to peak, signaling a near–term crisis across world economies that will cause massive dislocations. The counter view, held by international energy agencies and other antidepletionists, is that while there are always uncertainties about reserve estimates, it is most likely we have only used around a quarter of world reserves and that the outlook for the next 30 years presents no cause for concern. Oil supplies, they argue, will keep pace with demand, as reflected in the expectation that long–term prices (in year 2000 dollars) are likely to be around $30 per barrel.

I couldn't think of one political party in my country or indeed in any country at that time gutsy and honest enough to face the cameras and say, 'Now listen up, people, we've got a problem, here's what it is and here's a set of solutions which all of us have to work on together.' How galvanising that would be to a nation! But I was sure that wouldn't happen because I'm one of those cynical people who rightly or wrongly believe that people in governments don't automatically do the things that are right for their constituents. Unless it's good for business or good for maintaining their positions in power it isn't necessarily something a government will address. I felt zero confidence that I was living in a good and safe environment that would sustain me and my family into the future.

And if the government wasn't doing its homework, why weren't people at least being informed in the mainstream media? Journalists had just as much access to the internet as me, and far more research expertise. How was it possible that we were not being told that *within our lifetime and certainly in the lifetime of our children the world could well change forever?*

Why weren't people being given an opportunity to make up their own minds about all this conflicting information? Why weren't they being given the opportunity to prepare long in advance for the horrible possibility that Peak Oil and all it entailed was a very likely future for us? Why weren't our young people being encouraged and trained in all the things that they may need to know? Important things like trades, how to sustain themselves without the aid of supermarkets and technology and imports, how to make things, how to grow things, make do with things, innovate, recycle, how to stay healthy, become stronger. There would be just so much to learn and so little time!

Being a baby-boomer, I could reach back into memories of my childhood in the 1950s and remember my mother baking not from packet mix, but from basic ingredients, weighing out the flour and the other ingredients and then mixing it all up by hand. I could remember the baker arriving with his big wicker basket, putting fresh warm unwrapped bread on our kitchen windowsill. I could remember my grandmother growing tomatoes in our back garden. Even though I grew up in the city, I did know a simpler way of life back then. Before we had a washing machine, we had a copper and a wringer to do the laundry with.

My own children, on the other hand, know only a life of technologically assisted total convenience, a life of immediate gratification of needs. When the baby-boomers and their elderly parents are gone, so too will go all the life skills that were accumulated over the years.

With Larry at work all day, I had plenty of time to think about all these things, and plenty of time to search the internet. I had plenty of time to walk through in my mind what the future would hold.

There are indeed certain countries making preparations for the end of the age of dependence on oil. Iceland for example is moving to a hydrogen/geothermal economy and Germany is concentrating its efforts on developing wind power. Denmark is doing great things with methane produced from animal waste. Norway has been working towards sustainability in preparation for when their North Sea oil runs out. Brazil too is concentrating on these issues, producing transportation ethanol from sugarcane. Sweden has commenced a program to wean its population off fossil fuels over the next fifteen years.

America on the other hand has put on its military helmet and is dashing about the globe attempting to strong-arm its way into obtaining the last scraps of oil from oil-producing countries (albeit under the guise of bringing democracy to the masses or as part of their quest to conquer terrorism). Australia appears to be shuffling its feet, cap in hand, happily offering to sell its future-critical resources overseas, comfortable in the knowledge that it can puff along with coal burning and spewing pollution into the atmosphere for decades to come. What the Australian government doesn't mention is that coal cannot effectively replace oil. The conversion process that coal would have to go through to be a viable substitute actually uses more energy than it produces – this is what's called a 'net energy loser'. Australia is also proposing the use of biofuels such as ethanol (biofuels are made from renewable sources such as industrial waste or plant matter), but unfortunately the magical biofuels are also net energy losers. Even if we did go forward with biofuels, as MP Andrew McNamara points out: '… No other energy source [than oil] can fly planes or drive heavy trucks and machinery'.

Britain is convincing its people that nuclear energy is the way to go in the face of escalating oil prices, but nuclear power also produces the very same net energy loss as other alternatives to oil. Nuclear power has the added distinction of producing dangerous by-products that need to be stored for thousands of years. So, while the populace of many nations are being encouraged to believe that it is business as usual, our governments *do* know about the looming energy crisis. Quite simply, they don't want to upset the status quo, and neither do the mass media think it appropriate to tell people in plain language what is just around the corner.

In February 2005, oil expert Robert L. Hirsch published a report for the US Department of Energy on the peaking of oil production. The Hirsch Report discussed the likelihood of Peak Oil occurring and how soon we need to take mitigating action. The report states in its executive summary:

> The peaking of world oil production presents the US and the world with an unprecedented risk management problem. As peaking is approached, liquid fuel prices and price volatility will increase dramatically, and, without timely mitigation, the economic, social, and political costs will be unprecedented. Viable mitigation options exist on both the supply and demand sides, but to have substantial impact, they must be initiated more than a decade in advance of peaking.

This one little paragraph from a document of over 100 pages should have been banner headline news in every daily newspaper around the world. It wasn't. Search the US mainstream media for the government's follow-up actions as a result of the Hirsch Report. They are very hard to find. It is interesting to note that President George Bush and the former Defence Secretary Donald Rumsfeld both have properties that are self-sufficient and off the energy grid. I wonder why?

Governments don't want to come right out and say, 'Hey people, whoops – the well is dry – all gone – too bad so sad!' That isn't a vote-catcher and it certainly isn't what the stock market wants people to believe. After all, we are a consumer society and the process of globalisation and its ability to make money right now is far more important to the big end of town than abstract concepts like people's quality of life ten years from now. The acquisition of money is too important.

Eventually Larry and I reached a point in our research and our ongoing discussions when we felt we had enough information to actually comprehend the enormity of the effects of Peak Oil, if not for us, then at least for our children and grandchildren. We felt it was time to make some solid plans.

Maybe the one thing most clear to us in all this period was that science and government instrumentalities were not going to 'deal with reality' – we had to deal with our own reality in our own way.

Chapter Three

There was no way we felt we could simply sit by and do nothing about our situation in relation to Peak Oil. We were middle-aged and we wanted to ensure that our retirement would be at least as comfortable as our parents' old age had been. We also wanted to leave something for our children. That legacy was originally going to be our home and what was left of our retirement savings and investments or shares, again just as our parents had left for us.

We could see, though, that Peak Oil could destroy all that. It had the potential to change the whole way we evaluated our view of 'financial comfort'. We had been planning to invest our retirement savings so that they were managed by a professional fund manager. We'd wanted to ensure our money was continually growing and providing income, even when we became too infirm or doddery to pay the bills. But with the threatened economic changes that may affect us after the oil reserves have peaked, we suddenly didn't have the same level of confidence in investment schemes that we once had. We didn't know what industries would constitute a safe investment. We didn't know which investment companies were safe. What made it worse is that when we did consult a financial adviser, he hadn't heard of Peak Oil and its economic ramifications. That was a very disturbing moment for us. We endeavoured to enlighten him but I suspect he thought we were potty old greenies.

We weren't experienced in share trading or investing in things, and I suspect the majority of our peers aren't either. Without an investment adviser who saw the world through our eyes, we felt in a weak position, unsure of what to do or which company to entrust with our funds. It was one thing for our government to be looking the other way from the oncoming problems. Their main focus is to soothe voter confidence so they stay in power and keep their jobs. Similarly, maybe the media had to look the other way because doom-deliverers upset consumers, and media organisations only exist on advertising dollars. Financial people though – professionals whose job it is to peer off into the future and plant people's life savings in fertile fields – should know what is on the horizon, surely? They should have been telling *us* about Peak Oil and all its economic ramifications. We had a friend who was making a very tidy profit by speculating on the stock market, particularly in oil and gold, but we didn't have his expertise, nor were we willing to use the equity in our home to gamble the way he had done. We knew a rocky future was ahead, so to gamble on our security wasn't an option.

We were used to looking at our home as a reasonably good property that would have provided a good legacy for the kids to share after they planted us in the ground. But when we viewed it with Peak Oil in mind, its sale value lost some lustre.

If there was a major economic meltdown, putting lots of people out of work, and those people were not able to access even basic commodities, living in a major city would obviously become a nightmare and therefore the house might not get such a great price after all. There was a lot of equity tied up in that house that we desperately wanted for our children's future security, but if it lost its value that would leave them nothing.

We realised that we had to think differently about the future. What we considered to be financial comfort needed to be reassessed. For example, if we were just coping when oil was $1.20 per litre, would our finances allow us to cope if fuel went to $3.60 or $5 or higher? Rising fuel prices are like the tide coming in to a harbour. Everything in the harbour rises on that tide and everything depending on oil in our society is tied to basic oil prices. We wondered what those price increases would do to our ability to pay for ordinary, everyday things, and we worried about what those escalating prices would do to our retirement investments.

In the beginning, it hadn't really hit home – because like most people, when I thought about fuel prices, I automatically thought about the running of my car. But now I knew that increasing fuel prices affect everything in our lives. A friend of ours, for example, owns a removals business. When we talked to him about the cost of fuel, he said that because his business is trucking, as oil prices escalate, his prices have to rise. He believes they will reach a point where people won't be able to afford to use his services and he will simply have to go out of business. He told us that he could see this happening in the future and had already secured himself by buying a rural property that was some way down the path of self-sustainability.

I told Larry how the removalist saw the future shaping up and the exit strategy he had constructed for his family. We had speculated about how much or how little we should tell people about what we were learning because we kept running up against total apathy. It was a real problem because while we could read article after article and bounce ideas off Rick, we also needed other knowledgeable people in our own country to discuss what Peak Oil would mean in our own community, and help validate our ideas – yet people with Peak Oil knowledge were very hard to find. Larry began to guardedly use his corporate network to seek out anyone who might know what we knew so that we could share our concerns and maybe better understand what the future might hold.

After sixteen years of working for a very large organisation, Larry had developed an inner circle of colleagues to talk to. He talked with some of his work colleagues about Peak Oil and found a mixed reaction, just as we had found with our social network. Some rejected the idea outright. Others acknowledged the problem but said that they felt helpless to do anything. One responded to Larry's questions in a way that totally surprised and shocked him. This particular guy had been so aware of Peak Oil that some six or more years previously he had sold his properties and moved, along with a number of other families, to an 'intentional community' built west of Sydney. The homes that were built all circled an area of about two and a half hectares, much like the design of an old-fashioned English common. The land would be used to grow food. He even told Larry that close by was a butcher who was willing to process their killed meat for them. He and a bunch of his friends had seen the Peak Oil phenomenon, assessed it and acted on it long before we had even heard about it.

The organisation Larry worked for was primarily a food-processing and distribution business. Increasingly the profit of the business revolved around how well it managed its supply chain. They had made the concept of 'just in time' delivery into an art form. They didn't have giant warehouses storing heaps of goods waiting for orders to come in and be filled. Instead, goods on order were delivered to their receiving docks and were unloaded from the supplier's trucks straight onto their own delivery trucks. Furthermore, they were able to organise things in such a way that multiple suppliers' trucks arrived simultaneously at their delivery docks so that their own trucks could be loaded up with a neatly categorised variety of goods needing to be delivered to their own supermarkets. This provided rapid turn-around and timely re-supply. It also meant that they didn't need huge stocks of goods sitting in storage.

This very complex and finely tuned system had become a major part of their business success. Timing was everything. Any break in that supply chain had immediate and, in some cases, disastrous effects on the bottom line. Buyers flew around the world to tie up supply deals for cheap produce which was labelled as generic brands, undercutting homegrown produce significantly. Ships carried material to Australian ports. Trucks and trains moved goods to national delivery points and huge fleets of trucks then moved goods straight out all round Australia. Of course, to Mrs Average Shopper like me, a glitch in this well-oiled system meant frustration that the can of salmon I had come to buy wouldn't be on the shelf and I would have to go elsewhere to get it.

Larry worked in systems development and over the years he had been involved in developing systems in most areas of the business. The ability to move supplies and finished goods into and around the country was critical to his organisation's survival. In each section of the business, Larry could see that the effects of Peak Oil would cause loss, disruption and delay. We knew that in the future, this near-perfect system of food delivery may be compromised.

The same 'just in time' methodology was as prevalent throughout the manufacturing sector, with global parts supply lines. Peak Oil would have the same effect on those supply lines, which would become increasingly disrupted with shipping delays and parts supplier companies failing as fuel prices escalated.

We didn't feel that Peak Oil would one day be upon us with the same speed that a Tuesday follows a Monday. We speculated that the most likely scenario would be that slowly, life in the city would become more difficult. It may be so slow as not to be noticed on a daily basis. Prices would rise, perhaps more companies would wind down; more people would be out of work. Maybe some commodities would be too expensive in the supermarket, or there would be empty shelves as some things became unavailable; maybe there would be more violence or theft. The speculation was endless.

A thought kept recurring in my mind. I had read about people in Nazi Germany before the war. They stayed in their homes, hearing the news and seeing the development of a serious threat and they kept saying 'It won't happen. It can't happen!' But it did happen, and the Nazi regime swept them away. And here we were. We had gathered all this knowledge and understanding. Were we going to be like those people in Nazi Germany? Were we going to wait it out in the city until it was too late?

We gradually found that while the daily news carried little or nothing about Peak Oil, the number of people on the net that were talking about it and doing things about it and becoming active in discussion groups and chat rooms was noticeably growing. We found Yahoo groups on the net like ROEOZ (Running on Empty Oz) and ROECA (Running on Empty Canada – Rick's group) as well as many more. We signed up and read what other people were saying all over the world. It felt like we had unwittingly become part of some global counterculture – some sort of growing band of people who were waking up and stretching their minds and prodding each other into action. In vain we gave our friends these websites, hoping that they would read them and see what we could see. It didn't happen. But despite that, we couldn't stand still. We started to look at a couple of options in order to help us make some decisions about what we should do. We felt lucky, in a way. I was retired, and Larry was coming up for retirement. We had been looking at retirement options anyway. Maybe – unlike others we knew – we were simply in a position where we *could* look at options, and make choices for the future, as we had been planning for some kind of life change anyway. And so we looked at the pros and cons of the options we'd come up with.

The first option was: *Let's do nothing*. This was obviously a very attractive option. I didn't want to have all this knowledge in the first place, and a faint and tiny part of me didn't believe Peak Oil was real anyway. I wanted things to just stay as they had always been. It would have been wonderful to remain with our heads in the sand like our friends and children, ignoring the gathering black clouds, trusting in some fanciful belief in continuity and the altruistic proactive nature of a benevolent, caring government.

In this option, we would go on exactly as before. Larry would continue to work as long as he could, rather than retiring early. I would stay home and probably end up providing free daycare for my grandchildren. Larry would be able to contribute some more to our retirement savings. We would be in our idyllic little house and generally we would just muddle on. This would mean we'd be able to retain our involvement in our community and I could continue my pottery and weaving classes. I would be able to enjoy growing my roses.

We had begun to get involved in a local community garden and we could see that this could develop into another interest both of us could share. We would maintain our friendships with our social circle, and be able to enjoy having more time to do so. We could prepare for Peak Oil by perhaps investing in solar power for the house, growing a few vegetables in the garden, and paying more attention to recycling and conservation. We would be able to stay close to the kids and all the amenities we had grown used to.

While all these things were appealing, we worked through the drawbacks. One of those drawbacks was that Larry would have to keep on working. Although we had planned for him to work for another four years, we'd begun to think otherwise, now that his company was relocating so much further from our home.

We felt if we retained those four working years in our plans we might be leaving it too late for some things. If after Larry's retirement we wanted to do something else, something adventurous or physical or risky, or even moving to the country for some back-to-basics living if the oil thing got bad, our age might be a troublesome factor. More importantly, we felt that if the issues relating to Peak Oil did become a reality, we would not have any control over our lives. We would be totally dependent, as all city dwellers are, on the government, or on retailers and distant farmers for our most basic needs. If they couldn't provide them, we would be stuck.

We felt then that the worst thing we could choose to do was to sit and do nothing. If Larry continued working for four years, as we'd originally planned, we couldn't see now that the extra years would gain for us enough extra savings to ensure a comfortable income after retirement. We wouldn't be able to afford to travel or do anything much out of the ordinary. In fact, we felt to have the extra working years and not have that time together was a huge price to pay. But that was option one and it sat on the table between us as a serious consideration. Peak Oil may have been a big player in this decision-making process, but of equal importance was our financial future and also spending quality time together – with or without Peak Oil.

The second option was: *Downsize again to an apartment and invest the profit from the house sale in our retirement fund*. This option had some financial merit. We discussed whether we really wanted to be tied to the upkeep of a house and garden in the future when we were teetering about with walking frames and trifocals? If we sold the house, we knew we would get a good price. We had renovated it to perfection and it was as pretty as a picture with a lot of quality and style. We didn't have a mortgage so we could purchase a nice apartment still in our area and near the kids. The profit from the sale after the purchase of an apartment would go towards our retirement fund and provide us with an increased monthly income when Larry retired. Financially we would be better off, provided basic commodity prices remained the same.

On the other hand, by downsizing to an apartment, we would have nowhere for our dogs to roam about safely outside. We would be living in very close proximity to neighbours, which is a lifestyle we wouldn't enjoy. Importantly, once again we would be remaining under the control of the society in which we lived, with a real lack of options if the Peak Oil issues became a reality and caused increased prices and shortages of basic commodities.

While financially option two had merit, from a quality of life point of view it lacked a great deal. It was important for us to find a situation where financially we would be independent, and not be a burden to our children when we got old, and one which gave us pleasure and time together. We have always been at our happiest when we are doing things together. We are each other's best friend. And so this option seemed to be about removing both the freedom to live the lifestyle we enjoy, in a house with space for the dogs and a rose garden, as well as the possible option of planning for Peak Oil in a small way by growing vegies and moving towards solar power. Option two felt like compromises all round.

So, that dealt with both our 'do nothing' and our 'downsize' options. Neither option had enough positives of the kind we wanted or needed. We had to cook up another option that principally met our future financial security and freedom and quality of life needs, and also covered the issues relating to oil depletion. We constructed option three.

Option three: *Pack up and move to the country*. A move to the country would give us extra money to invest from the sale of our house, as we'd be able to purchase a cheaper property. A move of this magnitude would mean that Larry would have to retire early, which meant, on the plus side, that we would be together and he would not have the daily travel or stress factors associated with his corporate job.

We could develop some degree of self-sustainability by growing our own food and relying less on other people or organisations or the government to provide for us. This was a very attractive point. Moving to the country meant that our cost of living would be cheaper. We knew Larry would probably have to source some kind of work when we made the move, until we were established. Being in the country would be better for my health, and I could grow a million roses if I wanted to. I would have room to grow just about anything I fancied and certainly a lot of the things we needed. We would be out of the pollution of the city, away from traffic and aircraft noise, away from crowds and chaos. We would get more exercise, fresh air, fresh water and peace. We would be able to eat fresh homegrown food free from chemicals. We would be able to face new challenges together, meet new people, learn new things and immerse ourselves in a totally new experience. It sounded like an adventure.

On the other hand, the downsides of a move to the country were that we would not be close to our children and grandchildren unless they came with us. We would not be in close proximity to town shopping, or to medical assistance (which I frequently needed, as I have a degenerative spinal condition, and a few other serious health problems). Also, realistically, we would only have a window of about ten to fifteen or so years of fully active life before the farm work became a burden. This meant that we would have to use that time wisely. We would aim to find a suitable property and create self-sustainability in food, energy and water. In short, we wanted to find ways of providing everything that we were currently dependent on in the city. It would have to be a property that we could manage without relying on the heavy machinery used in traditional broadacre farming – run on oil – and without products such as herbicides, pesticides and artificial fertilisers – manufactured from oil or natural gas. It would have to have the capacity to support us, our children and their partners, and our grandchildren. It would be a life-changing experience, but then, so was the outcome of Peak Oil.

We mulled through the options over and over again, giving weighting to each positive and negative. If we were to measure this decision-making time in terms of cups of coffee and tea, we could have filled a swimming pool!

After countless hours of discussion, we decided that the idea of living in the country and sharing the time we have left together creating something that would benefit our kids in the years ahead was worth more than anything else. To have the chance to work together doing whatever we wanted was an irresistible component in the move-to-the-country scenario. When we stripped every other thing away, whether there were oil gushers in the middle of the Sydney Harbour Bridge, or Sydney were to turn into a scene from *Mad Max* or *The Road Warrior*, the element that was paramount in our ultimate decision to move to a farm was a fundamental one. We, as a couple, got our greatest pleasure out of two major things. The first was just being together, just hanging out together as my kids would have said. We are incessant chatterers; we laugh all the time, and kid around. We get a real kick out of doing things for each other. We have deep and meaningful discussions concerning just about everything.

The other major thing was caring for our family in a tangible way. To spend some years together working on a project that gave us pleasure and interest at the same time as creating something valuable for the kids had a powerful appeal. Having no one to answer to except each other sounded irresistible too. So, thanks to the discussions about our finances and the terror of the looming threat of oil depletion, we chose option three. We chose to move to the country.

We talked over our plans with the kids hoping that they would want to join us. They were locked in to their city lives for the time being, finishing university degrees, gaining experience in their jobs, and paying off mortgages. Three of our kids were still in the process of finding their life partners. None of them could really see themselves picking up and heading for the country. In fact, they were incredulous at first. I had put them first in my thoughts and actions for their entire lives. Now we were announcing that we were going to move away to a place in the country where we could set up a home with enough land to provide self-sustainability for the whole family. It was clear from what they were saying and how they were reacting that they were actually unable to conceive of a life other than the one I had programmed them to aspire to. Their disbelief that we would leave, and ask them to follow, just when their lives were seemingly blossoming was immense.

I thought hard about their reaction. I imagined what would happen if one day I woke up and on the news was a special bulletin put out by the government telling the truth about Peak Oil, and about the future of economic depression and depletion. I thought about what people would do and how they would react. The concept of having to change every facet of one's life and aspirations 'just like that' was outrageous. And in any case it would be impossible. The average young family wasn't in our situation. They had mortgages to pay off, maybe no savings, certainly heaps of bills. They had kids to educate and jobs that paid for their daily bread. They had their friends and their routines. They couldn't pull up stakes and leave the dependencies of the city for the country as we could. The thought of the chaos and the despair such a massive paradigm shift would cause was awful to consider.

The hardest thing we ever did was cross that great divide from what we had always known to be a 'sound and sensible' legacy to purposefully creating a new and different legacy for our kids. This one would be a legacy which was literally outside our sphere of real understanding, but which seemed to fit our emerging picture of a world that was going to be undergoing monumental changes at some point in the not-too-distant future. All our reading and all our research and questioning left us in no doubt that Peak Oil was an issue to deal with now, not to wait and see, and not to trust in any political decision-making or scientific possibility that may occur in the future.

We felt too that if we took this drastic turn in our lives, maybe, just maybe, some of our friends and family would take the time to check out for themselves what we had been talking about. We hoped that they would go to the internet and read for themselves about Peak Oil and finally realise that it is something that everyone has to face and come to terms with. Peak Oil is something that requires time to understand and time to develop new attitudes to, as well as time to grieve. Peak Oil requires people to take the time to think through all the issues that will arise, and make plans for overcoming as much as possible the changes and losses that are before us all. Moving to the country and becoming farmers was, for us, akin to going out and walking on the moon, but with our understanding of the situation, it felt like a choice we had to make.

The prospect of the country move was both wildly exciting and grippingly terrifying. We had absolutely no experience to fall back on and a huge learning curve to overcome. Once the final decision was made, however, an incredible blanket of calmness seemed to descend on us. It just felt right. The more we talked about it, the better it felt. If nothing else, we had faith in our individual and collective abilities to cope with such a big change.

I realised that we had finally arrived at the last stage in the grieving process over the ramifications of Peak Oil – the stage of acceptance. It gave us a focus and a goal to aim for. We felt that whether or not anyone else thought we were insane, we knew that we were doing something important for us as well as the kids. We kept discussing the negatives, the disasters, the 'what ifs', all the possible ramifications of such a life-changing move. It was important that we continued to play devil's advocate for each other as long as possible so that if we ultimately acted on this choice, we would be doing so with our eyes wide open.

We believed at that time that we had time to get established before costs began to rise too much and oil depletion began to bite hard. But we also believed that there was not a lot of time to waste. Our decision to move to the country met our major challenges head on. It would give us a more stable financial future and, should the results of reaching Peak Oil make life in the city untenable for our kids, they would have a safe and productive haven to come to.

We set about planning what we would do and how we would go about it. We were going to take our time, map out a schedule and learn as much as we could about which regional areas to consider and how to go about buying a rural property. We were going to be very systematic and very careful – after all, making such a huge change was not something that can be or should be done on a whim overnight. Also, being accustomed to dealing with projects in our corporate lives, we were determined that this one was going to be highly successful.

Suddenly, from the depths of fear and uncertainty, we had found a path to follow that we were really excited about. I can remember the evening we decided to do this. Larry said that we should shoot for December 2007 to be on a farm. That would give us about two years to make the change from city to country. I was happy with that. I knew I could deal with it in a measured way. Larry organised to take a week off from work so that we could make a start on our great two-year plan to look for a property. First step: research.

Around that time, there was a Country Living Expo being held in Sydney and we were really pleased at the thought of being able to go and have a look at all the different country areas being promoted. Also around that time, our local council and the University of New South Wales were holding an Eco Living Fair, with demonstrations of all sorts of energy-saving systems and devices. There was even an eco-friendly house to visit at the fair. The house had a garden that was designed based on the principles of a method called permaculture. That was interesting to us. We learned that permaculture was a garden design system that was first pioneered by an Australian called Bill Mollison. The principle of permaculture, according to Mollison, basically turns upside down the notion of man working the land, and instead, through his design system, gets the land to work for man. Mimicking nature, a permaculture-designed garden uses the natural world to do the work that farmers had traditionally done. In a permaculture garden, for example, you might find deciduous trees planted around a house, shading it from the sun in summer, and in winter, when the leaves fell off, allowing the sunlight into the house, cutting down on the need for energy-based heating and cooling systems. Permaculture gardeners design their gardens so that one plant's pests are eaten by a neighbouring plant's predator, eliminating the need for chemical sprays. We were fascinated with these principles and felt that if they really worked, we could perhaps string out those ten or fifteen years of farm working for a longer period before we got too old to be able to do the work ourselves. Permaculture, we decided, was definitely something we wanted to find out more about.

We then went to the Country Living Expo. There were stalls there promoting various rural towns and areas of New South Wales and we went from stall to stall hungrily gathering information like two children gathering up samples at a confectioner's exhibition. There were so many things to consider, and so much to see. It was overwhelming. At a stand for the Coffs Harbour Shire, a distinguished and friendly man introduced himself as a local shire councillor. We chatted to him and told him of our plans. He gave us some information and booklets and his card, and impressed us with his open, friendly, laid-back style. This man was to become pivotal in our lives more quickly than we could imagine.

At another stand we bought some books, one of which was to become a sort of 'bible' in our property search. It was a book called *Buying your Bush Block* by Allan Windust. This book, with its lists and snippets of fantastic advice, was just what we needed. Clearly Allan Windust had done several times what we were about to do and had learned all the things that we didn't know. We figured, why learn the hard way when you can learn from an expert what to do and what *not* to do when buying a property in the country.

We were excited. Here was something over which we had control, unlike the freewheeling Peak Oil roller-coaster we had been on for so long. We were off on an adventure that we had decided would take us about two years to achieve. At that time, we had no idea that our carefully laid out two-year plan would melt down to only six weeks!

Chapter Four

In the twelve years of our marriage we had never had a holiday together. With both of us working hard and raising kids, and with little money to spare, a holiday was a luxury we never seemed willing or able to afford. We had never even had a honeymoon. The idea of a week away to begin our search for the perfect rural property therefore had a special significance for us. It was going to be the honeymoon we had never had, as well as a working time visiting rural real estate agents.

In order to prepare properly for our working holiday, we stopped researching Peak Oil for the time being and began researching rural properties. We started with real estate websites, eagerly scanning photos of the properties and looking at what the properties were worth. In calculating what something in the country is worth, we learned that we couldn't just look at the house and the location as one would in the city. In the city we were in our element. We knew what to look for, which were the good and bad areas, we knew suburb values. We knew building styles and ages and what to be wary of. In the country, so many more factors make a property valuable.

We looked at properties that were cheap and then found that they either didn't have easy access to water, or the land was uncleared and maybe in an undesirable location in terms of bushfires, or the slope was too great, or proximity to towns was an issue. Some had been left to run down and others had been developed well. Suddenly we had to think about average annual rainfall and frosts and soils and a myriad of other natural factors. It wasn't sufficient to look at the house and say 'I could see my furniture fitting in there', or 'that's a pretty kitchen'. It was strange accepting that the actual house was not the principal factor.

The properties that had established orchards or crops or contracts for produce were more valuable. Properties that were certified organic and long-established permaculture-designed properties were of interest to us too. The size of the land was important but we weren't necessarily looking for something large – in rural properties, big may not always be better, we were learning. A larger property can mean higher maintenance costs, more water use, more heavy bush clearing or more cost in fencing. We looked at different areas, finding out which crops grew in those areas, and we looked at the surrounding towns to see what facilities they provided. With each search we were able to learn more and we greatly enjoyed this process – it was like looking into another world.

Our general mood had lifted dramatically because we felt hopeful and excited about our plans. At the same time as property searching online, I was investigating permaculture design. It had sparked our interest at the Eco Living Fair and we felt that this fascinating method of growing things was potentially ideal for us, as we were neither experienced farmers nor were we particularly fit and healthy. Permaculture was a design method that meant if we got it right, after the initial set-up nature would take over and do all the work for us. I found an internet-based course and signed up for it. The first few modules were emailed to me and very quickly I became engrossed and excited about the concept of permaculture. It was, it appeared, doable. I was very keen to work through the course and understand it better.

Even before we'd set out, *Buying your Bush Block* was getting dog-eared from use. Windust not only covered the essentials when it came to buying property, but he also gave more general information for the novice farmer. The list of 'skills you have to acquire or pay for' in the book was a bit troubling. There were skills in there that I didn't even know existed. 'Harrowing' for instance – I had had many harrowing experiences – usually at customer service desks in department stores. I had never considered harrowing to be a verb that one actually *did*! We knew that a monumental amount of learning was ahead of us, but at this early stage we were happy just to be tourists in the farming world.

Our initial holiday was booked for August of 2005 and we planned to do another one at the end of that year. We figured by that time we would have seen a lot of properties. Armed with our copy of *Buying your Bush Block*, we felt that with a bit of time and experience, we should be able to recognise a good property for our needs. At the back of the book was a checklist for purchasing a rural property and I dutifully typed up a copy of the checklist before our week's holiday so that we could use it when we were looking at properties. Lists – I loved lists – I was right in my element!

The Peak Oil Google Alerts kept popping up in our emails daily but by that time, we were well into an acceptance of what the future would bring, whether in five years or fifty. It was now just one of those things that we kept up to date with daily. We had our plan to become self-sufficient and live 'far from the madding crowd' and we were going to achieve it.

Our understanding of life after the end of cheap oil was that it was going to be similar in many ways to life during the Great Depression. We wanted to create for ourselves a productive, pretty and comfortable farm where as many of our basic needs as possible could be met through our own endeavours. A simpler way of life seemed to be the best option.

In preparation for our first sortie into rural Australia, Larry had bought a pile of maps and, together with all the hand-outs from the Country Living Expo, we began to eliminate the areas we were not interested in based on climate, proximity to amenities, and personal preference. We studied the maps to decide where we should look first. Things like climate, soils, communications, water and rainfall, a community and relatively easy access to a town with medical facilities and shopping were the broad issues of location. More specifically, we didn't want to be right on the coast where we would have to deal with potentially salt-laden sea air and tourist destinations and major roads. But we didn't want to be west of the Great Dividing Range either, where rainfall and pest plagues would be a problem. We didn't want to be too isolated nor too close to a major centre. By a process of elimination we decided on searching north of Sydney, and we chose to start our search in the mid-north coast region of New South Wales.

We wanted to find a location that was at least 300 kilometres from a major capital city like Sydney. We felt that was far enough away from a dense population to feel relatively safe and secure, something we'd learned might potentially be an issue from our Peak Oil research. Later, those feelings were confirmed when we watched the lawlessness that dominated

New Orleans in the aftermath of Hurricane Katrina. Living too close to a densely populated city could present real problems in terms of safety. At the same time we didn't want to be on an outback property hundreds of kilometres from a neighbour or a town, nor did we want to be close to a village where services and utilities were coming under increasing pressure. There had been a lot of press about the issues of drought and its effects on farmers.

My late brother had a friend who lived in a little town called Bellingen in northern NSW and we called her and told her we were heading up her way. We thought we would base ourselves in Bellingen and explore outwards from there. Bellingen is a pretty little town that has an annual jazz festival. This festival was being held during the time we would be there so we thought it would be great to see that, too, if we had time out from our travels.

My brother's friend Georgina sounded pleased to hear from us. She had been saddened to learn of my brother's untimely death and as I had never met her, it felt good that we were going to visit with her so that I could meet another of my brother's myriad friends. Georgina called a friend of hers who was a real estate agent and told him what we were looking for. He called us to say he would be happy to give us some advice. Looking back, this contact with a total stranger was another link in the amazing chain of events that was about to unfold before us.

In the lead-up to our departure, we began a process of information-gathering that was really fun. Because we had made this decision to 'deal with the reality' of a world with cheap energy on the downhill slide before it dealt with us, we wanted to learn how to live and work without all the trappings and dependencies of the twenty-first century. Our aim was to systematically downscale our way of living to one that was less and less dependent on energy or oil by-products. It was a lofty idea. We didn't know if we could achieve it, but it was worth a try and that was the plan.

We spent weekends visiting second-hand bookshops. We scoured their shelves for any old books that were about life before the age of cheap oil. We were looking for books about back-to-basics living. We wanted books that would give us guidance on old-fashioned skills. We found publications on how to make or do things like preserving and pickling, metal work, earth buildings, animal housing and husbandry, all manner of handicrafts, companion planting, growing herbs for cooking and medicinal use, generating power, carpentry, cheese making, solar power … the list went on and on. We had so much fun during these trips, combining book hunting with leisurely coffees or lunches and chatting about our finds.

One thing became more and more apparent. We realised how completely ignorant we were and how much there was to learn. We were such typical city folk, so cosmopolitan and 'with it'. What was glaringly obvious was the overwhelming volume of skills and information that modern city living has caused people to lose. Without those life skills we have evolved to a point where we are unable to live without the support of an army of retailers selling manufactured or processed or packaged goods. We have traded the ability to sustain ourselves for convenience, security, speed and immediacy. And that was all fine while we were living in the city, but we were awestruck at how unskilled we were and how unprepared we were to do things from first principles when we thought about our plan to move to the country and prepare for the effects of Peak Oil.

Those old books presented a way of life that was so full, so busy and so interesting, the richness was almost palpable. While it may have sounded romantic and quaint, and certainly healthy, it was obvious that the amount of work involved was tremendous. We were being given a glimpse of a lifestyle that was intimately tied to the seasons, to the earth and the elements. It was a lifestyle that relied heavily on one's skills, strength, endurance and knowledge, and a support network of family, friends and community.

I talked to Rick about all the things we were learning, and he told me about his childhood in rural Canada. He recounted a story of his mother's kitchen being crowded with women, all gathering together to help each other to make jams and preserves when the crops were brought in. Pots boiled on the wood stove and the women chattered and laughed as they worked. The house was redolent with sweet aromas and when they finished helping his mother, they would move on to the next person's place, with his mother going with them to do her share in return.

It was another era, another life, a life where people cared and shared and contributed to each other's lives in a way that is lost in our instant high-tech world. From our reading, we realised that while we may look back on that era as 'the simple life', it was far from simple, far from the 'good life' in one sense. We didn't really know if we were up to the task. People were used to extremely hard physical work in those times. Communities were small, and extended families, neighbourly assistance and working for the common good were part of the culture. That sort of community culture died with the development of the big cities, and the era of convenience. In its place came the nuclear family, and the rise of the individual – culminating in the kind of big-city life where a person can be lying dead in their apartment for six months without friends, family or neighbours having noticed. In a post-Peak Oil world, an old-fashioned support network and close cohesive community relationships would be vital, and we just couldn't imagine if that would ever be the reality again.

All the information we were gathering on the internet on how to do things provided us endless hours of discussion. Killing animals was a big topic.

'I can't see you caring for a chicken and then one day marching out into the yard and chopping its head off,' Larry said one night. 'It's just not you!'

I was quite indignant. Here I was studying hard so that I could be the next Ma Kettle and my own husband was denigrating my abilities even before we started.

'I *will* be able to kill,' I said, but secretly I too had my doubts. 'I know what I'll do,' I told him. 'I will give the chickens names that will make it easier for me. Let's say we have six chickens. I'll call one Maryland, one Schnitzel, one Soup, one Croquette, one Cacciatore and one Roast!'

We fell about laughing and came up with names for our other livestock. We would have a goose called Mrs Livy Pâté, a duck called L'Orange, two mules for hauling stuff that we could call Massey and Ferguson. Naming things had us laughing for some days.

The laughter kept a cover on the sharp edge of our fears about the coming years – the harshness of life after Peak Oil, the harshness of life in the country and the harsh reality that to sit down to a nice roast chicken dinner, we would first have to take a life.

Rick told us that even when he was growing up in the country, squeamishness was quite common. There were usually one or more people in the community who were fine with butchering animals and other farmers would call on them to come butcher their livestock, or take the livestock to them for butchering. His words made me feel a little less like I had two left farmer's feet when it came to doing the farming dance.

I became absorbed in my books on keeping chickens. The more I learned about these fascinating birds, the more Larry's words about me not being able to kill resonated. Chickens have personalities, and preferences; they have a social order. They need certain considerations in the winter and the summer and they like this or that to eat and this or that to do. To keep them healthy and happy the books gave me information on just about everything from how to treat scaly leg mite to what to feed a chook whose eggs have soft shells.

When I was in the supermarket one day about to buy a chicken for a Friday night roast, I suddenly realised that the clean, plucked and plastic bagged chook that I was about to buy had been a living, breathing thing that felt the cold in winter the same as me. As a reasonably intelligent middle-aged woman, I naturally knew that the roast I was about to make had once been a bird, but I had lived my entire life with a complete disassociation from the stark reality that to get that bird into the plastic bag and into the supermarket it had to first be killed by someone and then its beautiful feathers plucked, its feet and its head cut off and its organs pulled out. I can honestly say I had never previously taken a mouthful of chicken and pondered about its personality. I began to wonder if I would end up a vegetarian in the years to come simply because I couldn't take an axe to the neck of my little friend called Soup! Rick and Gwyn's daughter had become a committed vegan at age eleven after she became conscious of animal rights and animal cruelty. Why did I have to wait until my fifties to come to the same realisation?

Many times during the lead-up to our initial rural holiday I would back-pedal, fearful of the idea of leaving our home and the city. I would get angry that I'd ever heard about Peak Oil. I wanted to be blissfully ignorant of it, like our friends, but Peak Oil is like one of those ghastly big pimples you get on the end of your nose just before a big date – no amount of cover-up cream is going to make it go away.

My permaculture study was going well and by the time we were ready to leave for our holiday I had learned a great deal and had a good grounding in the design principles. This elementary information was going to (hopefully) help us choose a property with the ideal features for a permaculture farm. The day before we left, we took Maurice and Rebecca to the vet hospital to be boarded and when we went home to pack for the week we were as excited as two kids getting ready to go to their first school camp.

The drive north took us most of the day and when we arrived in Bellingen it was early afternoon. The town was sleepy and quiet and the bed and breakfast place we had booked had an old-world charm about it. We were to spend half our time there, and then, because there were previous bookings for guests going to the jazz festival, we were going to move to a self-contained holiday house with the magical name of Promised Land Cottages, just out of Bellingen. The Promised Land was the name of a really beautiful area to the north of Bellingen across the Bellinger River. It was lush, fertile open country that attracted celebrity escapees from Sydney. Unfortunately, the land was expensive.

We arranged to meet up with Georgina and her friend Wayne, the real estate agent, the next day and so we spent the rest of the afternoon relaxing and wandering about the little town centre. A fifteen-minute walk was all it took to cover the main street end to end.

Wayne met us early the next morning. Georgina had told him that we were there to look at rural properties but had no experience. Wayne had been born in the area and knew it intimately. He was a happy, warm and friendly guy who spoke extremely quickly. He didn't know I was deaf so he would chatter on happily with his head turned away from me as he peered off into the distance and in the beginning I had to guess a lot to work out what he was talking about. He got on very well with Larry and as we bumped and banged along unsealed country roads, he kept up a constant stream of dialogue that I hoped Larry would be able to recount for me later.

Wayne drove like a man possessed, as if he were late for his own wedding. His arm would wave out of the window at every passing car like the Queen in a motorcade. He knew everyone and they all knew him. He took us first to a farm that was currently on the market. The driveway was steep up to the house, which sat on the top of a hill. Wayne explained why it wouldn't be a good buy. The water tank beside the house was filled by a pump which was positioned at the bottom of the hill and across the road near a little creek.

'That little creek goes dusty dry at times,' he said, as he emptied a frog out of the overflow pipe on the tank, 'and there you are, up here with these lovely views and not a drop to drink!'

We wandered the property and as he walked, he would bend down and pull the odd weed out of the paddock. 'Fireweed! Always pull it out when you see it, eh?'

So we too got into the habit of recognising and pulling out fireweed. He explained about bushfires and soil and unsealed roads, about winds and the difference between summer and winter sun. He drove us to bush blocks that were uncleared, and blocks that were up tracks that would have daunted a mountain goat.

Wayne knew when every farm had last sold and what it had sold for. He knew what people were growing, what had succeeded and what had failed and why. With my new permaculture knowledge I was beginning to gain an understanding of the type of land that would best meet our needs and I was getting quite excited.

As Wayne spirited us about the countryside at breakneck speed, chattering and waving incessantly, a picture was forming in my mind of all the features that we should be looking for. Suddenly the road we were on sloped down to a wide, shallow but fast-flowing stream. We shot down the road and straight into the stream as if it were an airport runway. Water sprayed up on either side and Wayne just sped out the other side of the stream and onto the road again. Larry and I, strapped in by our seatbelts, were wide-eyed, but Wayne didn't miss a beat. He was in the process of explaining to us about floods and streams and frosts. A bit of water wasn't going to deter him from his lecture and he wanted to show us the other side of the stream … so why look for a bridge!

He showed us good dams and bad dams, he discussed the relative merits of chlorinated town water as opposed to fresh tank water from the roof (you need to factor in bat and bird droppings, apparently). He talked about fencing and river banks and the importance of knowing your neighbours well.

'Your relationship with your neighbours better be good. Don't get a place that shares access or water or whatever with your neighbours because if you have to share something and then that neighbour sells up or gets squashed under his tractor one day and a new mob takes the place, you just don't know if the new folk are going to let you do what you want. Neighbours are good for having a beer with at the end of the day, or helping you out, but you don't want to be depending on them. Some neighbours can be mongrels … real mongrels,' he said, nodding his head as if in agreement with himself.

We covered quite a few hundred kilometres criss-crossing about the Bellingen area with our travelling rural property guru, and our week's adventure was coming to an end. We were comfortable that we had seen enough real estate to come to grips with the area. More importantly, we were very grateful to Wayne for taking the time to teach us so much in such a short period of time. The trip had certainly been worthwhile. We both had developed a strong sense of what to look for.

Over dinner after our last trip with Wayne, I asked Larry what he felt was the best of all the valuable lessons Wayne had taught us. He stared off into the dimming distance of evening for a few moments and said, 'The best lesson I got from Wayne was to remember to drive with two hands!'

We had been given the names of a couple of people our age in the area and in the last few days we decided to call and make a date to meet them. They lived just outside of Coffs Harbour. We went to their home for afternoon tea and from the first hello it was as if we had known them all our lives. Nili and I shared the same feelings about kids and family and Pete and Larry seemed to gel, too. Their sense of humour and fun immediately put us at ease.

Nili and Pete had retired to Coffs Harbour after more than twenty years as cattle and sheep farmers. Pete had been a real estate agent in Sydney where he had met Nili, who had come to Sydney from Israel. They made the move to the country while they were still young and could relate well to the feelings that we were experiencing in making the transition.

Nili and Pete's knowledge about rural property was from a farmer's perspective rather than that of a real estate agent, and it turned out that they had lots of useful advice. They asked us where we were considering buying and we explained that we had only just begun our search. This past week had been a learning exercise in how to buy rural real estate, as far as we were concerned, so we weren't fixed on a particular area just yet. We explained that we had a two-year plan.

They told us that they had a friend, a very special old friend from their farming days, who would have lots of contacts for us and would be a very helpful person for us to meet. They arranged for us to meet him and his wife the following day. We were in for quite a surprise.

We met Nili and Pete the next day at a club on the beach at Coffs Harbour. It was a glorious bright sunny day and the gulls were squealing overhead in a gentle sea breeze as we waited for their friends. To our amazement, when they arrived we realised it was the shire councillor we had met at the Country Living Expo in Sydney! We couldn't believe it.

As Nili and Pete had promised, Rod McKelvey and his wife Pat were indeed a deep well of information and contacts. One of the contacts Rod recommended was the real estate agent who had been on the same Country Living Expo stand the day we met him in Sydney. He gave us his own business card and the agent's card as well, and told us to contact him if he could help us in any way.

We spent an hour just chatting with our new friends and laughed at the synchronicity of the universe – having met Rod in Sydney at the Expo and then Nili and Pete, and finding out that they were best friends. Rod and Pat were living in the Orara Valley north-west of Coffs Harbour and they recommended we take a drive up that way and have a look at the land there. They said it was a beautiful valley and worth our consideration. We agreed to go and after leaving them we drove up out of Coffs Harbour to investigate.

We were by this time fairly certain of what we wanted. The ideal property for us would have to be between four and eight hectares in an area with good rainfall, preferably gently sloping, ideally on a river or permanent creek. We wanted it to be on a sealed road, with mostly cleared land so we wouldn't have to do any heavy clearing, but still with some natural bushland. It should be in an area that would not be cut off from the closest town in flood times and the house should not require major work to make it liveable. Also, we wanted room to accommodate the kids should they decide to join us. Remembering Wayne's warnings, we knew that it should have its own access and water supply, a good dam and good fences.

Climbing up the slopes behind Coffs Harbour, the scenery was fantastic. The steep hills were covered with banana plantations that looked like well-combed green hair on a giant's head and Coffs Harbour was nestled at the bottom on a long fringe of white beach.

We drove into the valley. Farmhouses were dotted here and there in the green lush pastures or hidden in among thick natural bush. We meandered about, heading down side roads and dirt tracks. The countryside was open and sunny and the air was crystal clear. If we passed a paddock where a tractor was out dragging a slasher behind it, the smell of newly mown grass filled the air and was intoxicating.

There were For Sale signs on various places so we would stop and get out of the car for a better look. One farm we looked at had some possibilities; the land was gently sloping and it was on a sealed road, but we realised that the dam was situated midway between two properties. Remembering Wayne's dire warning about sharing things with neighbours, we rejected it. Another looked good but it was on a dirt road that had a steep dip that crossed a creek. We could see that in heavy rains the road would be under water.

It was early afternoon and we were heading back to the Promised Land Cottages in Bellingen when we passed another For Sale sign on a farm in Nana Glen. It was five hectares of undulating cleared land. At the road at the top of the property there was a strip of natural bush and at the bottom was the Orara River, according to the For Sale sign, although we couldn't see the river through the untouched bush strip. There was a circular dam near the bottom of the land. The rest of the property was like a park. A driveway from the road circled a pretty garden and led to a neat timber house with a wrap-around bull nose veranda. It was very pretty.

We noted the address and continued heading back. Both of us were a little dazed after seeing that place. It was very beautiful, in fact, too beautiful for this early in our search but we were mentally geared up to a long two-year search so although that little farm looked lovely, we let it sit in our minds as a place to look at and nothing more.

Back at the cottage, Larry called the agent that Rod had recommended and we arranged to meet him. We told him what we were looking for, and also mentioned the pretty place we had already seen in Nana Glen. He gave us some other addresses to look at and made an appointment for us to see the pretty one. The next day the agent met us at the gate of the five-hectare property we had asked about and showed us around. Larry and I couldn't look at each other. I had my checklist of questions and things we were looking for, and each question was answered in the affirmative. The house had four bedrooms and two bathrooms and a slow-combustion wood heater. Everything appeared to be in good condition. There was a shed with a tractor and ride-on mower and a stable for two horses. There were no access problems, or water problems and the property ended at the river bank. There was even an island. It seemed, according to our checklist, to be perfect.

We went on to see the other places the agent had recommended, but none had the appeal of the first one and each had some obvious flaw. Driving back to Bellingen it was hard for us to speak. We were both in a sort of trance. How was it possible that after only a few days we could find a place that met everything we had put on our list before we left Sydney?

Back at our cottage in the Promised Land, with evening fast approaching, we sat on the deck, barbecued some steaks and nursed glasses of red wine. Larry pointed to the neighbouring farmhouse. Beside the house, some distance into the trees, was an old rusted-out car body and right beside it a horse was grazing.

'Look at that,' he said, with the wisp of a grin. 'That ... is the future!'

The clear black sky was heavily filigreed with stars. The night sounds of the bush barely disturbed the stillness and quiet. The smell was clean and the air was crisp and cool after the heat of the day. It had been five days since we left Sydney and in those short five days, we had grown closer than we thought possible. We hardly had to speak because we were so at one with each other. We laughed a lot remembering our hair-raising drives with Wayne, and the strange coincidence of meeting Nili and Pete and their friend Rod who we had met in Sydney. What I remember most about that night, though, was the feeling of awe that from a chance encounter with Rod in Sydney, we had followed a path that led us to a farm we thought we may be falling in love with.

Sitting across the table from Larry, I was suddenly awash with tears. Up until we had met again after all those years and subsequently married, my life had been just plain hard. He had come back into my life and filled it with so much joy and so much fun and laughter and love. I said: 'I don't believe I could go on living any more if you weren't in my life. I just want you to know that.'

He raised his glass to me, took my hand and told me he felt the same way ... that our relationship had brought him so much richness and so much pleasure. He said his only regret was that his parents had not been alive to meet me: 'My parents would have adored you as much as I do.'

That night, enjoying our belated honeymoon, I looked over at my husband of twelve years and wondered what the future would hold for us. We were contemplating a life so different from the only one we had known. Could we do it? Could we trust each other to make this change? Could I do it? Would I feel as safe and protected with Larry out in the country as I did in the city? Larry had been the most incredible partner for all those years. Would this move to the country change him? Change us?

He had slipped effortlessly into the role of husband to me, father to my children and son-in-law to my aging parents. He had been by my side through three gruelling spinal operations and nursed me back to health. He had become the doting, caring and constant father-figure that my children had never known. He had become all things to each member of my family.

I had only ever seen him lose control once. At the time we had taken in my parents and my brother John and his wife to live with us. Larry had driven me home from hospital after an operation and I was in a lot of pain. He wanted to bring the car as close to the front door as possible but my brother's car was parked in the way. He called to my brother to move his car but my brother, who was going through a fairly severe breakdown at the time, couldn't be bothered. Larry sprang from the car and ran into the house. He picked up my brother, who was no lightweight, slammed him up against the wall and screamed, 'Don't you *ever* treat *my* wife with such disrespect!' and then he dropped him to the floor. John moved the car. Yes, remembering that time, I knew I could feel safe with Larry.

Contemplating the enormity of what we were going to do, making such a huge change in our lifestyle, I wondered if Larry, who was such an animal of habit, would make the transition easily. My fears for my own ability to make the transition were enormous. My health issues were great and I was just plain scared. That fear, however, was overridden by the fear of not making the move. I could imagine clearly how terrible it would be if we did nothing, now that we knew about Peak Oil. I would feel like I'd failed my family if we didn't act on the knowledge we had, and endeavour to secure our kids' futures with a place where they could be close to their food source, away from the confines and dependencies of a large city, if need be. With Larry, the one thing that I did feel certain about was his ability to protect me, and that he was strong enough to handle the physical work. Since the loss of my parents and brother, Larry had easily worn the mantle of head of the family. I trusted him completely and I hoped he trusted me.

We talked about the little farm we had found and reluctantly agreed that there was nothing we could do about it because we weren't ready. We had not even had our home in Sydney valued, let alone sold, and by the time it was sold no doubt the farm would be gone. One thing was certain; we were committed to making the move and finding a place just like the one we had fallen in love with.

We went to see it again at dawn the next morning and were more convinced than the previous day that it would have been really perfect for us. The open pastures were bathed in early morning sunlight and the gentle slope was ideal for creating a forest of fruit trees, as the slope was north-facing and somewhat protected from winds and frosts. We were sad we couldn't put a deposit down to secure it but we wouldn't have dreamed of buying something without first having sold.

Heading home, we became more and more depressed the closer we came to Sydney. The air became thicker with the smell of car and truck exhaust, the traffic built up and slowed, and the houses were too close together. It didn't feel good to be back in the crowded, hassled atmosphere of a big city.

Also, the closer we got to our home, the spectre of the chaos that Peak Oil could cause came flooding back into my mind, and I just wanted to escape again. Ahead of us was the process of selling the house, which would involve all the stress of opening it up to the public and keeping it pristine. I hated the selling process. The market was down so there was a likelihood that it would take some time to sell. We knew we would lose our favourite little farm to someone else. Still, we had learned a lot over this last week, and, having spent that time together with no distractions or demands on us from work or family or anyone, we had reconfirmed our commitment to each other and that gave a powerful boost to our plans.

During our first week home, Larry went off for his annual health check and blood test and I started the process of selling the house. I contacted the agent who had originally sold the house to us. I told him I was advertising it myself and that I would list it with him as well. A few days later I was sitting painting in my ceramics class when a friend walked in. I was surprised to see her because I didn't know she was taking the same class as me. She set herself up beside me and we both worked on our ceramic projects and were chatting quietly together. I said, 'Know anyone who wants to buy a two-bedroom semi? Ours is on the market.'

Without missing a brushstroke she said, 'Yes, me.'

My heart skipped a beat. 'Come and see it after class if you like.' I was trying not to sound excited.

She came, loved the house and wanted it. I couldn't believe what was happening. Her husband came to inspect it that night and also loved it and they agreed to buy it. Larry and I were incredulous. The agent had advertised it for a viewing for that weekend and here were friends wanting to buy it. Surely it wasn't going to be this easy!

At the end of the week, our doctor called. He wanted to see Larry. We were so caught up in the process of selling the house and reading all our back-to-basics books that it didn't occur to us that this phone call was in any way unusual. Larry made an appointment to see the doctor.

In the meantime, the agent was showing people through the house, and our friends who had originally wanted to buy the house decided against it but had told a friend of theirs about it. She had been looking for a place in the area for some time and fell in love with it. Then another couple came to see it as a result of my own ad and they too loved it. A few days passed with the two buyers coming and inspecting and discussing and um-ing and ah-ing and each making offers to our solicitor. And then it was over. We accepted the highest offer.

We were in a state of excitement. It had all happened so fast. And there went our two-year plan, just like that. We'd expected that it could take a very long time to find the right farm and then sell the house, but this was plain unbelievable. What it meant was that we could move to the country straight away. It wasn't quite what we'd intended, but I think something in us had changed the moment we'd arrived on the north coast, and neither of us questioned the idea of leaving the city this soon.

The house had been sold and I called the country agent to see if the farm we had so loved was still on the market. I had my heart in my throat as I called him.

'Yes,' he said. 'It's still for sale.'

Larry and I had decided on the price we were prepared to pay and so I made an offer and we waited impatiently for a response. If it wasn't accepted it meant we were going to keep looking and we were quite prepared for that. After a few tense days of phone calls to and from the agent, a deal was agreed upon and the farm was ours.

The kids couldn't believe that all this had happened so quickly. We couldn't believe it either. We really were going to leave the city in preparation for what might happen after oil production peaked. We were going to prepare for the future as we understood it. We were going to 'dig our well before we needed it' and we hoped that we could achieve it! We had no experience of country life except for the romantic notions fuelled by what we had seen on TV or in movies, but that wasn't important now. We would learn.

Then, just as we were hitting the heights of happiness, Larry went for his appointment with our doctor, Richard. I went with him. Richard explained that Larry's blood test results were unusual. His prostate was showing some unusual findings, much different from last year's result, and he would have to be examined. If Larry was scared he didn't show it. The doctor went behind the curtain to give him a rectal examination and I heard Larry say, 'Well Richard, after knowing you all these years, it looks like we are about to become very, *very* close friends!'

The rectal exam confirmed for the doctor that Larry's prostate was indeed enlarged and needed specialist attention. We were facing the possibility of the 'big C' – cancer! I reeled with shock but Larry just took the news as if he had been told he had long toenails.

Back at home, sitting in our pergola with hot tea, we were silent for some time and then Larry said, 'Darling, what is to be will be. I will go to the specialist and if it's cancer then we will just deal with it like we have dealt with everything else.'

I wanted to be as philosophical as him. I wanted to be as calm, but my heart was racing and I was just plain scared. Larry was the centre of my world. He had become the rock on which I depended for everything. Through the horror years of my parents' illnesses and subsequent deaths and my brother's untimely death, through the process of accepting the inevitable outcome of Peak Oil, through everything, Larry was the one who kept our lives 'steady as she goes'. He never got sick. I was the sickly one. When it came to infirmity, we had both come to terms long ago with the knowledge that my degenerative spinal condition would eventually get the better of me, and we had joked about getting me a fancy wheelchair with tractor tyres. Larry never even got a cold. And now the threat of cancer was hanging over his head!

Time hung suspended until the day we were to go to the specialist. We had exchanged contracts on the house and the farm, and I had booked to travel to Melbourne to attend a two-week permaculture course being run by the famous Bill Mollison himself at Melbourne University. None of these things seemed to matter any more. All I cared about was Larry and his health. He was as upbeat as ever and I marvelled at his ability to just deal with it.

Finally, we went to see the specialist, who arranged for Larry to have a biopsy. During all of this time, we had been in touch by email with Nili and Pete in Coffs Harbour and, amazingly, they were going through the same thing at the same time as we were. Pete had to have a prostate biopsy too. It just felt so surreal. Life was happening too fast and the coincidences were raining down on us like autumn leaves. But in its swiftness there was a quality about that time, a feeling of inevitability, some sort of pattern.

Prostate cancer generally is pretty slow-growing and doesn't usually run rampant through the body leading to early death, unless there are complications. But this knowledge did nothing for my fears – or for Nili's fears either – as we waited for the results of our husbands' tests.

I simply couldn't conceive of life without Larry, should he be unlucky enough to be one of the few who finds cancer and then suddenly is being planted in the ground. And to find this out when we were in the middle of the house sale and farm purchase – it was as if we were somehow being reminded about what is really important, about not ever taking each other or anything for granted. An old joke played back in my mind about a guy looking for a parking spot. He says to God: 'If you find me a parking spot I will go to church every Sunday for the rest of my life.' A moment later there appears the perfect vacant spot, and the guy says to God, 'Forget that last request, God – I just found one!'

The results of the biopsy were clear. No prostate cancer. Larry just took the results with the same calmness as he had the initial test results, while I wanted to dance and scream with relief. We called Nili and Pete to tell them and thankfully Pete's results were also okay. The journey we had been on that had ground to a halt during this health scare chugged back into life and we were moving forward again; only this time, we were moving with a new sense of resolve. Whatever life was going to throw our way, we would simply deal with it. It became our catchcry.

Just before I was due to leave for the course on permaculture in Melbourne, Larry was looking through his paperwork, sorting and organising things as he knew he was now definitely going to resign from his job. We had to put some definite structure to our finances immediately. We were shocked to find a document that was with his retirement savings papers that said his retirement age had been put up to sixty-five instead of sixty. He must have overlooked it when it originally arrived. That would have meant nine years of working life left instead of the four years we had been calculating. If there was ever a moment when we might have wavered about his early retirement, that document wiped it out. There was no way he wanted to work for the company for the next four years, let alone *nine* more years! The culture of the company was changing. They were bringing in more twelve-hour shifts, and compulsory security tags now had to be worn at all times so that management could track any employee during working hours. They would even know when their staff went to the bathroom! Larry could see that there would also be increasing pressure to outsource the IT work. He didn't want to be part of that culture change and definitely didn't want the extra hours of travel to their new location.

By comparison, the same five years spent on the farm would see us in a position where our fruit trees would be reaching maturity, our vegetable gardens would be well established and productive, and the enormous adjustment we knew we would have to make to country living would have been achieved.

We needed every moment from now on to get the farm organised and productive. I packed my bags and Larry drove me to the airport to fly to Melbourne.

Chapter Five

I arrived in Melbourne and our youngest daughter Missy met me at the airport. Taking the permaculture course and being away from Larry was going to be hard because we had not been apart for that long in the past. I had also become so accustomed to depending on him that I knew I was putting myself way out of my comfort zone.

I am no longer the type of person who enjoys meeting people or being away from the comfort, privacy and solitude of my home. Having spent more than a decade as a single parent, dealing with everything on my own and then working with people all my life both in the recruitment industry and earlier when I was nursing, I had, I felt, met all the people I had ever wanted to meet. Such intense focus on people had turned me into somewhat of a hermit, happy in my own company and my own space. To leave home and share my daughter's flat and live with her flatmates was going to challenge me. Also as a result of my preference for a solitary existence and long years driving myself wherever I needed to go, the challenge of using public transport to get myself to and from the university was something I was actually afraid of. The final challenge for me was going to be taking in all the information the course was going to give. I hadn't undertaken formal lectures for about thirty-five years and I was afraid that I wouldn't be able to handle it. But Larry and I had placed so much importance on this course for our future on the farm that I felt a great pressure to succeed. Permaculture promised to make our desire for self-sustainability a reality. Failure to master the information from this course was not an option.

Missy shared a rundown house with four other people. The three male housemates of the foursome were studying for their Bachelor of Circus degrees. Just the title of their degree made me chuckle. I had never heard of such a degree. I had been to circuses since my childhood but never considered that the clowns and jugglers and circus performers needed to be degree-qualified just to have pies thrown in their faces or to chuck armloads of bowling pins or machetes in the air. Missy's final housemate was a bright, attractive young woman called Sarah who had what an oldie like me would call a 'proper job'. It was the first time I had experienced living in my daughter's patch instead of her living in mine and her patch appeared to be much more fun. She warned me to expect the unexpected. It sounded a little ominous.

The house was littered with the sorts of things one doesn't normally find in a suburban home. There were black velvet-covered trays with cups and saucers glued on them in straight lines in readiness for a certain trick, a stop sign at the front door, a trolley in the hall on which juggling knives had been carefully laid out; witches hats piled higgledy-piggledy and riotously coloured bits of costumes everywhere. In the lounge there was an eclectic collection of furniture garnered from piles of discards from the streets. In the two weeks I lived there I often would wake in the morning to find strange bodies asleep on various pieces of furniture in parts of the room, although by evening they were mysteriously gone. I chose not to speculate on whether anyone in the house actually knew these comatose people who nestled in for the night and then disappeared in the light of day.

Missy told me she woke up one morning and walked into the kitchen to make her breakfast. During the night the kitchen table had become a creative canvas for one of her housemates. Fifteen differently shaped knives had been stuck into the wooden table – steak knives, butter knives, and big pirate swords used for juggling. What made it even more bizarre, Missy said, was that there seemed to be a tacit respect for the 'knife installation breakfast table' and so the housemates carefully placed their meals or groceries in and around the knives until the magic of the artwork had passed and one day it disappeared.

Sharing a home with people whose chosen profession is literally 'clowning around' is just an open invitation for almost anything to happen. Sarah returned home at four o'clock one morning to find her doorframe completely covered with sheets of newspaper. To get into her room she had to make a run at it and burst through the paper! It wouldn't have surprised her if she had found a cheering audience on the other side.

On another occasion, the guys managed to seemingly jam her door shut so that she would be effectively locked out of her own room. When she got home she naturally couldn't get in. She asked the guys to help her and they all gallantly endeavoured to help. They all tried a variety of ways to get the door un-jammed but to no avail. She left them to go and find some tools as they pretended to struggle to get the door open for her. While she was gone, they quickly unlocked the door and one of them slipped silently inside before they locked it back up again. Another frustrating hour passed for her until finally she managed to get the door to open, only to find when she swung it open, one of the guys who had been 'helping' her on the other side relaxing on her bed!

It surprised me that I was able to adjust effortlessly to carrying on a casual conversation with someone who just happened to be standing on their hands or eating my dinner while someone juggled meat cleavers beside me in the kitchen.

On the other hand I was so full of anxiety about the whole business of attending the course that I didn't know which of my fears to deal with first. Travelling by tram from one end of Melbourne to the other was a major one. I had visions of me getting on a tram and never being seen again. This was a fear I hadn't felt since I was a child. Rationally I knew it was ridiculous. I had lived in other cities, found my way through London and Toronto, and I was a mature, sensible woman but still, the intensity of my fear shocked me.

The day before the course commenced, Missy drove me along the route I would have to take on the tram to help me familiarise myself with the area. I felt as if our roles had reversed and I was the child while Missy was the parent. In the car, I looked over at my daughter and saw her through totally different eyes. She was my baby, but the person driving the car was a confident, urbane, beautiful and accomplished young woman, well used to adapting to new environments as a result of her years in Europe.

She had left us as a skinny young girl with a backpack that was bigger than her small frame and she had made her way in the world with ease. She had lived and worked in London, travelled around Europe and even worked in a refugee centre in northern Italy. Her ability to adapt like a chameleon to her surroundings gave her a cool, confident air that I admired. I used to have it once too but it had worn away over the years and now, in middle age, I was as nervous as a kid on the first day of school.

Because Missy is a psychologist, she was keenly aware of my fears and I could tell that she was dealing with me as she would one of her clients, with patience, good humour and positive reinforcement. Of all our kids, I felt that Missy would potentially be the one who would cope best with the inevitable deprivations that would occur when oil depletion put even the most basic commodities out of reach.

Another anxious thought I had was that because of my deafness, I wouldn't be able to hear the lectures. I hoped that I would be able to sit at the front of the class to make hearing easier, but at the same time, sitting in front was going to put me in a situation where I couldn't easily hide if I fell asleep or wasn't coping. I didn't know what to wear and didn't really know what to take with me. When I was unpacking in Missy's room, she actually fell back onto her bed laughing hysterically when she saw the pencil case I had brought. It was about the size of a large handbag and contained every possible thing a student might need. I had dozens of pens in all colours and styles, pencils, coloured pencils, stapler and extra staples, a hole-punch, liquid paper, ruler, post-it notes. I had gone to the stationery shop and stood there wondering what I would need and eventually chose one of everything I could see. She thinned down my supply to a few pens, assuring me I would manage.

On the first day of the course, I set the clock for two hours before it was reasonable to wake, because I was so afraid I would get lost on the way to the university and I didn't want to arrive late on my first day. My anxiety level was making me physically sick. Intellectually I was ashamed that I was having these feelings. I had always been the strong, independent, confident woman running a business and a home and now I was trembling at the thought of attending a course in a strange city. It didn't occur to me that I was brave enough to give away everything I knew and held dear in order to move to the country and start again; at this point I was solely focused on my fear.

I dressed carefully in what I thought was appropriate university attire of jeans and a shirt and hoisted my heavy backpack onto my shoulders. I felt ridiculous walking to the tram stop on that first morning. Here I was, a little, fat fifty-five year old woman, wearing what I had always considered to be 'young people's gear' and with a backpack that was definitely not Louis Vuitton! I was in the grip of absolute terror standing at the tram stop all alone. The streets were empty and I hadn't set foot on a tram since my school days in Brisbane in the early 1960s. I didn't even know how to pay my fare! Missy had told me about the ticket machines on the trams but it took me a few moments to press all the right buttons and get the right ticket. I felt stupid as I fumbled with coins and buttons to press.

I staggered to a seat and found that the backpack prevented me from sitting comfortably, so I perched awkwardly on the edge. I must have looked as though I was ready to spring up and flee the tram at any second. I scanned the streets as the tram slid silently along, hoping that I had caught the right one and was heading in the right direction.

The tram was filling with people, most of whom didn't seem to have the trouble I had with the ticket machine. In fact, as I watched them get on, many didn't even bother getting a ticket at all. Some read books while many wore headsets and were listening to music. I could neither read nor listen to music. I had turned my hearing aids way up to full volume to hear everything I could and I was too nervous to read or take my eyes off the passing streets and buildings.

It seemed to take forever to get to Melbourne University and because I didn't know which was the right stop, I got off the tram two stops too soon and had to walk with the heavy backpack weighing me down. By the time I arrived I was exhausted and then I had to try to decipher the map I had been given to find the right building on campus. When I found it, the doors were closed and I still had three-quarters of an hour to kill. I laughed at my own foolishness, and remembered the day my eldest son was going on his first primary school camp. He was so excited that he made me drive him to school at about 7 am for the bus which was scheduled to leave at 9 am! I figured maybe 'early arrivals' must be genetic.

I wandered off to find a coffee shop and when I got back to the building, people were gathered outside. They were an interesting looking group but I was at first too shy to approach them. I am notoriously bad at small talk. When I did eventually begin chatting to some of them, I was surprised to learn that many were from overseas.

Registration took a few minutes and I was issued with course notes and a name tag. I started to feel excited as I walked down the hall with all the other new students. The lecture theatre was steeply banked with seats and they were filling rapidly. I found a seat in the front row and to my horror realised that there was a camera crew setting up their gear. The whole course was going to be filmed! I sank as low in my seat as I could, but unless I sat right under the flip-up desk there was no way I was going to avoid being filmed.

I took out my notepad and a pen, and then another pen in case that one ran out, then decided I should have a pencil handy in case both pens failed. Anyone watching would have thought this strange little lady in the front row was suffering from some obsessive compulsive disorder. I was laughing at myself inside, but still went on with my preparations.

Bill Mollison, the pioneer of permaculture, sauntered in as if he were about to hang out at a backyard barbecue with a bunch of mates. He had a cup of tea in his hand, one of many which over the next two weeks would become the icon that symbolised Bill. He is a grizzly old white-bearded man, with an awesome intellect and a stage presence and delivery as polished and perfectly timed as that of Bob Hope. The humour with which he laced his facts riveted every student in the room.

Bill began by explaining the concept of permaculture. He told us that permaculture is a system of design that enables the creation of sustainable human environments. He had originally coined the word from *perma*nent agri*culture*. He added that there was a 'human' element to the word culture – and human cultures can't survive for very long if they don't have land for an agricultural system or food source which is sustainable or renewable. Permaculture embodies the relationships between not only plants and animals and birds but also all the things necessary for people, like houses, out-buildings, the supply of power and water, and a means of communication, and, finally, where all these things are placed in relationship to one another.

His explanation was very elegant and simple for such a complex design system and as he spoke, there were a lot of what I call 'aha moments' where I could so easily visualise the logical reasons for doing things a certain way. What I was about to study for the next two weeks with this fascinating rascal of a man was so vital for the successful creation of our self-sustaining property, I wrote down furiously almost every-thing he said. Later, reviewing my notes, I realised that I had also noted down his little asides, like his recipe for a Gin Buck

– two fingers of gin, one can of Sprite and fill with ice! I wondered when that would come in handy on the farm.

Bill proclaimed as he scanned the class: 'Now we are living in a dangerous system. We'll be out of everything very soon.' He then drifted into a side issue about twenty-one agricultural sprays that are poisons we all carry in our systems from herbicides and pesticides and how seven of them are cumulative. He announced grandly that we are 'walking disposal boxes full of heavy metals'.

On that sombre and worrisome note the lecture continued with an explanation of how coasts are no longer stable and the southern states of America are disappearing. 'Goodbye Egypt, Bangladesh, Texas, California. We have set up a system that will ultimately destroy itself!'

He described all the gruesome things that humanity has done which are literally killing our planet. These were things I had heard and read before, but hearing his explanations and facts made that knowledge come alive. He said that the carrying capacity of the planet is two billion people or less, but right now we numbered over six billion and there was much poverty and starvation.

'I have a very simple solution to the problem of overpopulation,' he said with a twinkle in his eye At that point he stopped. He looked around at each of the seventy students in the room. You could feel the tension rising. What was the next pearl of wisdom about to be cast before us?

He said with a smirk, 'I believe that one half of the world's population should eat the other half! That eliminates two problems in one go. It reduces the population and eliminates starvation!' While everyone laughed heartily, the message was still very clear and very worrying. What he was really alluding to was what naturalists call the law of 'survival of the fittest' and what economists grandly call 'demand destruction'.

Basically, demand destruction means allowing market forces to moderate demand by inflating the price of a commodity to a point where many people can't afford it. When that commodity is oil, the consequences are dire. I read an article about it on the internet called 'Demand Destruction: Who Gets Destroyed'. The author, Kurt Cobb, explained:

The heightened price of oil would certainly encourage conservation —
i.e., demand destruction — but that conservation might come in the form of
terrible hardship for millions and perhaps billions of people and possibly death
for many. That would give a rather gruesome connotation to the notion of
demand destruction. High prices would also encourage the development of
alternative energy sources, but that's assuming that world society does not become
so disoriented and chaotic that such efforts cannot actually be effected.

Larry and I had done our homework; we had evaluated Peak Oil and, basically, we didn't want to be part of the millions suffering terrible hardship, and we didn't want that for our kids.

Bill went on to discuss the problem of salinity. Dryland salinisation, where farming land gradually becomes unusable due to rising salt, is a massive problem in Australia: it's been called our worst environmental crisis. He finished the morning lecture with an announcement that the salting-up of rural Australian land is a political problem created by pumping rights being over-allocated, and farmers clearing away too many trees and forests. He then paused and looked about the room at all of us.

'The situation is curable,' he said and then paused, 'but only if there is enough of us!' By the time he suggested that it was a good moment to stop for a nice cup of tea, the entire student body was so depressed we would have gladly accepted a paper cup of cordial laced with cyanide, quietly held hands and lain down to die.

In the tea break I began to get to know a few of my fellow students. I was among the oldest in the class. Most of the other students were young, eager and highly motivated. They had come from North and South America, Vietnam, Burma, China, Germany and Scandinavia, New Zealand, the Netherlands, England – from all over the world – to hear Bill Mollison speak. Some worked in third-world countries with non-government organisations, some were involved in developing their own properties and some were concerned enough about Peak Oil, as I was, to seek an alternative way of life, living close to their food source.

For the rest of the day, Bill spoke fluently and spontaneously about the fundamentals of permaculture design. He challenged us constantly, and sprinkled his lecture with anecdotes about his assignments around the globe. He spoke like a keenly observant person, curious and vastly knowledgeable. I was in awe of all he'd seen and done.

Again, I wrote everything down. I later found that I had written in the margin of one page his observation that African women working in their fields don't bend their legs, but bend from the waist whereas Asian women do bend their legs. I'm sure, along with the Gin Buck recipe, this knowledge might come in handy one day … Larry certainly couldn't accuse me of not paying attention!

Bill had led a colourful life and had developed a strong and healthy cynicism for the honesty and integrity of governments, the veracity of religion and the real motives of big business and just about every other institution – and with good reasons that he was only too happy to share.

After the first day, I was both mentally exhausted and intellectually over-stimulated. My hand hurt from the constant writing and my belly ached from the constant laughter. Bill Mollison was a showman as well as an anarchist and a passionate and irreverent conservationist. But most of all, he was a serious scientist, an expert, and we were all hanging on every word he uttered. Underneath his hilarious stories was a constant message – the natural world is in trouble and unless enough people take the issues seriously, humanity will be in trouble. I was deeply affected by his words.

It occurred to me then that no amount of money, no amount of make-up or acrylic fingernails and designer clothes or sleek expensive cars or fancy homes with imported furnishings can mask who we really are. We are just mammals in the natural world and we need the same things that all mammals need. We need healthy food or we will die. We need clean water or we will die. We need fresh air or we will die. We need shelter and, because we are herd animals, we need each other.

I reflected on my life, my comfortable city life and how far away from natural and healthy it really was. I knew nothing about the natural world. Like everyone else, I had read about pollution and extinctions and forests being felled for wood chips and oil spills and I was beginning to feel ashamed that it had all been so 'ho hum terrible terrible, pass the salt dear, I like that sweater where did you get it!' for me until now.

Travelling home that evening, I took a long look at my fellow passengers as the tram gradually filled up. It was cold and everyone wore coats or jackets and scarves and beanies. But fashion at the time dictated that young women should have bare bellies and as I sat there I marvelled at the power of the dictates of the fashion world. Here were sensible, normal young women, well dressed in warm clothes, but with sweaters short enough to leave their bellies exposed to the elements. Clearly common sense is not as powerful as marketing. So we buy what is available to buy, we use what we are given; we conform so that corporations and governments can make money. And we do these things willingly because they are sold to us with a dream and a story, and that story is 'what we sell you, or get you to do, is in your best interests'.

I had just spent the day learning what is really in our best interests and it certainly wasn't what I was seeing on that smelly, overcrowded tram packed with people wearing ridiculous fashion, their hair and faces coloured with dyes, paints and powders – most of which would have been imported, and most of which would have been made from products that were derivatives of oil.

Outside the tram I saw parks with vast expanses of lawns which were neatly mowed and on which grew flowers and trees for the sole purpose of being looked at and admired. They too were of no value to the mammals that enjoyed them aesthetically. Somehow suddenly the city seemed like a ridiculous place of artificiality; a place that didn't support the inhabitants, but rather supported the companies that sold products that the inhabitants had to buy. And to get people to buy these things, they had to be convinced that they were good things even if they weren't.

So much marketing is geared to creating a need, and that is done by appealing to our fears and desires and lusts and dreams. Marketing doesn't sell products; it sells the fulfilment of dreams, and it promises results that are only achievable in our minds. The resulting disappointment then must be satisfied by the next product that promises to better satisfy that dream, and so on.

Bill Mollison had lived in the bush alone. He had lived in Africa and Asia and he had grown his own food, or gathered it from the bush. This two-week course could not possibly prepare me (and therefore Larry) for what we were undertaking. Discarding the life we led in the city meant more than just learning how to neatly tuck seedlings into the garden. It meant accepting our real place in the greater scheme of things, not following blindly the whims and wishes of our consumer society. At that moment, we had no idea about how to live outside consumer society. We were soft, ignorant and gullible.

Bill talked about soils and how it has taken five to six million years to create topsoils. There I sat, scribbling notes about soil and its properties, and a thought danced across my mind as my pen flew across the paper. A few short months ago I would have been fascinated about Oprah Winfrey's latest weight-loss tips – and now here I was hungering for more information about what constituted soil.

'Let the grass grow,' Bill said, 'then mow it and leave the grass clippings to lie there until the grass grows up again, and then mow again and let the organic matter layer up. Leave it there. Plant trees and never sell anything off a farm that can't walk off or fly off. Don't remove vegetation. It is the continuation of life on the farm.' He said that with vegetables and fruits, the scraps and spare leaves should all be composted and returned to the soil.

'Worms,' he went on, 'are wondrous things. Worms put on sixty tons of worm castings per acre per year. Darwin proved that worms create the soils of the earth. [Worm castings – or worm poop – enriches soil.] In the deserts their role is taken over by termites and rodents and dung beetles.' Bill's knowledge of and respect for the humble earthworm made us all rethink our opinions of these slimy wriggly things.

He talked about trees and water and how you can actually make gardens on concrete. He talked about seeds and animals and birds and whales and changing the level of acidity of soil. He talked about a good farmer being someone who grows worms and told us about a friend of his who 'employs six million worms on his farm'. He described jungles and explained about the importance of marshlands and plains and deserts. He painted brilliantly coloured word pictures for us of the exotic places he had worked all over the world where he had shown people how to create abundance out of nothing just by using the laws of nature instead of abusing them. Many times I found I had tears in my eyes. His anger and disgust would rise when he spoke about what genetically modified crops are doing to the natural world, and about the corporations who amassed great fortunes 'harvesting from misery'.

We are so ignorant and we are kept so ignorant about the food that is sold to us, the products that are manufactured for our 'comfortable lives'. In Bill's class, I felt small and old and ineffectual. We are, all over the world, the blind sheep that are herded and ruled by the very corporations that employ us. We wonder why we are all getting so sick, why we are getting fat, why our modern clever society is so corrupt, so morally bankrupt. Profit is more important than a healthy environment because profit is what keeps the economy going and a healthy economy keeps the corporations going that employ us. We are wonderful mice on magnificent wheels.

Bill spoke with genuine pride about his own farms in Tasmania and northern New South Wales and told us how he had planted them with thousands and thousands of trees to create what he called 'food forests'. The whole room was spellbound by his words and his knowledge and experiences. He was a man in tune with nature, a man who had spent his life with his hands in the soil. One student raised his hand and said, 'Bill, can you tell us please, do you talk to your plants?'

Bill looked at the earnest face of the young student and for a moment was silent. Then he answered him. 'Too right I do, my friend.'

The student asked 'What sorts of things do you say to your plants?' Everyone in the room was silent, leaning forward to hear the botanical secret that this man of nature was going to impart to us. Bill's eyes sparkled as he looked at the eager young man who had asked such a serious question.

He said, 'I say to my plants: "Grow you bastards or I will pull the lot of you out!"'

Bill was one of two lecturers. The other was Geoff Lawton. Geoff was all business. His understanding and experience with permaculture spanned twenty-seven years and he too had an impressive history of working all over the world, turning deserts into food forests, making prosperity and abundance where there had been only poverty and subsistence living. His passion and his knowledge were palpable and in his self-deprecating and gentle way, he made me feel that everything that he was teaching was doable even for someone as physically incapacitated as me.

I spoke to Geoff during the course and arranged for him to come to our farm and consult with us on the plans we would develop. We didn't have the luxury of being able to fail, I told him, and although Geoff was heavily booked with assignments in many different countries for the next twelve months, he did have a break in his schedule around Christmas so I made a firm booking. It made me feel comfortable that we would be able to have an expert in right at the beginning to get us underway.

Because I had to sit in the front row in order to hear well enough, I was often sitting with either Bill's wife Lisa or Geoff's wife Nadia. Both women were extremely knowledgeable and very friendly. I told them why Larry and I were moving out of the city and about our concerns for the future and the possible effects of the end of the age of cheap oil. I also warned them both that at some point during the course I was expecting to receive a phone call from my son telling me that I had become a grandmother.

We discussed Peak Oil at some length and they turned out to be as concerned about it as we were. For the very first time,

I found that I was not alone in knowing about this situation. In fact, all the students in the class were aware of Peak Oil, aware and concerned enough to want to find ways of mitigating the effects on them of a world after cheap oil. It felt amazing to be one of many, instead of alone with the knowledge of Peak Oil as Larry and I had been in Sydney. While the Peak Oil 'community' at that time was relatively small globally, it was growing rapidly thanks to the Yahoo chat groups on the internet like Running on Empty Oz and others around the world.

When people learn about Peak Oil, their need for confirmation and understanding is monumental. The drive to grasp the reality of it becomes a powerful force that will just not be silenced once you start to research Peak Oil. The chat groups allow people to feel that they are among kindred spirits, people who do not think that they are freaks. We went through it alone, except for Rick, but few are fortunate to have someone like him to lean on. As time passes however, and more information becomes mainstream news, more people will begin to see what we were seeing and hopefully they will band together for support.

The new knowledge I was gaining was changing me rapidly. It was a good change in one sense, because I knew that what I was learning was real and important and right. But in another sense it was stripping away from me everything that had constituted my security in the world I had grown up in, and in which I had raised my children. I was learning things that deep within me I somehow knew but had just always ignored.

The intoxicating drug of modern society was a powerful one and it was going to be hard to break away from it. I knew that instinctively, and in some sense I also knew that either we had to break away now, on our own terms, or at some later stage we would be forced to change – and that mightn't be so pleasant.

As the days passed and the lectures progressed, I found that a sort of broad overview of permaculture was crystallising in my mind. It is really very neat and very simple. Essentially a person using permaculture principles is using raw nature as a template. If you go for a walk in a forest or any tract of untouched bushland, it is immediately obvious that no one has gone into the bush and ploughed it up or watered it or fertilised it or sprayed it with pesticides. It hasn't needed trees planted or pruning or any other kind of external inputs.

The natural bush, an untouched forest, is a completely self-sustaining system. It doesn't suffer from drought or frost, it doesn't grow in neat rows, and every available space is used in some way. Trees or bushes or plants that don't do well together don't survive, but those that benefit from close proximity to each other do survive. The soil is alive and undisturbed and it is constantly provided with nutrients in the form of rotting organic matter from the trees and plants growing there. No one has to dig it up or plough or fertilise. Leaf litter, twigs and other organic matter just fall and rot and nourish the soil. Each tree or plant has pests and predators that eat the pests. Everything is in balance and everything thrives. It has adapted to the place it is in. All the insects and animals and birds that live in the bush benefit from the system and in turn return something to the system, perhaps their droppings or seeds that they spread, or by being part of the food chain. That system seems to have done very well for the entire life of the planet, so why not copy it – why not use the principles of nature?

A permaculture designer uses the same principles: let nature do the work and take advantage of the natural laws. In designing a property using permaculture principles, whether it is a farm in the country or a backyard garden in the city, each part of the system has to be connected to each other part and contribute positively to it. For example, small, shallow-rooted, shade-loving plants can be thickly planted with deep-rooted, sun-loving plants. Each contributes to the other's well-being. Beans can grow up cornstalks – so the corn not only produces corn, it also provides a living trellis for the beans. Permaculture planning ensures that everything has multiple uses and connections to everything else.

Thinking about the house we had sold in Sydney, the garden that I had loved so much was now, with this new knowledge, completely useless. The only 'connections' we had made were to grow a climbing rose on wires on one wall, and some sweet peas up the fence. Nothing contributed to the well-being of anything else, nothing was edible, and everything each plant needed had to be supplied manually by me. I was working for my garden instead of the other way around! Worse still, we had lawn! When I thought about the lawn with my new insights I realised that the lawn provided nothing except work and expense. It had to be mowed, it needed feeding and water – and in return? Nothing! I realised then that lawn, which does not grow in the wild but has to be cultivated, has only ever benefited the mower manufacturers, the fuel companies and fertiliser companies. Not only that but it uses precious water. I now knew that we could have achieved the same soft green carpet if we had put down other lawn-type things like native grasses or pennyroyal or dichondra or clover. Even better, we would never have had to mow!

As we hadn't yet moved to the farm, I decided to use our current place as a hypothetical project to try to work out how I would change a city yard into a more self-sustainable and productive area. I was amazed at just how much we could have done to improve it using permaculture. I had learned just how wasteful a city garden really can be, no matter how beautiful. You can't eat beauty and you can't eat a view and with food scarcity a definite outcome of the end of cheap oil in the near future, urban gardens are going to have to change rapidly in order for city dwellers to be guaranteed some food supply. In mentally redesigning our city garden I wouldn't have weeded and thrown the weeds into the green-waste bin to be emptied by the council trucks, but instead would have left the weeds in the ground and just covered them with cardboard as mulch so that they would rot down and replenish the soil. Pruning and clippings would have gone into a compost heap to be used later on the garden beds. I would have grown lots of vegetables in among the flowers. I realised that we didn't even collect our rainwater run-off, as it was piped straight into the stormwater system that is allowed to just run into the sea. Had we had a rainwater tank I could have watered the garden with rainwater and not had to worry about water restrictions which were in force at the time because of the prolonged drought. Even without an expensive rainwater tank, downpipes could have been cut and the run-off from the roof could have been captured in large bins and used on the garden.

Our yard wasn't big, but I now knew that I could have packed it with enough vegetable diversity to have fed us for an entire year. A total of only ten square metres is all that is needed to feed the average sized family. In the paved areas I could have had potted dwarf fruit trees, and on the fences and trees we could have grown grape vines or passionfruit or peas and beans or any number of fruits or vegetables.

I would have torn up the grass, put in stepping stones or a narrow gravel path and used all that recovered wasted space for growing food and flowers. And we had a very wide grassed area outside our fence boundary which could have been safely planted with bird-attracting native trees, or fruit trees instead of scrappy lawn that had to be mown.

Had I designed that small garden using permaculture principles, I would have been easily able to produce excess food that I could have given to my kids and my neighbours!

If people living in cities could only appreciate how important it is to live close to their food source, a great deal of productivity could easily be achieved if neighbours got together and planned a community fruit and vegetable garden. With that sort of involvement with one's neighbours, maybe people wouldn't be as isolated and insular.

When thinking about a design for the farm, I had to remember to make connections between environment, flora and fauna, and ensure I was making multiple uses of every section. Bill had explained that every element in the plan must serve several functions. A simple garden fence, for instance, shouldn't be installed just as a boundary marker. That is a single-function element. A fence can be used as a trellis to grow things on. It can also be used to reduce mowing by growing hedge-type plants against it, making it a barrier under which grass and weeds don't grow. A fence keeps animals or kids or marauding herds either in or out. It can serve also as a screen or a windbreak or shelter depending on the material used in its construction.

The multiple-use principle of permaculture can be applied to anything – a simple chicken for example. People have traditionally kept chickens for the eggs or meat but the keeping of chickens has many more benefits. Chickens do indeed provide eggs and meat, but just as importantly, they provide manure, and their natural habits can be put to work. Chickens scratch up and forage in the ground looking for insects, so they can be put to work to 'tractor' an area of ground, manuring it as they go. They then leave the area clear of grasses and weeds and also fertilised and ready for planting a crop. They provide methane and carbon dioxide and heat when they are in their housing, so plants in a greenhouse attached to the chicken house benefit from the warmth and gases produced by the chickens. And chickens provide feathers for stuffing for soft furnishings. So the simple chicken is more than an ambulatory roast dinner – it is a tractor, a poop machine, an egg factory, a future cushion and even an alarm clock if there is also a rooster!

The next thing we learned in the course was one I could easily relate to. It was to do with zones. This zone scheme is designed to optimise the space and placement of things to reduce effort. It's a farmer's version of common sense really. I have always prided myself on having a place for everything that is logical or sequential, so this idea really worked for me.

If zone zero is your house where ideally you want to be spending most of your time, then each zone out from the house should be placed with the most visited areas close by and the least visited areas further away. For example, taking that poor chicken again, the chicken house should be fairly close by, in zone one, so that when you want eggs for breakfast you don't have to put on your boots and trudge down the paddock in the mud. Better still, maybe you want to make an omelette with the eggs and you want some herbs and tomatoes to put with it. If the herb garden is by the back door, and the compost heap is near the chicken house, you can dash out of the kitchen door with last night's food scraps, dump them on the compost heap, whip into the greenhouse which is attached to the chicken house and pick a tomato, lift the lids off the nesting boxes (because you built the chicken house so that the nesting boxes protrude into the greenhouse and have hinged lids). You nudge mother hen out of the way, grab a couple of eggs, on the way back to the house grab some herbs, and you are back in the kitchen in an instant.

It reminded me of a day in my early childhood. My mother had hired a young country girl as household help. Her name was Effie and she was probably only fifteen or sixteen years old. This was her first job away from home and she was nervous and desperate to please my mother. One night early in her stay she prepared the dinner, carefully peeling potatoes and carrots, topping and tailing some beans and shelling peas. She put all the peelings and scraps into a bowl as she worked. My mother was sitting with me at the kitchen table. When she'd finished, Effie tucked the bowl of scraps under her arm and walked to the back door where she proceeded to fling all the scraps out onto our perfectly manicured lawn. My mother's jaw dropped and she stood up and yelled, '*EFFIE! What on earth did you do that for?*'

Effie nearly fainted. Her ruddy country pink cheeks drained to white and her bottom lip quivered as she said, ''Cause that's what me mum always does wif scraps.'

My mother was horrified but had the presence of mind to lower her voice a few decibels. 'Why on earth would she do that?'

'T' feed the chooks.'

'Effie,' my mother said, as her shock subsided into stifled mirth, 'we don't *have* any chooks!'

What poor hapless Effie had done all those years ago was throw vegetable scraps into her zone one which started right at her mother's back door! Zone one should contain everything you need to use or visit regularly. This zone should have the workshed, greenhouse, compost, clothesline, maybe a lemon tree, and the vegetable garden with salad greens and things most often needed.

Zone two would be well-mulched small fruit trees or a mixed orchard, trellises or terraces for specific plants, and hedges. Also in this zone you might put Clara the cow. We didn't intend having a milk cow. Just managing Maurice our Maltese and Rebecca, our Jack Russell, seemed enough of a challenge. Having a big mooing, pooing, and heavy animal like a cow was quite simply out of the question as far as I was concerned. (I had an urbanite's fear of large animals, and I didn't want any animals that were taller than me!)

Zone three would be unmulched fruit trees, other animals and a main crop. The woodlot would be here, for firewood, shade and windbreaks.

The last zone is zone four, which is natural bush. It is an unmanaged area.

To assimilate all that into my mind in terms I could readily understand, the house would be zone zero, the corner store for the bits and pieces we always need between shopping days would be zone one, the mall would be zone two and for those things one needs to obtain occasionally the city would be zone three. Aunty Maude and Uncle Horace, who you only visit at Christmas time because they live so far away, would be zone four.

The more I learned, the more I was anxious to move to the farm and put it in practice. It wasn't just the permaculture design course that had riveted me. In discussions with the other students, I found that the things they did with their land and the lifestyles they described were very attractive. There were two American guys there who lived with their families in the Santa Barbara desert and their lives seemed idyllic, simple and uncomplicated. They were gently spoken and extremely healthy; warm, uncomplicated people who laughed easily. They had purpose, and they were young men who were without pretension, completely centred and totally detached from the techno-gizmo-designer label artificial world of which my own kids were so much a part.

Another reason I was getting anxious to move to the farm was that the more I learned, and the more I spoke with people, the more I felt a real sense of urgency among a lot of them to get on and establish self-sufficiency. It takes time for trees to grow and soil to be re-invigorated. It takes time to learn about the land, the climate and the seasons. It takes time to acquire the skills required to grow and care for, harvest and preserve the food being produced. Learning to live off the land and with the land is not something that you can just 'do' one day when you realise that the cost and inconvenience of living in a big city is too great. By the time Peak Oil starts to affect you physically or financially it is too late. Too much time will have been wasted.

I wanted to get out there and get our place going so that when things did indeed start to get difficult, our kids would have a place to come where there was plentiful fresh food, a place that was a beautiful haven for them and their children. I knew that they wouldn't understand fully or appreciate what we were doing for some time, but that element of time was what was most precious.

A few days before the end of the course I got the call from my son Josh. He and his wife Tomoko had a baby son. My daughter-in-law is a quiet, confident and intelligent young woman, not easily ruffled or panicked. When she went into labour at home, she and Josh had been well prepared by their birthing classes and they had quite enjoyed the process. They had been confident that the labour was going well and they had plenty of time to get to the hospital. The baby had other ideas. Before they had a chance to get moving, his head was showing, and my son delivered his own son in their own bed. They called the ambulance and mother and baby arrived at the hospital together in perfect condition.

The description of the birth process which Josh posted on the internet for all the world to see was so beautiful and so special, it made me think about how the birth process, along with so many other things in our lives, has been made into a technologically dependent traumatic event. We have made the whole process into a medical drama that it doesn't need to be in most cases. In a post-Peak Oil world, medical facilities and medicines are going to deteriorate and, in a lot of cases, will not be available at all. Again I was reminded about how much we have to relearn about herbal remedies, basic first aid and self-care. When the 'old wives' are gone to God, along with their 'old wives' tales', whatever will we do?

I was grateful that Kimiyo and Takako, Tomoko's mother and sister, had been there to share that unique moment with them – but I wanted to be there too. I wanted to get home and see this new person who was the first of the next generation of our family. I wanted to share the joy with my son and Tomoko. It was because of him and future grandchildren that Larry and I were so motivated to do what we were going to do. But I was hundreds of kilometres away learning about earthworks and dams and swales. I was so filled with emotion I found it hard to concentrate. I kept thinking about my brother and my parents and how they would have loved to have met this new little man who carried their name. Missy, too, was anxious to meet her new nephew. We decided to fly home together one day before the end of the course. I found out that the last day was just the presentation of certificates, and Lisa Mollison assured me she would send mine on.

Missy and I were coming home to a changed family. No longer was it 'just us'. Here was a new man to meet. Granted he was a very little man, but he was all ours. Like all newborns, my grandson smelled delicious and he was soft and silky to touch. He was perfect and beautiful with his straight black hair and chubby pink cheeks. I was overwhelmed with him. When I held him for the first time, and looked into his cute little face, I feared for what his life would bring. By the time he was twenty and tall, hairy and hard-muscled, the world as we knew it would be totally changed. His parents, so proud and busy and focused on his every move and need, could not conceive of what lay ahead. With his delicate little body in my arms, I felt an even greater sense of urgency to get to the farm and bring all my lessons from Melbourne to fruition.

Chapter Six

So much had happened so quickly and it had been such a whirlwind of events that not all of our friends knew we were planning to move to the country. When I told them, their reactions were all much the same – disbelief, sadness, and some were envious but in an 'I couldn't actually go and do that' sort of way. I also called my cousin Coral and told her we had gone ahead and bought a farm and were leaving Sydney.

'You did *what?*' she screamed down the phone. 'You? On a farm? What do you know about farms? You can't do this! Your father would turn over in his grave.' She said I should have a good lie down and this madness would pass. 'You've gone and got brain fever!' she said.

After a few days Coral called me back sounding quite excited. 'You will never guess,' she said. 'Quickly, turn on the TV. There's a rerun of *Green Acres* with Zsa Zsa Gabor – quick – you could learn something!'

The next task was for Larry to resign. This was a huge step for us. We were giving up very good money and a company car, routine, security, everything that supported our life. We were casting ourselves adrift from what we depended on for everything. Frankly it terrified me and I assumed Larry felt the same. He had been a loyal, valuable and conscientious worker for a very long time. I wondered how he was going to make this major step.

For so many years I had counselled senior executives through the problems they encountered after leaving or losing a job that they had held for a long time. I knew the transition could be very hard. Larry surprised me though. He was buoyant and happy and full of enthusiasm for what lay ahead of us. The sixteen years served at his company could have been as lightweight as a sixteen-day casual assignment. His focus was so firmly on our future together on the land and his belief in the rightness of what we were doing was so solid that nothing was going to affect it.

His boss had known about the cancer scare and I guess she thought that Larry's decision to take early retirement had been precipitated by that. He didn't choose to enlighten her.

We had agreed not to talk about Peak Oil any more with people because they simply didn't understand and we'd realised from past experience that people were not motivated to ask questions or investigate for themselves. We knew that as prices started to rise and affect them in a direct way their interest may be spiked but until that time, there was just no point in mentioning it. Some of the people we had told believed that a magical solution would materialise, but most, I think, just couldn't accept the vision of a life utterly changed through chronic oil shortages. Our understanding was so different to others, and by this stage we were tired of being considered lunatic harbingers of doom.

Larry's workmates gave him a big farewell party and I was invited along. It was very moving to hear all the wonderful things that people said about him and to see how much respect he had earned from his peers. It had all happened so fast: he had to work another four weeks, and then it would all be over.

After Larry had worked out his notice and had finished his corporate life forever, I booked us both into a St John Ambulance first aid course. We felt this was an essential part of our preparation because we were going to be living so far from medical assistance.

Tony, the instructor, had an amusing but very professional delivery and he showed the class how to put slings on arms for all manner of hideous breaks, and how to bandage cuts that were bleeding profusely or what to do with bandages when some gruesome object was still protruding from a wound. He made it all so jovial we could have been using the bandages to dress up for a Halloween party as Egyptian mummies.

He also told us how to treat burns and stings, and then he began to talk about snake bites. At this point I started to get a pang of fear. Spiders and bees and wasps were things I had encountered in the city. They were never pleasant encounters but I coped with them as people do. Of course I knew that snakes were 'out there' but they had never shared space in my life. Now, in that class, I was faced with a fact of farm life that made me feel very uncomfortable.

Unless I covered the entire farm with a glass dome, I was going to face a snake at some point. But I was finding it hard to face the brutal realisation that one of us could actually be bitten by a snake and the other one of us was going to have to remember what to do. I could deal with the thought of all manner of wildlife, but legless things and things with too many legs seemed to hold little allure for me.

The reality of where we were going to set up home suddenly took a very sinister turn in my mind. Living in the country was no longer fluffy bunnies and moo cows, home baked bread and rosy apples fresh off the tree. We were leaving the relative safety of the city, three minutes from a medical centre and five minutes from a major teaching hospital. We were going to be a long way from such help and we were going to have to rely on each other in an emergency. The things Tony was teaching us were hugely significant.

Once again, I was writing notes furiously, taking in everything Tony said, because I realised that this was actually life and death stuff. Tony was talking about crush fractures from falling under a tractor, drowning in dams, fatal anaphylactic shock from bee and wasp stings, and racing to get antivenin for a snake bite. He told us about one fellow who was working outside a country town who was bitten by a red-back spider. The farmer called his doctor in the nearest town but the doctor told him he didn't have any antivenin for the bite. For us, always surrounded by all manner of help and assistance, to hear of a doctor who didn't have supplies was a terrible realisation.

I must have looked worried, because Tony made a joke about red-bellied black snakes being more afraid of me than I am of them. 'But,' he said with a grin, 'watch out for brown snakes because they aren't afraid of you, and they will chase you!'

Everyone else in the class was having a good chuckle at that but I knew that if anything other than a very angry snail tried to chase me it was bound to catch me. Just the thought of it was making me break out in a sweat!

The worst moment of the course was when we were learning CPR – cardiopulmonary resuscitation. I had learned it when I was a seventeen-year-old junior nurse, but it was so long ago and at seventeen, death is just a word. It was Larry's turn to be the patient and he lay on the floor with his eyes closed. I was in the team that was supposed to resuscitate him. My team had to leave the room and then come in and 'find' the patient unconscious and not breathing on the floor.

We came into the room and there he was on the floor. It was exactly like a movie when the scenery and the crowds fade out and only the main character is on the screen. I took one look at him and tears welled up in my eyes and my heart began to pound. We weren't in a building with a team of first aid students, and Larry wasn't lying on a carpeted floor pretending to be unconscious. He was lying in long grass in our paddock, his heart and his breathing had stopped and I was alone. I had to save my husband! I could hardly see because of the tears, and I felt absolutely terrified. It was so real I couldn't breathe properly.

I tilted his head back hard to open his airway, cupping his chin with my trembling hand. The woman inside me was screaming, *'Don't die! Don't you bloody die!'* I fumbled to find the right place on his chest and began to do the chest compressions with the heel of my hand. I counted. I breathed into his lungs and turned to watch his chest rise as I had been instructed to do and all that time I was silently screaming at him *'Don't die – I can't live without you. God help me! Don't die, darling.'*

Scenes raced through my mind. What if I found him in the paddock and I didn't have my mobile phone with me? Do I leave him and run to get it? Do I start the CPR and just hope it revives him enough for me to then leave and call an ambulance? What if the neighbours aren't home? What if they are home and can't see me in the long grass? What if he is lying in a snake-infested area?

The CPR seemed to take forever. I was completely oblivious to my other team mates and the roomful of people. Tears were streaming down my face. When we had 'resuscitated' him and he got up off the floor I was completely drained and shaking all over. It took me a while to calm down again, but the intensity of the fear and the stark pictures of Larry lying on the ground are still in my mind.

Tony was a friendly easygoing guy and during the break when everyone went up onto the roof for lunch we started talking with him. We told him that we were doing the course because we were going to live on a property a long way from doctors and hospitals and we also told him we were doing it because we wanted to be self-sufficient way ahead of the Peak Oil issue. His eyes sparkled and he proceeded to tell us that he had been off-grid and self-sufficient for the last ten years. He told us that his house, including all modern appliances, two computers and four televisions, was all powered by a windmill and six DC3 aircraft batteries. Once again, we had run into another person who had seen this calamity coming long ago and quietly done something about it. We took his details and he took ours and we agreed to keep in touch. After the contacts I had made in Melbourne at the permaculture course, we seemed to be running into all sorts of people who were as well versed as we were about Peak Oil. It was like belonging to a secret society. No one was talking openly, but they seemed to be making their own quiet moves way ahead of time.

The first aid course was sobering and disquieting not only because of the isolation of our new farm, but because of the realisation that in years to come, there may not be medical assistance in easy reach and there may not be the drugs or equipment we have always taken for granted. That is a hard thing to contemplate. But a lot of drug manufacturing is highly dependent on an abundance of energy and no matter which way I thought about it, the age of cheap energy is coming to an end. One of the hardest things about that idea for me was that we don't even know the half of it. I think getting your head around the magnitude of the number of products and services that won't be available, or will only be available at huge cost, is almost impossible. I know that over 300,000 products are dependent on oil … but it's hard to reconcile that number with the things we use and eat and need in everyday life.

Every time I tried to get my head around the Peak Oil issue, I felt more and more glad that we had chosen the path we had. It seemed to us that each step we took towards leaving the city felt like the right one. Now we'd finished our first aid course, our nights were consumed with reading back-to-basics books, or learning about some aspect of agriculture, or how to make things. We were completely engrossed in our new learning process.

We were now free to focus our attention on the task of moving house. I began to sort and pack our belongings and many times during that process, sitting alone in the house, I would break down and cry. Once again I was going through the stages of grieving for what we were losing because of this outrageous oil situation looming some time in the future.

We were the baby-boomers, and together with most of our generation, we had lived a life of incredible affluence compared to the lives people had led before the advent of cheap oil and all the marvellous things that came from it. Now that way of life was not just threatened, it was earmarked for a place in history as the 'glory days of the age of oil'. Everyone on the planet was going to be affected. Everyone, no matter how rich or poor, no matter how clever or ignorant. Sooner or later, enough people were going to learn the facts and rail against the inevitability of crumbling economies, shortages, unrest and perhaps wars. We just didn't know if it would be in the next five years or the next fifty.

I didn't want this knowledge. I didn't want to be the only one of my group of friends who knew about it. I wanted to be just as ignorant, just as contented and just as trusting as my friends. But I wasn't; and it hurt me and scared me and disappointed me. I was once again in a lonely place. I would wander about the house, remembering the fun we had when we had gone out and painstakingly chosen the leadlight folding doors to match the front door and the leadlight hall light. I remembered the days of pondering over colour charts for the wall paint, and the materials for the curtains. I remembered the thrill of seeing each little part of the house being remodelled and beautified.

I looked out at all my healthy, bushy and blooming roses. I could hear the echo of the laughter of my family around the dinner table. I walked out onto the street and looked down to where my daughter's house was and remembered how we had daydreamed together about the day she would be standing at her gate and I would be standing at mine as her child was allowed to walk 'up to Nana's place' for the first time. The tears flowed down my face unchecked. This was the last thing I could ever have imagined and it was breaking my heart. Even my own children didn't really understand how life was going to change for them.

And now we were packing up our lives, packing up our possessions and our memories. We were leaving town, leaving the only life we had ever known and throwing ourselves, in our mid-fifties, into a lifestyle that was totally foreign to us. What kept me going were the constant reminders of why we were doing this – the Google Alerts about Peak Oil arriving in my email inbox every day. We would read them and discuss them and file them away. It was somehow compelling to receive these daily confirmations that what we were doing was necessary, as hard and heartbreaking as it was. Frankly,

I needed the constant reassurance. I needed a lot of reminding that giving up everything I knew and was comfortable with, everything I loved, was for a good reason.

The emails were growing in number and from sources all over the world, and the messages were the same. 'Sit up and take notice, people – oil is a finite resource and it is running out!' I couldn't understand why our friends and our kids were not receiving them and reading them. Maybe our diligent reading of them was made more palatable because we had Rick to turn to for confirmation and discussion and to bounce our thoughts off. His book was finished and would soon be on the market. *Oilephant Down* by Richard Embleton would join the growing list of other books available in stores and on the internet about Peak Oil.

During the packing, the sorting, the talking and reading and crying, still the nightly news and the daily papers were devoid of solid information that could have and should have been out there. Petrol prices were rising; *that* was in the news, but the real reason for it wasn't. My anger was mounting at the government and the people in powerful corporations who knew, as we did, about Peak Oil but chose to do and say nothing.

There was so much to do and so much to think about. My list mania came in handy and kept me focused. I had lists of things to organise for the Sydney house, lists of things to organise for the farm, lists of people to notify, lists of things to buy, lists of things to clear out, lists of medical, dental and hearing-aid things to organise. My mind never rested. During the day I was doing chores and ticking them off my lists and all the while I was thinking of more things to achieve.

At night I would study my permaculture books, or chat to Rick on the internet. Larry and I would sit together for hours questioning our decisions, reviewing and fretting over details and what-ifs and maybes. The simple question, 'Have we done the right thing?' was repeated over and over and in different ways.

'We *have* done the right thing!'

'Have we done the *right thing*?'

'Boy, have *we* done the right thing!'

'Are we too old? Are we too stupid? Are we wise?'

There was so much to come to terms with. When the price of oil became higher and food and commodities became more difficult to find or afford, I would have to learn how to do things I had never done before. I would have to learn how to make things from first principles. Each night I would lie in the dark and wonder about the simple things. Would we grow olives for olive oil? And if so, how do you get the oil out of the olives? What about peanut butter? We could grow peanuts but how do you make the nuts into butter? How does one 'roll an oat' for porridge or make a kernel of corn into a flake? I knew I could make tomato ketchup, but what about salt? And what about flour? I doubted that we could grow wheat in our area but if we could, and I learned how to grind wheat into flour, what do you add to it to make it self-raising flour? I had seen corn growing in Nana Glen, so maybe I would have to learn how to grind corn for flour. But I didn't know what to grind it in and I didn't know if I would have to dry the corn first before grinding it. I had seen butter being made, but had no clue how to do it myself. Would it come to that in time?

How had I got to this age with such ignorance? I thought about our favourite mid-week meal — simple spaghetti bolognaise. Open the packet of pasta, boil it up with a bit of salt then brown the pre-minced meat, open a bottle of spaghetti sauce, pour on the sauce, add some garlic from the jar in the fridge door, a bit of wine, some dried oregano and basil from a jar and hey presto — a quick easy meal. But what if I couldn't buy a packet of pasta and had to make it myself? And the minced meat wouldn't be as easy to obtain as walking into a supermarket and picking up a plastic-covered polystyrene tray. I would have to grow the tomatoes and basil and garlic and other herbs to make the spaghetti sauce. The greatest loss stemming from the end of cheap oil was going to be convenience.

I was operating on two levels. On the surface I was excited at the prospect of a change of lifestyle, a move to the peace and serenity of the country with the man I loved. I was also terrified, harbouring fears about the life I was leaving behind, the oil crisis ahead, not to mention snakes and spiders and creepy nasty things that didn't like me as much as I didn't like them. And then there was the bucket of fears about my own inadequacy, my ignorance and my poor health. I don't believe that Larry was questioning himself as much as I was. He is a carefree spirit, the kind of man who will happily open his mouth and let Fate spoon in whatever it wishes. I fervently wanted to be like him. But my nature is the antithesis of his. If there is nothing to worry about, I worry about why there is nothing to worry about!

One activity on my list was a task I was putting off for as long as I could. When I got the removalist to quote on our move, there was only one thing he refused to put on his truck. It was our compost bin. It wasn't a closed bin, but an enormous tub that we had made out of a commercial chlorine container rescued from the local public pool. The original container was about two and a half metres tall and about a metre wide. The pool people were going to cut it up and dispose of it so we brought it home and cut it in half. One half made an enormous planter which we had put in our pergola area to grow palms and ferns, and the other half was used as a monster-sized worm farm composter. It was teeming with worms that munched up all our food scraps.

The original idea had been that we would use the worm castings on my roses, but now that we were moving I wanted to take the entire thing, worms and all, to the farm. The removalist told me that as compost was combustible, he was prohibited by law from carrying it on his enclosed truck. That meant only one thing. We were going to have to get all the worms out and put them in a normal worm-farm box for the trip north. It meant shovelling out the whole container and picking all the worms out by hand. While I love the 'concept' of worms making our scraps into their lunch, I had never actually taken to physical contact with them. It had always been a sort of arm's-length relationship.

We had kept them for so long we felt they were too valuable to us to think of leaving them behind. In retrospect of course it was a ludicrous situation but we set up a plastic table and, with masks on our faces and gloved hands we sifted through the composted material shovelful by shovelful, lifting the worms out and plopping them into the box. About halfway through the process we had enough worms to start a factory, so we bagged up the rest of the compost and worms and took them over to our son's place for his garden. Had we given him a barrel of $100 notes he couldn't have been happier. His thumb has always been as green as mine and his garden is a delight.

Having got the dreaded worm job out of the way, I turned my attention to water. I had been worried about the water situation we'd be facing, because our farm didn't have town water. All my life, water was just there in the tap, as much as I wanted. Now we would be dependent on rainwater. I'd need to think much more about how much I was using, especially if the drought continued, and so I decided to experiment with water. For one whole day, I kept a bucket in my kitchen sink. It was a ten-litre bucket and I wanted to measure how much

I used in one day of ordinary housework. My experiment showed me that in one day, just from washing my hands between tasks or during food preparation, I filled the bucket. Just one day's worth of a few seconds at a time of hand washing, and I used ten litres of water. That evening, I ran a bath, and instead of draining the water I left it there so I could measure it. In the morning I took my ten-litre bucket and emptied the bathwater onto my garden, one bucket at a time. The bath held over 200 litres of water. Carting it in ten-litre bucket loads out to the garden was a heavy chore but after that exercise, I had a different attitude to water. Not only is it easy to waste, it is heavy to carry, and if the rains didn't fall on our farm roof, we wouldn't be collecting it in our tanks.

Each time I flushed the toilet or put on the washing machine I would think about how precious water is. I decided to stop using our dishwasher after that experiment. It seemed like a huge waste of water and power when seven litres in the sink and a bit of effort on my part would do the job just as well. Sydney was in the grip of water restrictions, so why waste water with appliances that I could do without? I was going to deliberately have to get used to doing without a lot of modern conveniences, so I might as well start right away.

Little by little in meaningful ways, I was coming to realise how cosseted we were living in the city, and how attractive it is to not have to think about these basic things. I also realised how dangerous that blind comfort is. Australia has about twenty million people. If each of them used ten litres of water a day just to wash their hands, that's roughly equivalent to about 30,000 backyard swimming pools going down the drain each day. What shocked me even more was learning that in Sydney, water usage per person, whether adult or child, is calculated at 500 litres per day, but in the country, where people are more conscious of the need for conservation, water usage is calculated at only 150 litres per day per person. Basic values between city and country in such things as water conservation are worlds apart.

During our packing and organising process, I had many questions about connecting utilities to the farm and about farm insurance, which is different from city insurance. I needed also to get referrals for various trades and services we would need. We found Rod in Coffs Harbour to be an absolute godsend, able to answer all these questions and dispense advice with good humour and patience.

Rod put me in touch with some organic farmers whose property was not far from our new farm. Jim and Connie proved to be incredibly helpful and knowledgeable and knew all the local people we would have to know or consult. They had moved to Nana Glen twelve years before from Melbourne. Jim had a very successful career in logistics, purchasing and management in Melbourne and since their move to Nana Glen, they had amassed a wealth of experiences in organic farming which they were happy to share with us. Their willingness to spend time on the phone with me, their advice and consideration were something that we were grateful for and surprised about. Happily, we were to experience this many times as we met more of the people among whom we were going to live.

Another person I needed to talk to was a local plumber called Bill Edwards. Bill and his wife Diane had moved from Sydney eight years before, and were living in a little village close to Nana Glen called Coramba. Bill had been a plumber in Sydney, as well as a professional photographer with a very successful career. (It just goes to show that all sorts of people *can* make the change.) I didn't know it then, but Bill would become a good friend in the months ahead. He was as helpful and friendly as Jim and Connie and spent considerable time on the phone teaching me about water and water tanks and LPG gas cylinders. He even gave me advice about getting the dogs started on tick medication before we arrived. Bill explained that the ticks in the area were really bad and the only sure way to avoid losing our precious Becky and Maurice was to get them started on a systemic insecticide.

I took the dogs to the local vet and asked her to prescribe a course of the medication Bill had recommended for ticks. She looked at me in horror. 'I wouldn't recommend that,' she said. 'It's a very strong organophosphate.' She looked at me as if I had requested we feed the dogs arsenic. 'It is too strong and totally unnecessary.'

I explained that we were going to a tick-infested area but still she wouldn't agree. She recommended we just use the drops that go on the back of their necks. Then I rang the vet in Coramba that Bill had recommended. The receptionist was a lady called Judy and she spoke to me on the phone as if we had been old school chums. She confirmed what Bill had told me. 'You have to get them onto a systemic insecticide at least a week before you arrive,' she said.

We chatted about dogs, and Becky, our Jack Russell, in particular. I asked her about snakes and she told me that Jack Russells are the number-one victims of snake bites because of their inquisitive nature and their killer instincts. I mentioned that I had learned in my permaculture course about a particular bush called mugwort that snakes don't like crawling through. I intended growing a lot of it around the farm. She asked what it was, and puffing out my chest with pride in my newfound knowledge I said, 'It's a herb called *Artemisia vulgaris*'. I thought I sounded very botanically authoritative.

'That may be,' she laughed, 'but around here we have found that the things snakes like the very least are shotgun pellets and long-handled shovels!'

I had no intention of getting close enough to a snake to use a shovel – mugwort would have to do for me. And as the ever-helpful Bill painstakingly explained septic systems to me several days later, I realised that here was yet another process, just like planting snake-repelling herbs, which used nature to work for us.

I had heard of septic systems, of course, but had never lived with one. What went down our toilet went into a parallel void as far as I was concerned and I really didn't want to know about such things. The farm was not connected to a town sewer system, though, so I knew I would have to become knowledgeable about our new septic system. Bill told us that we would not be able to use chemicals in the house as they would kill the useful bacteria in the septic tank. This was a blow to me. Blue toilet water that smelled fresh and looked like the sea had always been part of my bathroom cleaning routine. I had always used cleaning chemicals that would kill just about anything from Ebola to the Black Plague. Now I would have to find the right products to suit our septic system and learn to think differently about germs altogether. It had just not occurred to me that the word 'septic' means to decompose through the action of bacteria.

I sadly waved goodbye to my blue loo, and searched around for a shop that specialised in eco-friendly products. We found one on the north side of Sydney. It was a fantastic place; the proprietors Graeme and Doris sold products for cleaning the house, washing dishes, washing ourselves and our hair, toothpaste, deodorant, laundry detergent and even shampoo for the dogs, none of which contained chemicals that would ruin the bacteria in the septic system. They had eco-friendly make-up and even house paint had we needed it. The shop smelled magnificent.

We bought a bulk supply of everything we would need, right down to insect repellent. Graeme and Doris were really interested in what we were doing. We spent a lot of time talking to them and found out that they were members of the Permaculture North group in Sydney. Apparently that group is very active and involved in permaculture especially for city living. It was good to learn that permaculture was becoming popular as it would be very necessary in the times to come. Graeme even told us that he had wanted to attend the same permaculture course that I had done in Melbourne but couldn't spare the time away from the shop. They were yet another couple who were switched on to the issues of Peak Oil and also climate change. We left their store with cartons of products ready for our new life.

Maybe the best item we bought from Graeme and Doris was a brilliant device for removing unwanted guests from the house. It was a long shaft with a pistol-grip handle that, when depressed, caused plastic filaments to fan out at the end. The filaments then close over any unpleasant interloper that doesn't speak English and has an unreasonable number of hairy legs. The said interloper can then be deposited unharmed back into the great outdoors from whence it came. It was the niftiest thing we had ever seen but I hoped I wouldn't have to use it often.

We knew when we eventually made the move to the farm we would not be able to just drop into the nearest shop for whatever we needed as we had in the city. Going to the shop would mean getting into the car and driving twenty-five kilometres to town, so we knew we would have to learn to think ahead and anticipate our needs more carefully.

One product that I found myself giving serious thought to was toilet paper. I had never given a single thought to so basic and yet so essential an item in my entire life but suddenly it was a precious product I devoted considerable mental energy to. I guess the only people who actually do devote thought to toilet paper are the manufacturers, although I was later to discover from Rick that toilet paper is a frequent topic of discussion on the Peak Oil online groups. I wondered where it was made and how it was made and how far it had to travel to get into the stores. Mostly I wondered what we would do without it if it was not available.

Six billion humans on earth require some form of rear-end cleaning and currently 83,048,116 rolls are used every day. That's 30.6 billion rolls per year and 2.7 rolls per second. No matter which way you look at it, that's a lot of trees being felled for wiping one's behind. I had seen a reality show on TV about people living as the Pilgrim Fathers did and one thing they didn't have was toilet paper. The people on the show had to use leaves when they went to the 'bathroom' among the bushes. I was horrified. I couldn't imagine anything worse than being stuck on the farm without toilet paper. To assuage my loo paper anxiety, Larry and I went off to a bulk supplier and bought two huge bulk packs of rolls. I was temporarily content. Leaves may one day be all that I have to rely on but for however long toilet paper is available, I am going to hoard it as if it were gold. I could imagine a very healthy black market trade emerging in toilet paper if things got nasty.

In ancient Rome, those good folk used a brine-soaked sponge attached to a stick to clean their behinds, and that stick was used communally. I didn't find that an appealing option when compared with my triple-ply rolls. Colonial Americans used corncobs, although eventually the corncob was superseded by old newspapers and catalogues. The *Old Farmer's Almanac* and then the Sears catalogue used to be made with a hole in one corner so that they could hang conveniently in the outhouse for use after a good read. One American manufacturer in the mid

1930s advertised his toilet paper as being 'splinter-free'. I assume that most people are like me and don't dwell on toilet technology, we just retire to the little room and high-tail it out of there without pondering how life would be without such a place, and without that soft splinter-free roll hanging on the wall.

The other product I was concerned about was plastic. Plastic is made from oil and one day would be too expensive to buy. I bought up as many plastic containers as I could without the store detective tapping me on the shoulder and suggesting I needed a psychiatrist more than I needed storage solutions. I figured that while they are cheap and plentiful, I should hoard them along with my wonderful stash of toilet paper. Although there are now plastics made from plant material (how, I have no idea) the massive infrastructure it would take to use that as a total substitute for oil-derived plastic does not currently exist. And just how much critical food-producing land can we afford to turn into acreage to produce substitutes for oil-derived products?

Underpants received similar serious consideration. All the underpants I owned were made in China and were cheap. As the price of fuel rose, it was obvious that the price of all our imported goods would also rise and I didn't want to run out of underpants. I guess as one gets older these commodities tend to hold a particularly prominent place in one's mind. But then, from a woman's point of view, all our comfortable and well-designed personal sanitary products are going to be expensive, or not available, in the long term. Reverting to ways of old to cope with the monthly cycle is as unpleasant to think about as the old Roman sponge-on-a-stick scenario!

As I organised my stocks of these priceless commodities, time was slipping away. The items on my to-do lists were almost all crossed off. It was really happening. We were almost ready to leave. Josh and Tomoko invited us to their home for a farewell barbecue with the whole family. Josh is a gourmet cook, and so it was no ordinary barbecue; it was a feast of meat and seafood, salads and fresh vegetables and fruit, all beautifully prepared and presented. It was held in their garden beside their robust and thriving vegetable patch.

When Tomoko's mother Kimiyo had come from Japan for Jasper's birth, she and Josh had plotted out and prepared the ground, enriching the soil and packing the area full of a wide variety of vegetables and melons. Under Josh's care the garden had flourished. It looked beautiful and the lunch table was covered with food, much of it homegrown.

We had a wonderful barbecue. It was typical of our family. There were constantly several conversations going on at once, noise, laughter, music, and more food than we could possibly eat, everyone happy and busy and moving around, arms passing plates across other arms passing plates.

I held my baby grandson in my arms and fought against the urge to cry. As I looked into his eyes, and breathed in his beautiful baby smell, I thought of all the first achievements and milestones I was going to miss in his life. His first teeth, his first words, his first steps – all precious, fleeting moments that I would never see. But our resolve to be prepared for Peak Oil was powerful. Even knowing we'd miss the joys of watching Jasper grow could not dissuade us from our dream of self-sufficiency.

All our intense and ongoing study and research and knowledge of what reaching Peak Oil would mean had by this time left no question in my mind about the importance and wisdom of early preparation. All the articles we'd found on the internet, all the books we had read, stressed that one vital point: early preparation.

We felt that if we could achieve a productive farm within the next ten years, we would have done something special and important for the family we loved so much. The loss of constant contact and involvement with our wonderful, warm, colourful and funny family was less painful than the thought of not being in a position to help them as price increases and shortages of basic needs began to affect them and cause them extreme hardship. We loved them too much to just let it all happen as the years ticked by. Knowing we could have or should have done something but didn't do it would have been more painful than anything.

My cousin Coral had brought us going-away presents: hats with corks on strings around the brim to keep the flies off our faces in the country. Everyone was happy and laughing, taking photos and making jokes, but underneath all the frivolity there was a feeling of stark disbelief. I felt a heavy, dragging sadness looking around the garden at all my family, the people I loved most in the entire world. I couldn't hold back the tears. Everyone was being so bright and cheery and encouraging but at the same time they were all as shell-shocked as we were that we would actually pack up and leave them. It was a bittersweet day.

As we drove away, I took a look at the tree Josh had planted in the front garden. It was a Norfolk Island pine tree that we had grown in a pot and kept with us for years. When he first left home some years ago he had taken the pine tree with him and nurtured it. Josh had finally planted the pine tree in the ground several months ago to mark forever the place where Jasper had been born. Thinking about it caused the tears to stream down my face again.

On our last day, the huge removal trucks rolled up to our house early in the morning and the men came in to pack the furniture and carry out the boxes. As each room was emptied of our belongings, the house we loved so much was becoming 'just a house', just rooms. The things which made this house a home – the pictures, the bits and pieces that had meaning just for us – were gone.

As the truck doors were slammed shut on that last day, they closed an era in our lives. The clang of those huge metal doors is a sound that will stay in my mind forever. It was over. On 10 November 2005, city life for us was finally over.

Chapter Seven

No matter how organised you are, no matter how carefully you plan and anticipate every possible element, Murphy's Law invariably kicks in to remind you that if there is even the slightest possibility to slip up you definitely will. I had been so proud of myself on the lead-up to that last day. I had thought of everything. My lists were completed. We had bought a blow-up mattress on which to spend our last night in the house, as we had to finish cleaning before we left and our bed had been packed on the truck. I had remembered one set of bed linen, one set of towels for our last shower, cleaners, mop and broom and disposable cloths to clean with and a garbage bag for their disposal. I had remembered the kettle and mugs and tea and coffee, a little milk, travelling clothes, a sedative for Rebecca, the more excitable of the two dogs, snacks and a plastic box of water for them to drink on the long journey north, their leads, and some doggie poop bags. With my preparations we could have been about to drive from the South Pole directly to the North Pole. I had lists, I had pillows, I had even kept our permaculture books and course notes because I couldn't imagine any fate worse than losing those if the removals truck had an accident and all our other possessions were burned to a crisp.

That last morning we woke early, showered and dressed and finished the cleaning. No matter how many 'oh just let me do this' moments, finally there was nothing left to do except pack our little car and leave. That's when Murphy's Law kicked in. By the time we had loaded our bags, pillows, bed linen and dog bedding and treats, the little car was bulging. All the last-minute things had nowhere else to go but piled up by my feet and around me in the front seat. But I had not thought about the brooms and mops! So, with the dogs secured with their doggy seatbelts in the back seat on top of the pillows and towels, we had to make room for the broom and mop handles which had to go between the dogs and through the front seats, where they rested against my shoulder. It was fine so long as I didn't want to move at all. It was like being an astronaut strapped into a space shuttle but without those bags for bodily relief built into my clothes.

Our new life in Nana Glen was ahead of us and our city life was fast disappearing into the distance behind us. Rebecca was like a teenager on ecstasy at a rave party. She was in the back seat dancing as hard as she could whether the music was playing or not! The car trip was her idea of dying and going to doggy heaven. She waited until we were flying up the freeway until she decided that her bowels required immediate evacuation. She really did try to make her toilet exercise as silent and discreet as possible, but in a tiny car with the windows up and stuff packed to the roof, what gave the game away was the unmistakable aroma of an active canine colon! Out came the doggy-poop bag and the garbage bag. By moving the mop and broom handles down a few centimetres, and twisting myself sideways and sliding up by pushing with my feet on the bag of water bottles and a pillow at my feet, I was able to reach the offending offering and bag it up without having to get Larry to stop on the freeway. I couldn't decide whether to stash the little treasure, toss it, or save it for the compost at the farm. It took me the next hour to unwind myself and settle again into my astronaut position but I will always be grateful to her for pooping on her own pillow and not on ours.

That November day was hot and sticky and bright. We stopped every two hours to stretch our legs and let the dogs out to give them a drink and a run around. We had sedated Rebecca (although being a Jack Russell, only a sledgehammer would have knocked her out completely), but she was at least manageable. Maurice, being the grand little old man that he is, was snoozing on his pillow happily as if he had spent all his life travelling hundreds of kilometres a day squashed in a tiny car and fenced in by broom handles.

As Larry drove, he would periodically ask for a drink of water so I would reach down for the bottle at my feet. Or he would want a snack so I would reach down for the bag of treats at my feet. Or he would want a cigarette which I would have to light for him. Rebecca was in perpetual motion, looking at everything that whizzed past and if she could have spoken she would have been saying 'Are we there yet?' at every opportunity. Her acrobatics would get both dogs tangled amid the leads and brooms and pillows and I would have to screw around and untangle them. Or I would think of something important and have to add it to my list which was in my bag at my feet. If the trip was a long and scenic one, I don't remember it at all. I was so busy I had no time to enjoy it, or consider the ramifications of it, or daydream about our future. I was like a harassed flight attendant with a planeload of party-goers! By the time we arrived in Coffs Harbour I was as exhausted as if I had walked the whole way.

We were not going to the farm directly for our first night as the farmhouse was being fumigated and the removalist's truck was not arriving until the following day. I had phoned around and found a motel in Coffs Harbour that accommodated travellers with dogs. It didn't feel like we had left the city for good yet, perhaps because all the organising and activity had dulled the fear and there was too much to think about.

Early the next morning, Larry went to the real estate agent's office and picked up the keys to our new home. We drove the final twenty-five kilometres in a state of high excitement. We arrived a few moments before the removalists, and just in time to greet our new friends Nili and Pete. They arrived with a huge basket filled with roast chicken and salad and sultana pound cake for lunch to welcome us and also a cooking pot full of spaghetti bolognaise for our dinner.

Although we had only met them personally twice in our lives, they were as warm and as caring as family. Since that first day, that is exactly what they became to us. Nili became the sister I never had, and Pete and Larry quickly became best mates. I had been given four gift-boxed, rose-patterned mugs by a friend I had visited when I was in Melbourne, and when the mugs were unpacked, I told Nili and Pete that these four mugs were to be our own special mugs, never to be used for anyone else but us four. The first of our new traditions was in place.

On that first day, while the men were carting in our furniture and all the cardboard boxes, Nili and I supervised and directed, unpacked things and sorted. She had a confident strength about her, a tough exterior perhaps, but a warm and sweet nature and her confidence and calmness rubbed off on me.

I looked around us and wondered if I would ever find anything again. The removalists had left and the house was full of boxes and furniture. The chaos was total. At that point Pete suggested to Larry that the best way they could help us was to get out of our way and take a walk around the perimeter fences and check over the property. I didn't know it then, but at that moment, old-fashioned rural gender duty-segregation had begun. Larry agreed, and said he particularly wanted to show Pete the river at the bottom of the property. It was beautiful native bushland with a little island in the river, but it was shielded by a thick forest of tall trees so we couldn't see it from the house.

The farm was just a huge horse paddock. Nothing was growing out there but grass. Before we bought the farm, the idea of a blank canvas on which we could create our own food forest had seemed perfect. Now as I stood on the veranda and surveyed my new domain with its backdrop of forested mountains and a foreground of green pastures, I realised just how much work was ahead of us. For this farm to grow so much as a pea we would have to put it in the ground … and there seemed to be a mighty lot of ground out there. Coming from a home and garden totalling about 300 square metres, the five hectares of the farm seemed to roll on into the distance like I had suddenly put the wide-angle lens on the camera. Of course, in comparison with the farms around us that were ten or fifty or 100 times as large, ours was a tiny snippet of land. I looked south down the Orara Valley, over the pastures with cattle lazily grazing under the hot November sun. It seemed that we were far from the worries and fears of the coming oil crisis.

Nili and I sat on the veranda and had tea in our new rose mugs and talked as if we were old friends catching up on the latest news. She made me feel at home. Pete had brought with him some fencing wire and star pickets so he and Larry could make a safe little dog pen for Maurice and Becky until we could secure the boundary fences. We didn't want Becky running amok around the expensive horses and cattle of our neighbouring farms.

Pete showed Larry how to make the fencing and it was done in a matter of moments. We were to learn that Pete had expertise in just about everything a farmer should know, although after twenty years on the land, we shouldn't have been surprised. Quickly erecting a temporary fence was nothing to him, but for Larry, whose only manual skill had been punching a keyboard for thirty years, each task he undertook under Pete's patient and good-natured guidance was a new one. I could tell he was having fun. This was 'real men's work'.

It was going to take some time to get the computer set up and attached to the internet so for the first time in many months we were going to be without the daily updates on Peak Oil. In a way, it was a relief to be free of that constant feed of information, but not to be able to be in regular internet contact with our kids was going to be tough, although we had their upcoming visit to look forward to. All the kids were planning to spend the Christmas–New Year break with us on the farm. It gave us about five or six weeks to get settled before the house would be filled with the laughter and banter and noise of our family again, and the sheer joy of my sweet little grandson.

Nili and I walked around the little above-ground pool in front of the veranda and to my horror there was a big blue-tongue lizard sunning itself a few feet from our legs. Nili assured me it was harmless and as I looked at it I consoled myself that it did at least have four legs – not eight legs or no legs – so it couldn't be all bad. I discovered later that spot was actually home to a whole family of very polite blue-tongue lizards. They seemed totally indifferent to our presence and we were purposefully indifferent to them. They all have very benign, quite attractive little Mona Lisa smiles on their shiny faces, and they would look me right in the eye as if to say, 'Good morning, now would you please watch where you are going, this is my breakfast table you are standing on here!'

In the late afternoon as the sun set Nili and Pete went home and left us to settle into our new home. Evening stole quietly over the valley and the night sounds of the bush began. No traffic, no sirens, no planes, no music, no sounds of neighbours' voices; only frogs and crickets broke the silence. The air was sweet and fresh. We sat silently with our tea. We had arrived in our little patch of paradise.

The next day I had my head in a carton of crockery when I heard a female voice outside calling out 'Helloooo'. A smiling face appeared on the veranda and she introduced herself.

'Hi. I'm Lindy, I live over there.' She pointed to the white house on the north hill. 'I just wanted to welcome you. I didn't want to come over right away. Just thought I would give you a bit of time to settle in. Here, these are for you.' She handed me a dozen eggs which I thought was a very neighbourly thing to do.

These were the first eggs we had ever had that had come directly from chickens to us without the intermediary steps of government egg authorities and supermarkets. Lindy had wandered over with her old dog Ben. When Becky saw this huge raggedy old farm dog in the garden her reaction would have done justice to the arrival of a hungry lion. She couldn't bark like a normal dog, such was her fury at this intruder; instead she screamed and darted from spot to spot on the veranda trying to attack Ben. Had he been interested, Ben could have used her as a toothpick. In Becky's desperation to be given a clear run at ripping Ben's throat out, poor old decrepit Maurice wandered into her line of sight and so Becky set upon him out of frustration. We had to prise her jaws off him. It took Maurice three days to recover from Lindy's welcome visit.

I invited her in and before she stepped into the house, she slipped off her shoes and walked in barefooted. While her action registered with me, I just thought she must like to walk in bare feet. She sat at the kitchen counter and told us she had a herd of cows and horses but she actually made her living as a lawyer in town. She seemed extremely nice and helpful, telling us about the previous owners and about the land and the area. She didn't stay long, but just long enough for us to feel that we may have struck it lucky and found ourselves a really agreeable neighbour.

Not long after Lindy's visit, I heard another welcoming 'Helloooooo' and this time it was our neighbour from the south side.

'Hi, I'm Sandra. I just thought I would come by and introduce myself. Here's some eggs.' Our egg supply had just increased by 100 per cent. Before Sandra came into the house, she too slipped off her shoes as Lindy had done.

I gathered that walking into a house with the shoes you were wearing outside was not the done thing. And for good reason. After tramping about in the dust or mud or chicken poop, walking it into the house isn't the most sanitary thing to do, and causes the lady of the house extra work. It was something that we quickly came to adopt too. Our work boots are left outside the front door and our slippers or sandals reside inside the door. Neither of us would dream of walking into the house with our outside shoes on. It created a joke between us because invariably Larry would put his boots on and then remember he needed something inside the house and I would have to go and get it for him. When our first visitors arrived from Sydney a few weeks after we were settled,

I couldn't help noticing with some amusement that they didn't take off their shoes before entering our house.

When Sandra arrived, I was in the process of cooking some corned beef in a big pot on the stove. Sandra is an attractive, confident country woman quite a bit taller than me. She has an energy about her, strength and an easy laugh. We talked for a while and she proved to be as laid-back and pleasant as Lindy. Sandra and her husband Malcolm both worked in town and also grazed cattle. Sandra had been brought up on the land and when I told her our plans to get chickens and ducks and geese, she offered to teach me all I would need to know about the chickens. While I was checking the corned beef she came around the counter and gave me some tips about the cooking as well. And when the corned beef was cooked, it was the best corned beef I had ever made.

We arranged to visit Jim and Connie, the organic farmers with whom I'd had long phone conversations in Sydney before we left. Their forty-hectare property was a short drive away on the same road as our farm. We were looking forward to meeting them as they had been so full of advice and encouragement to us. We had brought some small gifts with us for them. Connie met us and invited us onto their veranda where she served tea and cookies and dips and chopped-up vegetables from her garden. She and Jim showed us around and they told us about the Landcare natural resource management work they were involved in and their organic farming course. They were very prominent and well-known members of the community and they were more than welcoming.

As we sat chatting, wallabies were grazing beside the house and a fat shiny black hen came sauntering out of the bushes looking for Connie to come and give her some feed. A butcherbird landed on the railing looking for a share of our afternoon tea.

On a large portion of their property they grow hardwood trees in partnership with the state forestry but the gardens we could see were beautiful, and the whole area was lush with fragrant flowers and bees and butterflies busy at their work. Their garden was clearly the result of many years of care and attention. We knew that this couple, along with all the other people we had met since arriving, were going to become friends. As we left, Connie darted into the house and came back with something in her hands. She said, 'Here, these are for you.' I took the proffered gift and realised that she had given me two dozen eggs.

Driving back home, I said to Larry, 'I feel terrible. We haven't got one thing that we have produced to give to people. So far the only thing we have produced on our farm is omelettes!'

The house was slowly getting sorted out. What I wanted to achieve before the kids came for the holidays was a completely organised and fully functional home. I sent an old lounge suite to be recovered and called a curtain company to come and fit and hang the curtains that we had brought from Sydney. We bought new bedroom furniture for all the spare bedrooms and called a pool company to come and show us how to maintain the little above-ground pool. Larry hung all our photos on the walls and also painstakingly hung our collection of porcelain rose plates. Orchestrating the unpacking and purchases seemed to take forever. I was quite nervous during this time. I wanted everything to be perfect for when the family arrived.

One evening our talk drifted to what we should name the farm. We wanted a name that would reflect the true character of the place, not as it was at that moment, but what it was to become. It was certainly paradise even in its present unproductive state. The views from the veranda of the forested mountains and the green fields fringed by the river trees were like a postcard.

The objective for the place was to create a permaculture food forest, as well as a safe haven for our family. We mulled over a variety of ideas and rejected them all until we came up with a name that sat well with both of us. We finally decided to call it 'Eden Forest Permaculture Sanctuary'. It was certainly a very grand name for a horse paddock that boasted just one old gum tree in the middle, but it embodied all our dreams. We went to bed that night tired but content. We were home in our one-tree forest.

As each new day dawned we seemed to feel an ever-increasing level of enthusiasm. There was a feeling of 'rightness' about us being there. We knew we didn't know anything about living in the country but we had begun a meaningful adventure.

We were finding rapidly that differences between city and country living were quite dramatic. We were up at or before dawn each day, waking naturally without an alarm clock. That alone was a big change. We had both lived with an alarm clock all our working lives. Now we didn't even have to wear watches. On the farm, work continues for as long as there is light to see. We eat when our tummies tell us we are hungry and we sleep when we are tired. Time doesn't mean anything more than light and dark, or season to season. It felt somehow more natural.

Each dawn was so different from the one before and each was so beautiful and so perfect that if an artist had committed each one to canvas I doubted that anyone would believe they were real. In fact, there were some mornings when I would come out onto the veranda and the sky and the early morning light and mists would be so awesome that I would laugh out loud all by myself. It was as if God was just fiddling around with outrageous 'beginnings' just like the ever-changing opening credits of *The Simpsons*.

In the city if I woke early, I would be in the house, not seeing the sky and the gentle silent way a day is born. That beauty would be hidden from me and my focus would have been on taking a shower or making a coffee and getting ready for work. Now, watching the dawn became a special time, a time of silence and peace. My body was starting to change its pace and slow down and I began to enjoy the sense of calm as I watched the sun break each morning. It was a gentle and peaceful way to start the day. At night the only light on in the valley was ours and the only sound was the frogs. Their songs lulled us to sleep. Night rains played timpani on our tin roof.

Dawn became the time we would sit together and plan each day. Larry had a blue clipboard and mine was pink. We would list all the things we had decided needed doing and we would then work out together in what order things should be accomplished. The list of tasks was enormous, but we were following a plan, which made it slightly less daunting. The first place to attend to in a permaculture farm is zone zero – one's house. The house had to be made comfortable and functional and there were a number of things we were discovering that needed urgent attention.

The master plan was to turn our one-tree paddock into a fully productive farm which would produce as many of our basic needs as possible. This would involve attempting to grow as many varieties of vegetables and fruit as we could. We also planned to grow things like coffee and tea, trees for firewood, olives and sunflowers for oil, cork, and various things for weaving, such as flax and willow, rushes and kangaroo grass – we were going to try everything.

For us to achieve all that was necessary for the future we had to have a very clear picture in our minds of what we wanted for Eden Forest. By nature we are both very goal-oriented people, and our corporate lives had refined that ability and sense of direction. So we wanted to set out our objectives very clearly and formulate a step-by-step way of achieving them.

Our ultimate objective was to be self-sufficient and to systematically disconnect ourselves from dependence on external inputs for energy and food. We also wanted to develop or hook into local community connections. If we could achieve both of those things to the greatest degree possible, then we felt that when life started to become more expensive and more difficult as oil depletion bit in, we would have given ourselves the best chance of living as comfortably as possible.

We worked out a set of descriptors, a sort of mission statement for Eden Forest that we felt would take us at least five and possibly ten years to achieve. There were eight points on it:

Number one was to create a comfortable and safe home that would be welcoming, organised and functional. We wanted our home to be a comfortable and pleasant place where we and anyone visiting or staying would feel at ease, a place where all needs were met.

Number two was to create a useful workplace. This would incorporate a safe and well-equipped workshop, farm and production facilities, a library and archive area, a learning centre and research area. We would need a greenhouse and processing shed for whatever we produced that needed packing or drying or processing in some way.

Number three was to become our own primary produce source. We decided that we wanted to grow only heirloom fruit and vegetables. The vegetables that supermarkets and greengrocers sell are varieties that travel well and are uniform in appearance. They are often ripened artificially or stored for long periods, and taste and vitality are of secondary importance. Chemical sprays and chemical fertilisers are used to grow them. Heirloom vegetables, on the other hand, are grown from seeds that have been collected and saved and passed down through families and growers who are not contracted to big multinational companies. These vegetables grow the way they have for hundreds of years, without genetic engineering, without any artificial processes. They taste different – always better – and they are natural. We had read a great deal about seeds and we knew that large multinational seed companies sold seed that needed to be continually bought each year because they were bred in such a way that they didn't self-seed. It was a neat idea for a large corporate organisation to make more and more money because farmers had to continually repurchase from them each season.

We also wanted to develop areas of the farm that would allow us to grow vegetables and also fruits that were not normally grown in our area. That would mean developing particular microclimates in certain parts of the garden to meet the specific needs of the plants and trees we selected. As well as the fruit and vegetables, we wanted to grow herbs, nuts and berries, run chickens, ducks and geese, and cultivate fish in the dams.

Number four was to create a business structure which would be the instrument through which we would make an income. That income we hoped would come from sale of primary produce, from education through courses we would both run and from the value-adds we would develop from our primary produce such as jams, preserves and pickles and any other useful things we could think of which we might be able to learn to make.

Number five was to be our social source. We wanted Eden Forest to be a hub of networking locally, a place where we would entertain and provide input to our local community. We wanted it to be a communication centre.

Number six was to continue our research into permaculture, food and power production, observation of our land, the weather, changes or unusual events, and the recording of those observations, reading and learning, discussion and debate.

Number seven was to create a nature reserve. We wanted to get involved in land care and river care, and turn our property into a forest that was free of invasive weeds and pest trees, where native vegetation on the perimeters of the property would flourish. We wanted to plant bird-attracting native trees and plants everywhere.

Number eight was the creation of Eden Forest as a model of self-sustainability. We wanted to perfect the recycling process and renewal practices. We wanted to achieve energy production, independence and efficiency, and be able to power our house and our machinery by ourselves. We wanted to demonstrate the value of multiple-use ethics – using cornstalks as trellises for beans to grow on, letting the chickens clear and fertilise the soil, making compost from garden clippings rather than using fertiliser. Most of all, we wanted Eden Forest to be part of a viable local interactive community.

Each of the points on our mission statement required a great deal of thought and a timeframe and budget. They may have seemed lofty ideals to achieve, but they were what put fire in our bellies and got us out of bed and raring to go each morning.

We knew we were going to make lots of mistakes and suffer a lot of failures. Long before we could possibly teach permaculture, we knew we had to experiment and earn our stripes the hard way – by doing it – and that would take time.

If we succeeded, but the deprivation following Peak Oil didn't happen after all, we knew that our list of objectives, our mission, was still a great one, and one which would keep us occupied, learning and active and busy together as a team for years to come. From a purely commercial point of view, the development of Eden Forest along these lines would increase its sale value if we or the kids wanted to opt out. So no matter what happened in the future, we were going to work hard together to create a wonderful and interesting place to live and work.

Chapter Eight

Creating a comfortable and safe home ought to be relatively easy. In our home in the city that meant getting Larry to push the furniture around the room several times like a revolving scene-change at the theatre until I was happy with it. He would grumble and grunt and get frustrated after the second or third turn around the room but we would get there in the end.

Unlike our previous house, the farmhouse possessed some idiosyncrasies. For reasons that simply defy logic, the boards of the veranda had been laid so wide apart that our chair legs kept falling through. Regularly we would be sitting at the table talking one minute, and sprawled out flat on the veranda the next, with the chair legs having to be extracted from the gap in the boards. It was a most inelegant way to carry on a polite conversation with new neighbours, especially if we happened to have glasses of wine in our hands! Maurice and Becky also had trouble walking on the wide-spaced boards.

Without careful navigation their little legs would disappear up to a hip or shoulder. A few times when Maurice had been dozing in the sun on the veranda, the name tag on his collar would get caught between the boards and the poor old guy would be unable to lift his head. He would grunt and moan and we would have to rescue him. It was very distressing for him to be tethered by the neck to the floorboards. We also feared a visitor would come and fall and hurt themselves and we would be sued. The veranda was a high priority item to get repaired.

Another immediate and major task was securing a proper water supply. I had asked Bill the plumber to visit Eden Forest before we had arrived to assess the water tanks. He had told me that we would need new tanks as the capacity of the ancient ones currently in place was insufficient. Bill's opinion concurred with the information I had read in *Buying your Bush Block*. The book said that to last through a dry spell an average family home should have storage capacity of 60,000 litres of water. Our capacity was way below that and so I had arranged for Bill to put in new larger tanks. We didn't know at that early stage that not only were the tanks insufficient, but the guttering and downpipes didn't actually marry up to the tanks. We learned, during the deluges of the rainy season to come, that most of the water from the roof ran down the downpipes and straight onto the ground and flooded around the yard, or leaked in a streaming curtain of water ribbons right out of the gutters. Or that's what we thought was happening, anyway. What we subsequently found was that whoever put the downpipes in from the gutter had a small lapse of concentration and forgot to actually cut out holes in the gutter for the water to travel down the pipes. It was a shocking waste of precious water when one's only source is rain. But I guess it was no more of a waste than in Sydney where rainwater is piped out to sea while the dams that provide the city's water supply get emptier and emptier.

When Bill came we liked him immediately. He had a wonderful craggy smile and a wicked sense of humour and to our surprise he was quite well acquainted with the principles of permaculture, even bringing us a copy of Bill Mollison's textbook to show us that his was old and dog-eared from use. He arranged delivery for a new 'squat' which is what he called the new tank, and he and his offsider began preparing the old tank for removal. He called in a quiet young fellow called Jamie who wore a cowboy hat down low on his brow. Jamie drove a bobcat and was going to excavate and prepare a level site near our machine shed to place the old tank. The whole thing was going to be quite an exercise.

On the same day we had Bill and his team working away on the tank, I had arranged for a man to come and fix the gas cooker. It had a fan-forced oven and when I turned it on for the first time one night, I thought that Larry had gone completely mad and was out in the blackness of night mowing the lawn! The noise, to my hearing-impaired ears, sounded just like a two-stroke mower. When I realised that the racket was coming from my casserole in the oven and not my demented night-mowing husband I was horrified. Our intention was to replace the oven with a wood-burning one, but that was way down on the list of things to do. For now the 'mower oven' would have to suffice.

I had also arranged for a local TV guy to come and get our set working. Geoff the TV man came and explained that because of our isolated location some of the free-to-air channels would be unavailable to us until the time the channels began to broadcast using a digital signal. He tramped around on our tin roof, making noises in the house like Santa and his reindeers, endeavouring to improve our reception. He fiddled with our extra antennae and eventually we were able to receive just one commercial channel, the ABC and SBS. Having always had cable TV in Sydney, this was a big come-down, but what we didn't know at that stage was that as time went on, we would be so busy during the day and so tired at night that our addiction to cable TV was going to diminish dramatically.

While Geoff was up on the roof he happened to take a look at the chimney attached to the slow-combustion wood heater in the kitchen. He told us that the chimney had been installed incorrectly and so he had fixed it, and as an added bonus he'd even cleaned it for us. He said it was a surprise that the place hadn't gone up in smoke. At times like this the helpfulness of these country people was almost overwhelming. Everyone seemed willing to go out of their way for a stranger.

Neil the local computer fellow showed up on the veranda amid all the comings and goings of trucks full of crusher dust and blue metal and water tanks and bobcats and TV antennae and clanging and banging. Becky didn't know who to bark at first and eventually gave up and went to sleep beside Neil at the computer. This country life was just too hectic for even her to handle.

I learned that day about a very important country tradition. Everyone who sets foot on the veranda happily accepts the offer of a cup of tea. I felt like I was running a café! I had never made so many cups of tea at one time in my life. The cup of tea and the accompanying piece of homemade cake were enjoyed with a good deal of chatter and joking and kidding around and then, as quickly as they all assembled on the veranda for their 'smoko' break, they were all gone again, back out into the hot sun, working at their tasks.

It wasn't just the older men who came to work at the Forest either. We employed a nineteen-year-old called Brent to slash the paddock because the ride-on mower that had come as part of the property was broken and needed repair. This young fellow tore about the property as if he were a racing car driver. I had my hand on my chest watching him, thinking that any moment his tractor would flip over and trap him underneath. But it didn't. He survived and gladly accepted the offer of a cup of tea.

Brent told us that our part of the river may have platypus living in it but if we see any we should keep it secret otherwise the Department of Platypuses or some such government body would come out and fence off our access to the river. This was exciting, although less so his suggestion that our dam probably had eels living in it.

During our cup of tea with Brent we told him all about Peak Oil. He was very interested and we played the *End of Suburbia* DVD for him. He was white-faced when it ended. After he left, I said to Larry, 'I wonder how many nineteen-year-olds in the city would sit and have a cup of tea and just shoot the breeze with a couple of boring old people like us?'

As the days marched on towards the Christmas holidays we were learning a lot about our land and what we were learning was quite thrilling. For instance, we learned that the top of the property has about three inches of topsoil before you hit clay, but the bottom end towards the river is deep rich black soil. We were learning about the rains and water run-off across the land and the winds too. We would be able to turn these observations into usable information when it came time to formulate a formal permaculture plan.

Every part of the farm was becoming familiar to us and we spent a good deal of time walking around just looking at everything and noting the little things about it that could be important to us. One thing disturbed me. On the front of the machine shed someone had nailed up the skull of a horse.

I found this disturbing. Looking at a dead horse's head every day was spooky. I begged Larry to remove it and give the skull a decent burial. The skull was nailed up very high and so he found an old metal ladder, climbed up, and removed the poor sun-bleached skull. He then ceremoniously buried it in the black soil down by the old dam. Directly after the ceremonial burial, which I watched from the veranda, the skies opened up and it rained like Noah was about to visit. When the deluge abated we found that one of the workbenches in the machine shed had sunk into the mud. Maybe the horse's head burial wasn't such a good idea!

When Jamie had cleared the land behind the shed with his bobcat in preparation for the relocation of the old water tank, we discovered a pet graveyard complete with little crosses with names on them. Jamie bulldozed the brush and small trees in order for the guttering on the shed to be replaced so that we could capture the rainwater in the old relocated tank. We were going to use that tank water to irrigate our future vegetable gardens. Behind the shed was dark, rich, aromatic soil.

While all the activity was ongoing outside, I was occupied inside the house unpacking more boxes. I saved all the packing paper and stripped off all the tape that had been used to seal the boxes and collapsed them for storage in the shed. Cardboard and paper were important to us because we intended to use it all as mulch for when we set up the vegetable gardens and planted our trees. By effectively shutting off all light to the grass and weeds by covering them with cardboard and slashed grass, photosynthesis ceases and the grass and weeds die. There is therefore no need to touch the soil. No back-breaking digging or weeding or ploughing. I had learned that to dig the soil was not only a waste of time and effort, it was also damaging to all the teeming bacterial and fungal life that gives the soil its vitality. That suited me very well. Building garden beds above ground was going to be far less stressful and difficult for us and it was going to keep the ground happy too.

We had agreed that from day one on the farm, we would be diligent with saving water, recycling everything and re-using whatever we could. Two lidded plastic bins were used for food scraps which we would use to start a compost heap, and only plastic and non-recyclable things were put in the big garbage bin.

We were frankly shocked at the amount of plastic packaging and non-recyclable items we have always taken for granted. Certainly in the city we were used to a recycling system, but in a mindless way. Here we became keenly conscious of every scrap of anything that we used and by being so aware, we were amazed at just how much garbage the two of us could generate. When I thought about how much garbage twenty million Australians must generate I was aghast. It made me cross thinking about the whole packaging and distribution process of most goods which virtually forces us to accept non-recyclable waste. We had adopted Bill Mollison's motto, 'everything that once lived can live again'. Paper, cardboard, food scraps, hair from my brush, floor sweepings, tea bags, in fact, anything that was once living – all these sorts of things go into the compost.

We endeavoured to think of multiple uses for as many things as possible. We saved all our plastic soft drink bottles so that they could be filled with water. With a spike-spout on the top they can be up-ended into the ground beside new baby trees when planted so that each one has an individual watering system during the dry season. In Sydney we would just have thrown out the polystyrene packaging from the computer. But with our focus on recycling as much as possible, we saved it to use for tray containers for raising seedlings or to store tools.

Everything we do is either governed by the looming threat of Peak Oil or stems from the permaculture principles we have adopted, so our every task, every action is deliberate and thoughtful. The dishwasher that was in the house when we bought it has been swapped for an upright freezer that Nili and Pete had used on their farm. Something as simple as washing the dishes is done now with awareness of the importance of water conservation, and the washing-up water is poured on the garden.

Frankly, while seeming to be giving up a lot of things that made life easy in the city, we are actually gaining a great deal by doing things differently, thinking about things differently. The process of having to purposefully think about what we are doing instead of just following life-long routines more suited to a different time and a different place is challenging. In the city if I accidentally poured something down the sink that maybe shouldn't have gone down, I would think 'oops' and that would be it, because the consequences wouldn't have been obvious to me. Nothing would have changed in my immediate world. Here a down-the-sink-oops moment can kill all the bacteria in the septic system and we would feel it drastically – or at the least, we would smell it drastically. All actions taken here have a direct and immediate impact on us or our comfort, safety or our future success at growing our food. When you live in the city you can *pretend* to care about the environment, but when you live in the country you are a *part* of the environment so you don't have the luxury of pretence.

It is curious for instance that we are both feeling so wonderfully alive. We don't feel sluggishness in the mornings, or fading-to-grey in the evenings. We sleep like logs and wake up like five-year-olds with ADHD. It could be just that everything is so new and exciting, or it could be the oxygen-rich, pollution-free air which gets a good wash and sparkle in the afternoon rains each day. Maybe it's the lack of chemicals in our systems or maybe it is a combination of all these things. Certainly the lack of city stress must play a part. And there is something mystical and magical about being so intimately involved with the land and the trees and the birds and insects and the weather. We are very keen observers of the weather now that we are part of the countryside, part of the scenery. Rain in the country means our food gets to grow another day. Rain in the city only meant 'take the umbrella so that when we get out of the car at the restaurant we won't get wet!'

We were driving back from a day's shopping in Coffs Harbour one day and as we climbed the hills behind the town, the mountains were capped with fluffy mist and low, grey, rain clouds that made the tree-covered ridges look like portly, heavily bearded gentlemen with grey angora beanies pulled down low over their eyebrows. It would have been just another pretty piece of scenery before, but now I know that when the portly gentlemen are wearing their beanies that way, our property is in the grip of heavy rain, which means run-off, soil erosion, flooding of the immediate house surrounds, maybe power failure – lots of things that directly impact on our lives. We pay attention to the wind direction, the sun's path and even the shadows on the ground, mentally marking off where they begin and end as this will influence our planting.

Our strange permaculture methods are a novelty to the local farmers. They must think of us as those two new city galahs who have probably never spent longer in the bush than the time it takes to have a picnic. *Here they are, going to cover their farm with cardboard and hay and grass clippings instead of getting out with a good old ripper or a plough on the back of a heavy tractor!*

We had been the odd ones out in the city, with our dire predictions of a future without oil, and now we were the odd ones out in the country with our cardboard mulch. We had become accustomed to being the only two soldiers marching in time to the music. We hoped that one day the rest of the parade would lose their iPods and hear the same beat we were marching to.

Christmas was fast approaching, which meant that not only would the family be arriving but it was also the time when Geoff Lawton, my permaculture lecturer from Melbourne, was booked to come and consult with us on our farm design. He was fitting us in before jetting off in the new year for overseas assignments and a Peak Oil conference in New York where he was going to be keynote speaker, so his time was very precious. We needed to get some aerial photos showing the contours of the land so that we would be ready for Geoff when he came to consult.

When the aerial photos and contour maps arrived, Larry and I spent hours poring over the plans and getting a feel for how we will organise all our planting. We were like two kids helping each other with a huge school project. We couldn't decide where we should site the chicken house and greenhouse and where certain orchards should go. We had to consider where to build the swales (terraces or ditches) and dams and ponds to capture or divert water run-off, and what to plant as windbreaks. We ended the evening feeling extremely ignorant and awed by the amount of knowledge we had to acquire in order to make this a happening thing. But one thing was certain: we knew that we were doing the right thing and we knew also that permaculture was the right way to achieve it.

While all this speculation and planning was going on, we received an invitation to a Christmas party at the old Coramba pub. We felt quite overwhelmed because it was an invitation-only affair for the people of the valley who were involved in Landcare or other committees, and were instrumental in advising the Shire Council about our area in some way.

The people we met were interesting and welcoming. At our table there were the owners of the local timber mill and we asked them about their work. One of them told us that good timber was getting harder and harder to find.

'There was a time here when a farmer would plant trees especially for his grandson to fell,' he said, 'and his son would do the same for his grandson. That just doesn't happen any more. Makes our job more difficult.'

It was a sad indictment on the ways of modern farming that people no longer provided for future generations in this way. And it is a practice we are going to have to return to after Peak Oil, and should be returning to now in preparation for that time.

It was a lively party and speeches were made about the achievements of the past year and the plans for the coming year in the valley. It was lovely to feel such a strong sense of belonging after only a very short time in the area.

I am constantly surprised, pleasantly so, about how easy it is to meet people in the country. It may be that people have more time, or it may be just the way of country people, but everyone is so friendly. A call to the energy company resulted in me having a laugh and a long chat with the customer service person. I was surprised to learn that electricity supply is more expensive in the country than it is in the city. She explained that was because of the longer distances; more poles and infrastructure are needed for fewer people. We talked about the farm and chickens and vegetables, and she told me she knew our place and passed it often. I invited her to drop in next time for a cup of tea. When I rang a government department about dam water storage capacity the man who took my call ended up introducing himself as Alan, and then inviting Larry and I to his farm to meet his wife and look at his pecan trees. If I had made the same calls in Sydney and the operator invited me to go look at his pecan trees I would have needed a passport and a course of malaria tablets.

We did go and visit with Alan and his wife Denise. Their farm was beautiful enough to be opened to the public. The pecan trees all stood in neat lines on very flat green land and everything was in perfect order. Their gardens were verdant and they were in the process of restoring the old farmhouse. Alan taught me to use two bits of wire to find water. At first I didn't believe it was possible. Larry tried it and nothing happened, but when I held the wires I was totally amazed to see them swing inwards all by themselves when I walked over one of their water pipes that was buried in the ground. We left their farm with the promise of having them over to our place in the near future.

Since arriving on the farm we have only drunk rainwater. There is no fluoride in our bodies, and thanks to our eco-friendly shopping trip before we left Sydney, no organo-phosphates in our detergent, washing powder, toothpaste, soap or shampoo, and no insecticides.

To cope with creepy crawlies and flies in the house we bought special chemical-free products from a catalogue. The fly situation was an issue until the products arrived, but when they did, I wondered why we ever used aerosol poisons before. The fly eradicators for example are quite simple. They are compostable sticky strips that attach to windows and trap the insects. After a while you just remove the strip, bury it and replace it.

Before the family arrived Larry went into town to buy a truck, which we would need for carting all the things we would need for the farm. He had never driven a four-wheel drive before, let alone bought a truck, but he managed to find a Space Cab with an aluminium tray back and drop-down sides at a good price. It was a manual gear shift and he hadn't driven a manual since his youth. Watching him drive it in the beginning was like watching someone wrestling with one of those trick walking sticks that keep collapsing. His gear changes were miserable, drawn-out operations that made the engine and me wince. We would grind up and down the hills to town, freewheel to stops, heave along in the wrong gear, and meanwhile Larry would be happily motoring along enjoying the scenery or talking to me, completely oblivious to the internal conniptions of the long-suffering truck. We would pull up to our destination and the truck and I would both sigh in relief that the torture was temporarily over.

When we had to haul the trailer behind the truck it was more of the same. No matter how hard he tried, Larry just could not master the art of backing it up without the trailer jack-knifing in the opposite direction to the way he wanted it to go. In the beginning he would get me to do it and although I didn't know any better than him how to do it, I think the truck was so delighted to have me changing its gears without ripping its throat out that it just did what was required in sheer thankfulness.

Larry's other major purchase was a chainsaw. He did better handling that, but the owner's manual that came with it was so full of safety warnings I seriously considered hiding it from him. Pete gave him his first lesson. Nili and I stood some distance from them, full of trepidation, as Pete showed Larry how to switch it on and hold it and all the basic handling techniques. Then they decided to give it a real try by cutting down a tree. Pete selected a suitable tree for the lesson and with the calm and deft hands of a skilled surgeon he showed Larry how to do the first cuts. Nili and I looked at the tree they were attacking, and then in unison turned our heads to scope out where the tree would fall. We could see that the tree was going to fall directly on a young and healthy-looking grevillea.

Nili told Pete he was in danger of wiping out the shrub. Pete looked over to the shrub, thought for a second, looked up at the top of the tree, back at the shrub and went on cutting. The tree fell, and the last leaf at the top of it fell six inches short of the shrub. Nili and I stared at each other open-mouthed. From that moment on, in our eyes Pete became a kind of retiree's version of Crocodile Dundee.

The amount of learning is endless, and although it's exciting, sometimes it's daunting too. After the purchase of the truck and chainsaw, Larry is feeling tooled-up enough to attack one of the tougher jobs, finding ways to power the place without being on the grid. His nose is perpetually in a book called *Switch* by Jackie French, which explains how to create systems for power, sewerage and water. He spends hours researching various options on the internet as well. My job is to design the planting and chicken hotels so I am also reading a Jackie French book, this one called *Companion Planting*. Also on my reading list is *Trees and Shrubs for Eastern Australia*, Bill Mollison's huge permaculture text, and *A Guide to Keeping Poultry in Australia*. It's like living in a twenty-four-hour school.

Every day something new and exciting happens. I know there is a little frog in our bathroom. I saw him hop in there early one morning but I haven't had time to rescue him yet. Since changing our little above-ground pool from chlorine to a peroxide system the amphibian inhabitants are partying hard every night and venture up on to the veranda at any opportunity they get. Their music is what we go to sleep to. Well, Larry does, but when I take out my hearing aids they could be croaking the *1812 Overture* through froggy megaphones and I probably wouldn't hear them!

Chapter Nine

The 'Nana' part of the name Nana Glen is a Gumbaynggir Aboriginal tribal word meaning small lizard. Nana Glen's proud symbol is of the *Gehyra nana* lizard which, I am led to believe, is the village's mascot. It appears to be a vapid little nocturnal gekkonid creature with webbed toes and the dubious distinction of having two tails. I didn't know if two-tailed lizards were a particular genus of lizard or if they were a genetic anomaly of the area in which we have made our home. I wondered if maybe this area was an old nuclear waste dump and things with two tails were the unfortunate result of a most unfortunate history.

There are a lot of things I don't know. Many years ago for example, I was told by a Middle Eastern gentleman in a moment of unrestrained passion that I was worth 150 camels. To this day I don't know whether I am a woman of incredible worth or a great bargain! I guess all people view things differently.

Country people certainly view things differently from city people. Their priorities or maybe their focus is just different. I was taking my afternoon tea on the veranda and reading a copy of the rural newspaper called *The Land*. The paper featured articles on issues that have far-reaching consequences not just for the farmers or producers but ultimately for city consumers too. In contrast, more of the articles in city papers tended to be about violence or other crimes and anything that could be sensationalised.

There is very little in the city papers about the issues of the land. It's curious because after all, what would city people do if all the country folk just took care of themselves and their local communities and didn't truck stuff into the cities? It made me realise how ignorant or maybe even arrogant I had been in the city. I had never cared if farmers were screaming for help during the drought, or when prices for their wool or meat or whatever they produced were being undercut by imports. I didn't care because my good old supermarket was always bursting with more than enough of everything I wanted. And the supermarket was able to provide me with imported produce that was so much cheaper than the homegrown variety, and to me at that time it was more important to have low prices than something homegrown. The long-term ramifications of that never once entered my head. Now viewed through my new 'country' eyes, and through Peak Oil eyes, it meant something very important to me.

Country people have a different sense of what is of value, too. They know that to enjoy a glass of orange juice you first have to grow the tree and then you have to wait for the fruit to grow. They know that sometimes your tree will bear lots of fruit and you will benefit from all the work it took to grow it and they know that one fearsome swipe of nature can mean no fruit or the loss of the trees themselves. There's an intrinsic respect for things that city people like we were are completely unaware of. There is a precarious and tenuous hold on pure hope in everything they do. And there's a 'wait and let it happen' sort of approach to things, an appreciation of slowness. In the city, if I wanted juice I only had to call 'Waiter!'

The country women we have met so far are strong, smart, savvy women. They are as comfortable mending a fence or riding a tractor as they are making a sponge cake. They are as adept at helping a calf being born as they are at tending their own children. Their hearts are big enough to help out a sick friend and steeled enough to put down a suffering animal. These are inspirational women. You don't mess with them; you respect them. They don't suffer fools gladly. I wonder if I will ever become like them. They are adaptive, and practical, unfettered by the façade of affluence, whether they are wealthy or not. They will always walk into your house in bare feet.

Now that we were actively changing our lifestyle from city to country in preparation for Peak Oil, I was realising that just learning how to grow tomatoes and make my own spaghetti sauce wasn't nearly enough. What had to go hand in hand with the lifestyle change was a change in the way I thought about things, my expectations and aspirations.

In the city I had been a typical consumer. I was accustomed to living a life many would consider privileged. I regularly had my hair done at the salon and I had my acrylic nails done every three weeks. I didn't have to scrimp and save for things, and I regularly bought new clothes. We ate out a few nights a week and entertained regularly. I often sent my ironing out to a service, or had cleaners and tradespeople in to do work for me. Certainly I had worked very hard and for a long time, but I had done so, I realised, because I was living up to a standard that my parents had set. It was a way of life, a measure of what constitutes a successful person. Success was measured in terms of wealth, status and possessions. One's home had to be in the right location, one's car ought to be a particular type. Art collections or clothing and jewellery, private schooling for your kids or holidays overseas were all yardsticks to be measured by.

But what would happen in the future to those societal measures and standards? If a severe recession or depression hit, as the forecasts predicted, money wouldn't cut it. You might have lots of money but you can't eat money. Sure you could buy something to eat, but only if it was available to buy, and then only if the person who had it attached any value to the money you were offering. Maybe money would be replaced in value with knowledge. Maybe it would become more important to have skills and expertise. Maybe among the 'have-nots' there were the skills and knowledge that the more well-heeled in the community didn't possess.

I thought about some of my friends and acquaintances who were very wealthy. How would they manage in a super depression if their assets and investments lost all their value? I realised that in the years ahead, it wouldn't just be physical hardship and deprivation that people would have to deal with. It would also be an emotional hardship. So much of our way of life would have to be redefined, re-ordered or re-invented. How we define ourselves or measure our success may require adjustment.

One's perspective is always governed by one's experiences and view of the world. It may be the little things, the little perceptions that will need re-evaluation. For instance, Nili and Pete came to dinner one night and were sitting at the kitchen bench talking with me while I prepared the food. Their long life on the land had taught them to place a very high value on water conservation. I was focused on entertaining them in the manner that I always had, using nice things for serving food on. I had been brought up to entertain that way. I had some dips that I was about to spoon out of the plastic containers into attractive new gold-rimmed serving bowls. Nili put her hand on the back of mine as I was about to spoon out the dips.

'Are you crazy?' she said. 'Do you have so much water that you can afford all that extra washing up? Do you really think we will think less of you because you don't serve a few spoons full of baba ganoush in a fancy bowl? Save your water, use the plastic containers. The food will taste the same.' And of course Nili was right. She automatically evaluated what was more important – was it the water or the touch of refinement? Clearly the water won out.

The question of redefining the ways in which we think after Peak Oil has bitten in was one I mulled over in my mind for some time. I contacted Rick on the computer and thrashed it out with him.

'Talk to me about the concept of personal success in a post-oil world. Currently we measure success in terms of money and possessions and status – will that change?'

Rick thought for a moment and responded, 'Tough question.'

I continued. 'For example, I have a number of friends who are wealthy, well groomed, and socially well connected. They are seen at all the right places; they go to all the best events around the world. They are considered successful. But will the parameters of that definition change in a post-peak world?'

Rick said, 'The woman of the future will be rough, muscular and able to hold her own with physical work. She will be adaptive and brave.'

I didn't much like what he was describing. It sounded somehow unpleasant. It smacked of broken fingernails and scruffy hair. It definitely didn't sound like perfume and silk underwear would be on the agenda.

'So we will have to redefine words like success, I guess. Will our concepts have to change?'

'Absolutely!' He shot back. 'We will have to forget comfort, and wealth will definitely be redefined and will have nothing to do with money. You have, as a result of your move, become incredibly wealthy by tomorrow's standards.'

That didn't give me comfort. 'Do you think that maybe success will be measured in terms of knowledge and skills in the right things, in survival things?'

'You're right there. The things you are learning in Eden Forest are the right things.'

I had been feeling so overwhelmed at the sheer amount we had to learn, it was only a small measure of comfort to hear Rick say this. I was perpetually worrying that we wouldn't have enough time to acquire the knowledge necessary. I felt old and stupid and ignorant. I told Rick: 'Larry thinks that life will be just like it was in the Great Depression in the 1920s and 1930s, happy families coping on less, living a simpler life. He doesn't see it as the end of the world as we know it. I have a different view. If I look at things through the eyes of my children, I certainly see the end of their world as they know it. They didn't live through the Great Depression.'

Rick explained that there had been many other factors involved in recovery from the Great Depression. There was a world war, and an economic growth spurt that brought about so much development that there was a six-fold increase in energy use from pre-depression times. 'That situation is not going to repeat itself. Recovery from a depression comes about through growth. There will be nothing to fuel a recovery after the shit hits the fan this time. And the other big difference: this depression will be global, really global.'

This conversation with Rick was depressing me greatly. My own hope is that there is a possibility that after a period of time, a thinning out of the population from starvation and wars, and a hard bite of reality for many, a new lifestyle will emerge that will not be as absolutely black as it was when the crisis really kicks in initially. But I do think Larry is fooling himself if he thinks that there will be the same world order as there is now. There just won't be the same social structure, the same parameters to define things with.

I told Rick about a Google Alert I had just received. It was about Peak Oil–aware personal investment which will encourage research and development of alternative energy sources while helping individuals prepare for global economic weakness. Again, I was trying to somehow put a positive slant on things.

He said, 'Yes, I saw it. Look, money can be made now by investing in the right things, but that money is going to have to be liquidated into survivable tangible assets that will survive the economic collapse. Things like land that will produce food.'

The problem with talking to Rick on the internet is that we live in different time zones on opposite sides of the world so one of us is always exhausted and about to go to bed while the other has just woken up and is all bright-eyed and bushy-tailed. Our conversation ended and I headed to bed feeling very depressed. I fell into a fitful sleep and had a nightmare.

I woke up sweating and shaking and lay awake till dawn thinking. I'd dreamed a farcical dream where John Howard was about to address an audience on his solution to the Peak Oil crisis, but was shot in the eye by Kerry Packer before he could say 'something visionary' as he'd promised. There really was no one in Australian politics who was going to lead the country with vision. There was no one in power with guts enough to make some really monumental changes. No one was strong enough to stand up to the 'big end of town'.

So did that mean the solution lay with the little people? The problem was of course that most people won't make the changes in their lives in time. They won't see what's coming because they are too busy just trying to stay in the rat race. The only thing Larry and I could do was go on with our plan to make Eden Forest a reality and hope that, as time went on, enough people would become aware of the potentially civilisation-changing crisis to do something positive about it themselves.

Although I'd felt depressed after my doom-and-gloom conversation with Rick, and even worse after my carnivalesque dream of John Howard and his Peak Oil solution, a few things turned up that made me feel that all was not lost. In late November there was a short item on the ABC's *Catalyst* program presenting the Australian Peak Oil issue. The description of the program asked 'How prepared are we for the real oil crisis?' We taped the program and added it to our little library of information. The fact that this was now being shown on the ABC made us wonder if this was the beginning of the breaking of the news into mainstream media. We hoped so. Not very long after that program went to air, another one was advertised. This time it was a CNN docudrama titled *We were warned: tomorrow's oil crisis*. We asked Nili and Pete to tape it for us, and put that in our library too.

Then a few weeks later, another docudrama was aired on SBS, this time a French one called *As It Happened: 2013 Oil No More*. This film explores a scenario in which there are only two years' oil supply left – the oil companies had simply been lying about their reserves in order to keep their value high. The result is worldwide chaos. Clearly the black reality of the oil situation *was* getting through to some people, and they were using drama to hopefully make people think, imagine what could happen, ask questions and do their own research.

I decided to put my head down and make a charge through the huge line-up of things I had to learn. Baking our own bread was the first thing I wanted to tackle.

Chapter Ten

The rains of early December had produced waving fields of waist-high grass. Our next door neighbour, Malcolm, offered to come over and slash our big paddock. We were very sceptical that he could get the tractor over the soggy land but Malcolm just barrelled around like a crazed bull let loose in the paddock. His huge tyres sent up sprays of water and if the slasher picked up a small log or something else hard it just crashed and clattered until it had finished chewing it up and spitting it out. The paddock took five hours to mow and when it was finished it looked like the grounds of Buckingham Palace (with mud).

We were to learn about the reality of the December to March rainy season but at that time we had not been at Eden Forest long enough to appreciate what the 'rainy season' really meant. The rains that came in the first few weeks after our arrival were only a tiny sample of what was to come.

With the rain and mud around the farm, my Wellington boots became my favourite footwear. Although they were in chic black, they did lack some panache – but they had a special quality. They had a way of sucking themselves onto my ample calves so that getting them off became an exercise in physics. They adhered like a vacuum seal to my legs and when I took them off I would get the same sensation as an amputee: I could still feel them on long after they were off, even though they were sitting outside at the front door and my legs were inside the house. But they allowed me to slosh and squish around the property like I did when I was a little kid with those stupid ankle-high yellow rain boots my mother used to make me wear.

If only my parents were alive to see me on a farm. My father particularly must be looking down at me in amazement. His idea of roughing it was to begrudgingly accept three-and-a-half star accommodation. He was the only man I ever knew who was so uncomfortable in the great outdoors he would even stand up at picnics. My parents' presence is very strong here in the house as we are surrounded with their precious things: my father's beloved grand piano, furniture, some crockery, photos, statuettes and wall plaques – symbols of their lives and the influences they had on both of us. It is comforting and homely to have these things around us, and I believe they are vital to our emotional well-being in this new life. For us, those things were symbols of the continuity of our family, and they were important in making us feel really at home. As we get well past Peak Oil and things begin to deteriorate and people begin the inevitable and required adaptation to a new way of life, there will be a tremendous psychological need to have links to the past and special mementos of the lives they will have been forced to leave behind.

I wanted to make an effort to engender more of that homely feeling and I was keen to become expert at all the things that contribute to that sense of order and competence in a secure and well-run home. First and foremost, I was determined to start making bread on a regular basis. I imagined the house sparkling clean and filled with the delicious aroma of freshly baked bread. I had visions of myself in a gingham apron with a bib front and aromatic apple pies cooling on the windowsill.

I had given up using our microwave oven and that was relegated to the shed. I had given up my huge all-singing, all-dancing top loading washing machine for a tiny front loader that uses only a fraction of the water and power. I had given away the dishwasher – and now I wanted to give away buying bread.

It may have appeared that we were depriving ourselves of simple luxuries or conveniences way too early, long before recession or deprivation from Peak Oil became a reality, but there were good reasons for doing so right away. We wanted to survive and prosper and be as happy as we could be in a world suffering from the end of cheap oil. We had learned enough to know that it will not be easy. Making the transition early and by our own choice meant that we could make these adjustments gradually and in a considered, ordered way. We didn't want to be forced to deal with a dramatic upheaval that required us to have to absorb everything all at once.

For us there was only one thing that was going to make it possible. It wasn't going to come down to our preparedness and the move to the farm, or learning new skills, or hoarding mountains of toilet paper. It wasn't about learning to pickle cucumbers or learning to grow vegetables. It was all about our attitude. Surviving anything is about attitude, about a state of mind that can cope with any given situation. We knew that if we believed strongly enough that we were going to cope, we would. My friend Rick has a good maxim for situations like this. He says, 'If nobody tells you that you can't succeed, you will.' If we believed that we could be happy with less, we knew we would be, in spite of the deprivation of recession.

We wanted to be comfortable just making do with things, and being creative. People who have survived recessions, wars, natural disasters, major catastrophes, or horrific accidents or illnesses survived because of their attitude. Perhaps it never occurred to them they might not survive it, or perhaps because their determination to survive was in overdrive, any doubts or fears were eliminated. We felt that, having lived a certain way for over fifty years in comfort and ease, we didn't want to find ourselves miserably having to adjust and change and do without when we were in our sixties or seventies. We wanted to have the sort of 'can do' attitude that would carry us through hard times with the same contentment and happiness we had enjoyed in the good times. The huge amount we would have to learn and change would have been totally daunting if we hadn't adopted a positive attitude, had plenty of time and handled things one step at a time.

So while Malcolm was roaring about in the paddock and Larry was in town shopping, I set about teaching myself how to make my first loaf of bread. I also put on a chicken to roast with all the trimmings. I wanted the evening to be a demonstration of my burgeoning country homestead persona. All that would be missing would be the white bonnet. I had a clear vision in my mind of two fat, fluffy, hot, crusty, poppy-seed-covered plaits of bread fresh from the oven. I carefully followed the recipe and felt so virtuous and God-fearing I was almost going to find a scarf and cover my hair, and swap my jeans and T-shirt for a long skirt and a shirt with modest sleeves! As I worked little clouds of flour rose and then settled on everything. My hair and clothes were dusted in white and rivulets of doughy perspiration ran down my face. The kitchen had a pale haze in the air.

I kneaded the dough and punched it down just as the recipe told me to.

'So this is what you did with your time, old girl!' I muttered to my dead grandmother. 'And all my life I thought you spent your time wearing an eyeshade and playing poker!'

Finally after I had plaited and twisted and seeded the two loaves I put them in the oven to bake. I was sweating and my arms ached but the yeasty smell and the feeling of accomplishment were marvellous. I shouldn't have felt so proud – after all, a lioness doesn't get all puffed up with her own importance after she downs a water buffalo. She probably just thinks, 'Okay, that's lunch over with – now what will I give the kids for dinner?'

The joy was short-lived. The loaves came out of the oven exactly like Turkish pide bread. There were no plaits in sight. They had somehow cooked themselves out and the two loaves lay in their tins like flat tan bricks. My vision of those two fat, fluffy plaited loaves burst like a balloon stuck with a pin. When Larry sat down to the table for dinner he ate a large piece of the heavy flat bread and mmmmed and ahhhhhed as if I had presented him manna from heaven. The man is a saint, I tell you, a bloody saint! The bread was definitely not from heaven. I am thinking of making a few hundred of them and building a retaining wall. My vision of myself as that competent country earthmother went as flat as the bread!

While we were getting more settled and starting to feel at home, Maurice and Rebecca were settling in well too. They no longer barked at the horses and cattle next door and were becoming quite laid-back about people arriving on the veranda, unlike the frenzy they were perpetually in back in the city. Because medication for ticks is so important here, they have gotten into a morning drug-taking routine. It was quite simple to get them into the habit. I started giving them first a little snippet of dried liver treat and then for the next treat the tablets are shoved down their throats and then I'd follow that up with another hit of liver treat to finish the procedure. Now when they wake up in the morning the pair of them line up in the kitchen as if they are addicts on a methadone program waiting at the clinic door. The tick medication they take is an enzyme which requires a very energy-intensive manufacturing process to stabilise it into the tablet form. I wondered which would go first – the dogs or the availability of the medication.

We were finally down to the finishing touches to the house before the kids arrived. We bought new bookcases to take our considerable library and Larry stained and varnished the shelves. There was enough space to unpack the hundreds of jazz records that my father had collected since the 1930s. We had carted boxes of them with us every time we moved and because we didn't have a turntable that played 78 rpm records, the boxes of records were always like an albatross around our necks. Before we left Sydney we decided that we either had to get rid of the collection, or find a record player and take the time to listen to them and enjoy them.

Before we'd left Sydney I'd searched for an old player and eventually found an advertisement in a newspaper. The person selling the turntable lived in the north-west of Sydney in an area which is noted for its expensive homes. We drove out to collect the player and as we searched for the address we were struck by the size of the estates. We looked at these places with their acres and acres of bowling green lawns and their ornamental trees and wondered what they would become in the years ahead. They were perfect for producing food but it was difficult to imagine these wealthy landowners turning their hand to such tasks. It was funny; now *I* felt like the wealthy landowner, although of course we'd already reduced our lovely lawn to a muddy mess, thanks to Malcolm and his tractor.

I was looking forward to being able to implement our permaculture plan. We had organised all that we needed to before Geoff Lawton's arrival, which was now just a few weeks away. We knew after he'd surveyed the property we'd be doing more than borrowing Malcolm's tractor – we would be calling in the earthmoving equipment to make dams and cut in swales on contour in order to catch or divert water to where we wanted it to go so as to 'put water to its duties' as Bill Mollison would say. The earthworks would have to be immediately followed with planting nitrogen-fixing legume trees to enrich and prepare the soil and create shelter and support for the fruit trees that would come later. Finding the right location, sheltered from the ravages of inclement weather, was intrinsic to our success in fruit growing. Weather had become a daily focus. In my mind I was constantly planting stuff and then pulling it out and repositioning it. It's fortunate that it was only happening in my mind!

One afternoon I was watching the early news on TV when a weather warning streamed across the bottom of the screen. The warning said, 'Severe thunderstorms, flash flooding and damaging winds.' I became quite alarmed and double-checked the weather site on the internet and sure enough there was the warning.

'Don't panic,' I told myself sternly. I went into the bathroom and filled up a big plastic bucket with water so that if the power failed we could still flush the toilet – the water pump for the tanks is powered by electricity. I then filled the kettle and lots of bottles with water, switched off the computer and unplugged it, cleared everything off the veranda which wasn't nailed down, and made sure the torch batteries and mobiles were charged. I even did my hair and dressed neatly in case a violent lashing of wind came by, gathering me in its path and flinging my lifeless body over the mountain and into another town. I wanted them to say, 'Shame she died so young. Nice outfit though!'

Once everything was prepared we sat on the veranda and ate our dinner, watching the lightning in the distance, feeling the calm before the storm. We didn't talk much. The heat was hanging in the still air like a heavy curtain all around us. Then it started to sprinkle a little, a puff of wind touched my skin … and that was the end of the storm. I felt like I was waiting for a bus at a stop that had been decommissioned. The bus just never came! Frankly I was furious. I had done such a brilliant job of preparing for the damaging winds and the severe thunderstorm I was quite let down. Little did I know what storms were to come!

One morning I came out onto the veranda to have my coffee and found the floor thickly carpeted in white. I stared at the floor quite shocked. Then I realised that the white carpet was thousands and thousands of wings of flying ants. They were *everywhere*. Maurice was attempting to drink from his water dish and kept stopping and sort of back-washing his tongue as dogs do so well when you try to give them something they don't want, like a tablet. The water was clogged with ant wings. I felt I should be issuing straws to both dogs. The house, too, was littered with wings. Apparently about twice a year we are visited by swarms of flying ants. I had a mental picture of a terrible lot of ants walking along wingless, muttering 'helluva way to travel'.

Winged things have dominated our conversation of late. Lindy's chickens have taken to coming into our yard each day around three to take their afternoon tea. Their visits have given me a chance to observe them at close quarters and contemplate how it will be when we are ready to house our own chickens. It's also made me wonder again whether I have the capacity to kill and eat a chicken I have raised. After days of watching Lindy's birds going about their little lives, having their disagreements or their trysts, clucking with delight when they found a fat morsel in the grass, I had to admit to Larry that I didn't think I would be able to do it.

The chickens remind me of a band of mischievous kids who have zero respect for anything. Lindy has too many roosters and not enough hens so automatically there are going to be disagreements, but it's the nature of the disagreements that amuses us. Through the fence they come, hurrying down the slope into our yard to do their shopping, hens clucking and roosters cock-a-doodle-dooing even though it isn't dawn. They come in very purposefully and proceed to scratch about and gobble insects. They chatter to each other and mutter to themselves and they squabble incessantly. Chickens are very political and also not all that pleasant with each other. The roosters are compelled to take proprietorship over the hens and when there are more roosters than hens, well, right there you've got your own little tribal war.

One afternoon we watched one very vocal rooster, a handsome black fellow who looked like he was wearing a white lacy collar falling down to his shoulders and a very jaunty red floppy hat over one eye. He had taken a fancy to a browny-red hen and wanted to have his wicked way with her while she was busy with her tea. So he availed himself of her ample pleasures, hopping aboard as she pecked about in the grass. That caused another rooster, a scrawny white and black guy, to scream his indignation and rush over to dismount the offending gent. Wings flapped and voices were raised and all the time, the little browny-red hen continued to peck in the grass while these two men were fighting over her charms. She had that 'Sam, the ceiling needs painting' air about her. They could have killed each other and I think she would have just stepped over the two dead suitors to get at the bugs in the grass. I thought to myself, 'You go, girl!'

There is actually a lot of blatant sex happening on farms – it's a veritable hot-bed of lasciviousness. The cows that live to our south are having a rocking good time at the moment. Malcolm next door told me about his bull, a big black brute with twelve wives. Seven of the twelve wives have just given birth and he is still methodically working his way through their bedrooms. But Malcolm said he prefers to do his 'work' at night (I am talking about the bull here!). Apparently the bull doesn't like anyone to see his bedroom antics, like some corporate CEO jealously guarding his patents. I wish I had night vision glasses – I would love to see that hulking great animal in full 'voice'. What can I say – Malcolm has very happy cows. Very happy, smiling, contented cows.

Malcolm is a wealth of information. He told us about a very clever tick removal trick with eucalyptus oil. Apparently if you find a tick on your dog, you put eucalyptus oil on it and the tick screws itself out backwards and falls into a swoon and dies right before your eyes. I had heard that tea tree oil is used to combat head lice so it probably has similar properties and effects. We had sent away for special tweezers to deal with the ticks, and the vet in Sydney had instructed us to grasp the tick with the tweezers and twist to the left. I guess ticks screw themselves in clockwise and have to come out anticlockwise. (Do northern hemisphere ticks go in anticlockwise and have to be taken out clockwise? One tends to have more time to think about completely useless bits of information when one is puttering about on a farm!) Anyway, Malcolm said not to grasp them with tweezers as they will inject their poison right away, just dab with eucalyptus oil and watch the fun. Malcolm's idea of fun needs a bit of an overhaul, I think.

Natural products like the eucalyptus oil and the recipes I had gathered for making my own cleaning products figure greatly in deciding what we have to plant. Recipes for just about everything needed around the home abound on the internet and in the myriad of back-to-basics books we have collected.

Cleaning the kitchen one morning I had an interesting internal dialogue with myself. One of the advantages of deafness is that I can be very alone with my own thoughts. Sudden sounds don't interrupt my train of thought and unless I am wearing my hearing aids I don't bother with a radio or TV. I become completely absorbed in a sort of one-woman monologue. In this way I can do a lot of thinking while I am involved with a chore. I was road-testing my new chemical-free cleaners and was very pleased with the results, except for one thing. I guess I am conditioned by years of using harsh chemicals to automatically associate the smell of those chemicals with cleanliness. The kitchen didn't smell of anything in particular with my new cleaners, and I wondered if I had done a good enough job.

I thought about the time before big companies sold harsh, toxic chemicals to make one's home a stronghold against bacteria, and figured that millions of people must have lived without these products. For sure I can live without them too, I thought. Then another part of my mind popped up and said, 'Yes you dizzy old broad, but in days of old life expectancy was only to thirty or forty … people were dropping like flies from a hideous range of infectious diseases.' That led on to another part of my mind saying to me, 'Well *duh*! The global population is on a boat that only has two billion seats and there are currently 6.75 billion of us on the boat! Sooner or later the boat is going to sink!' While I was wiping down the benches I was suddenly plunged into an internal political punch-up about the value or villainy of keeping people alive as opposed to the process of natural selection weeding out excess humans.

I was making myself quite angry just thinking about how ridiculous it was that our way of life has led us not only to serious overpopulation but also to such over-indulgence and carelessness that we are becoming more and more unhealthy, more obese, unfit and full of poisonous chemicals. Cancer, heart disease and diabetes, among a line-up of other diseases, grab us and send us off to our graves. Instead of endeavouring to prevent illness from developing by changing our sedentary, cushioned lifestyles, we turn to the medical and pharmaceutical professions and say 'Fix us!' Those professions of course have burgeoned into billion-dollar industries and now there is a pill or a jab or a spare part or an operation for just about everything.

We prop up society with expensive drugs, keeping alive millions of people who have, in effect, created their own ill health through poor diet and lack of simple physical movement. Of course I am one of those people too – a victim of clever marketing and my own gullibility. We eat chemically treated foods laced with additives and artificial colours, sugar, salt and other preservatives. We drink chemically treated water and we breathe chemically toxic air. And what's more, we *pay* for all that stuff! That may sound stupid, but what is even more stupid is that we actually continue to do it. But we want to live forever and we expect the doctors and pharmacists to come up with the magic solutions to achieve it. When they don't deliver, we sue them. What a cockeyed system!

By the time I was up to cleaning the stove, I was having a raging stream of consciousness about overpopulation, euthanasia and the increase in serious illnesses at younger ages. I'd remembered a segment in Rick's book about the now proven links between chemicals, decreased immune system function, and the chronic rise in childhood asthma, and had convinced myself that all the chemicals in our environment were definitely contributing to the world's plethora of woes.

I started in on cleaning the fridge with a paste of bicarb soda and lemon juice with a touch of vanilla to make it smell nice. I was so angry with myself and the world, I was scrubbing away furiously at the fridge shelves as if they were smeared with glue. What was making me angry now was the realisation that I was on the farm, hundreds of miles from my family because I believed we were heading down a dangerous path to an unstable and difficult future. And why? Because despite a vast amount of information about pollutants, climate change and oil depletion and its consequences, governments and corporations were steadfast in their determination to maintain the status quo, keeping businesses chugging along, keeping people buying and consuming and getting sick for as long as possible just to make a buck!

That hallowed consumer society we live in and the city life that everyone wants to preserve at all cost came into stark focus in my mind when I remembered walking out into the vegetable garden earlier in the day and idly eating a strawberry. It was fresh and sweet and juicy and had been picked about two seconds before it was being consumed. But instead of insisting on the real thing, we readily buy strawberry *flavoured* food and drinks and give them to our precious children. The ingredients that go into making that strawberry flavour are just mind-boggling: amyl acetate, amylbutrate, amyl valerate, anethol, anisyl formate … and that's just the ingredients starting with A! Altogether there are forty-six separate ingredients in strawberry flavouring.

That is the ingredient in just *one* of the artificial flavours and enhancers we have been only too willing to ingest. We are so ignorant of what we actually put in our bodies, because we are not only discouraged from finding out, we are seduced into buying things by brilliant marketing and lulled into passivity by ludicrous labelling laws. And all so that we are kept in the cycle of consuming, consuming and consuming that keeps the economy growing. A growth economy is more important than causing cancerous growths in our bodies, apparently.

We have become chemically dependent in all aspects of our lives and what is so immoral is that the *long-term* build-up of many of the substances we consume via manufactured food has only ever been tested for the *short term*. The average human home is hugely chemically toxic. We are not told about the chemical treatments given to carpets and materials, finishes or adhesives. We know about some things – cleaning agents and the like, which we keep in childproof cupboards, but so much of what we use is toxic and we are quite unaware of it. We trust that the minimum levels set by our governments of exposure to toxins are correct. We trust blindly, and then wonder why there is so much increase in disease.

As I scrubbed, I was thinking, 'Maybe the frenzied desire to make lots of money was the modern capitalist man's version of going to war. It's a socially acceptable form of war. If man didn't have the overwhelming drive to grow wealth, he would have nothing else to do with his time and energy because all the hunting and gathering is being done for him.' In the place of 'real' work to do, we have become obsessed with possessions. Like bowerbirds, we gather 'things'. Larry and I had found a bowerbird's mound when we were staying at the Promised Land Cottages in Bellingen. Bowerbirds have a propensity for anything coloured blue. On the mound was a blue plastic clothes peg, a torn piece of blue plastic, a blue plastic baby's pacifier and a bit of blue nylon string. I remember thinking that even the poor bowerbird will have to change its ways when blue plastic things are no longer manufactured, because there isn't much that is blue in nature except the sky.

Unlike bowerbirds, though, we aren't content with just any old things. They have to be bigger and bigger, faster and faster, then smaller and smaller, better and better. We frantically invent things for people to buy, but then build in obsolescence so that people will have to buy them again and again. Or else we invent a new fashion. Last year's black is this year's brown. The more 'things' we possess the happier we are. We kill ourselves with work to make more money so we can acquire more things. We surround ourselves with possessions as a sort of mantle of success.

Paradoxically, the more things we have, the more committed we are to defending them and protecting them. We become prisoners to our possessions, unable to break free of them for fear of losing them. How strange that would seem in the eyes of our hunter-gatherer ancestors or a modern-day Kalahari Bushman. We are like madmen on a fairground ride that has got stuck on fast forward and we are so enjoying the ride that we have lost sight of the fact that it is going to ultimately kill us.

I always enjoy these internal dialogues. In the privacy of my mind I fulminate on the woes of the world with the zeal of Erin Brockovich, and invariably these thoughts spill out into a conversation with Larry when he comes in for his dinner. On this particular day, he had gone out to work around the farm and had left me happily starting on my chores. He returned to find me flustered and furious. Larry knows the signs and listens to me with patience until the rage is spent and then he quietly and lovingly tells me I am stark raving mad. And then we just laugh.

I told him about my homemade cleaner experience and then we speculated as to how much of an impact chemicals have had on our own health. I'd always suffered from frequent and severe asthma attacks and headaches, which had lessened a little since we'd moved up here. Could this have anything to do with the fact that we'd dispensed with all the harsh chemicals we used to have in our home? We also noted that since being here I have not had to visit a doctor yet, whereas in the city I would need to see the doctor about every two or three weeks. I wondered if there had ever been a study done on the frequency of doctor's visits just because they are in close proximity. Now that we are only using natural eco-friendly cleaners for the house and ourselves I can only speculate on what element of city living was causing me to be so sickly.

The other eco-friendly device which is working very well is my fly trap on the veranda. It fascinates me that flies actually fall for this thing. Then again, maybe the flies are just like us, drawn to sweet-smelling chemicals that kill us. The flies walk in at the top, toddle down a cone-shaped tunnel with a hole in the bottom and then spend several hours or days walking around the cone until they drop dead and plop into the water in the bottom of the container. Why they don't go back out the way they came in is beyond me.

The trap originally was on the table but as the medium in the water at the bottom 'matured' (and believe me, it was not like fine wine) it became necessary to find a more suitable place for it. The problem is that it has a very 'rich' smell, obviously to attract the flies. We hung it on the wall above nose height which didn't entirely solve the problem; occasionally a gentle breeze will carry on it an aroma akin to a very unfortunate horse with a terrible case of flatulence.

Deciding what herbs to grow that will be useful in the house either for cleaning or medicines or cooking is just one piece of a puzzle. The other one is learning how to dry or extract oils or process them and how to use them all. It got me thinking of all the other things that we are going to have to grow. I thought of rubber trees and oak trees that can be used to make cork, papyrus reeds in the ponds to make paper, melaleucas to extract tea tree oil, horsetail for silica for making soap and cleaners and more.

I emailed each of the kids to ask them what they wanted us to produce at Eden Forest and got back a flood of emails with their preferences. Among their lists were McDonald's trees, KFC trees, pizza trees, make-up trees, trees that grow iPods and lingerie. Their suggestions were hilarious and they had a great time at my expense. Underneath the ribbing though, each in their own way has at some point expressed a level of gratitude that Larry and I have undertaken this herculean task for their future well-being.

Chapter Eleven

As time goes on we have been giving some serious consideration to whether we should rethink our previous ban on having animals that are larger than me. Having a milk cow has now moved to the 'maybe' list but goats have also been nudging at the corners of my mind. Without a cow or a goat we will potentially be without milk for our coffee in the future unless someone close by in our valley is doing some milking. And even then, with the rules and regulations that govern all areas of primary industry, a local producer currently can't sell directly to us anyway.

Local and state laws currently inhibit or prohibit the development of self-sustainability. It is a point causing immense frustration to people who are becoming Peak Oil aware and who are trying to set up their 'earthship' or create eco-villages or campaign for changes in their community. The current legislative agenda is so geared to supporting corporatism and consumerism that anything aimed at self-sufficiency, and especially a self-sufficient community, is going to run into substantial hurdles and roadblocks. These simply cannot be overcome while ever the official line is business-as-usual. Self-sufficiency robs from corporations and corporations must be maintained at the expense of people. Corporations maintain governments and people in government want to keep their jobs. Discourage consumerism in favour of self-sufficiency and you discourage spending.

Thinking through our basic needs and putting things in place on the farm is crucial to us. The problem with having a milk cow is that she needs to be milked once a day whether you need the milk or not; for her to produce milk she has to have a calf and for her to have a calf, she has to be courted by a bull. It's not like going to the store every few days to get a bottle of milk when you need it. A lactating cow needs constant emptying.

Goats have the same problem but goats also unfortunately have a bad reputation. It seems that goats have a propensity for getting into trouble. They can get out of just about any fence that isn't electrified, eat everything that is before them whether edible or not, and manage to either hang themselves, get stuck in places that don't fit goats, or garrotte themselves on wire fences. Goats, generally, do not march to the beat of human drums. But cows and goats share some very attractive qualities. They produce milk, meat and leather. It's just a crying shame that chicken skin is not considered a fashion accessory and chickens don't have milkable breasts, because I would be a happy woman if they did.

These livestock decisions were important because they have a bearing on how we will develop certain areas of the farm. Larry was working on a grid plan so that I could work out the orchard planting on paper for our two smaller paddocks. I was working on the seed purchasing for all the vegetables, fruits and native trees, which was quite complex because I wanted to lay out the beds so as to take advantage of nature's way of pest control. Certain plants have to grow with certain other plants and so it is quite a chore working out where everything should go. Once the decision is made to plant tomatoes, then you know to plant basil or some other similar herb close by, as these are companion plants which help each other resist various pests. The continuous use of petrochemical pesticides and herbicides has made the pest population more resilient and as these chemicals become too expensive to use, we have read that plagues of pests will make agriculture harder. We have to grow 25 per cent more than we estimate we need just to cope with the loss to pests, so 'companion planting' has become an imperative in the hope of reducing that loss as much as possible.

We seem to be spending hours each night poring over books and plans and graph paper. Not only are there the permaculture principles to think about, but of course there's also a correct time to sow each different variety of seeds. For newbies like us this involves masses of material to research just to get started. We drag ourselves to bed exhausted each night.

I got up one morning after a particularly late night and it was one of those dawns where a guy behind the distant hills gets out his slingshot and catapults the sun into the sky accompanied by a drum roll and a big boom *tish*! And there was light and it was good – a direct quote from the great book. It was the kind of morning that pumps you full of zest and ping. This was the day I had set aside to make breakfast cereal so that we could stop buying packaged cereal. A baby step, maybe, and it's only an interim baby step, but it is one more step towards providing for ourselves. I found a recipe for toasted muesli and carefully added all the ingredients into our 'to grow' list so that in time we would be growing and drying our own ingredients, as well as making the muesli. It was very easy to make and when it was finished we ate it still warm from the oven. It was delicious and the house smelled wonderful from the roasting honey and juice-coated oats. I couldn't help wondering why I had never done this before. As each fresh batch was made, I became more and more elaborate with different ingredients, until we were bounding out of bed in the morning just to have our homemade muesli.

Every time I tackle making something new from first principles instead of buying processed foods, I am struck by how simple most things are to make by hand. There are probably two reasons I haven't tried making these things before. Firstly I have been conditioned by marketing and advertising to go out and buy foods without even trying to make them myself and the second reason is one of time. It has always just been more convenient to pick up a packet of something than make it from scratch. We were always so busy. But why were we so busy? Mostly because we were working long hours in order to pay for things we wanted to buy. And over time things were more and more expensive so we had to work longer and harder to pay for them. Somewhere in that 'mouse in a wheel' situation maybe we forgot what we got onto the wheel for in the first place.

All our lives we have done what we thought was 'work for a living'. It is just what everyone does. But were we really *working for a living*? I reasoned that we still have the same basic needs as our ancient ancestors – air, food, water, shelter, warmth, sleep, sex, order, belonging to a family and achievement. What had changed was that in our society, in the modern urban context, all our work is indirect and disconnected from our needs. We work for money to pay an invisible army of others to produce what we need for us. So in fact, we don't work for our living, we work for the consumer society so we can buy back what we need. A new layer has been added, a layer on which we have become totally dependent.

In a self-sustaining lifestyle, work is directly connected to our needs. You use what you produce in its rightful season rather than relying on that invisible army and so working for a living becomes literal rather than figurative. But isn't it great to have that invisible army slaving away doing all the hard stuff while we do other stuff that doesn't break our nails? Theoretically maybe it does look pretty attractive. Why cook when you can eat out? Why dig the dirt when you can go buy a lettuce? As oil prices rise and therefore the cost of everything else rises, people won't be able to afford to eat out or buy lettuces. We will be forced to disconnect from that invisible army and go and do our own digging.

I clearly remember one night in my early childhood when my family was watching our new television. We were the first in our street to get a TV and it was a carrot that my parents dangled to ensure my brother and I had done all our homework. I remember that night so well. We were watching our favourite show, *The People's Choice* with Jackie Cooper and a basset hound called Cleo. An advertisement came on for some arrowroot biscuits. My mother had always baked biscuits and cakes but the ad for these biscuits was so compelling she was desperate to have some even though she knew they were dry uninteresting things that needed butter and jam to make them palatable. First thing the next morning she scurried down the road to buy a packet of them. I guess from that first TV ad we just kept on getting sucked into the buying vortex and never got out. We gave up our right to being innovative and creative in favour of convenience. The other thing we didn't realise back then was that by opting for convenience we were giving up important basic skills and a bit of pride in personal achievement. Perhaps they were even greater losses.

After breakfast one morning, I was settling down to do my tasks and suddenly Larry came back to the house. He looked crestfallen. I asked him why he had such a long face and he told me that his beloved ride-on mower had finally given in to chronic mechanical melancholy and had died. I had a rather unpleasant flash of me on all fours with a pair of scissors out in the paddock cutting the grass! The mower breaking down may not sound like a big problem but someone had told us when we'd moved up here, 'There are only two seasons around these parts – winter and mowing.' And he was right. If you mow in the morning, by evening the paddocks have a five o'clock shadow and by morning it is time to mow again. If you stand quietly outside you can almost hear the grass growing. Larry loaded the mower onto the trailer immediately and we took it off to Derek the mower-fixing man.

Derek has a Major Mitchell cockatoo called Hobo the Traveller. Hobo lives in a huge cage outside Derek's workshed. The shed and surrounds are a tumble of metal and bits and pieces and boxes and mesh and pipes – the detritus of a man content in his tinkering. I liked Derek. He had a firm handshake and looked right into my eyes as he smiled and introduced himself in a broad English accent. He called me 'lass'. I liked that too. No one had called me lass in fifty years.

I liked it less when he told us how much the snakes love it in the grass around his workshed.

'One of 'em spent a few hours slithering about trying to figure out how to get in to Hobo's cage. Hobo would have made a tasty morsel.'

The tasty morsel kept saying 'G'day' to me and bobbing his head up and down, before climbing very purposefully all the way from the back of his huge cage to come right to the front just to ask me how I was. 'How *are* ya, g'day, hello' – nice bird, right neighbourly!

Derek took the ride-on into his mower hospital and told us he would call after he had examined the patient. Since that first visit, Larry, Derek and Hobo have become good friends. Derek is what is known as 'a good bloke' in the Australian vernacular and he laughs heartily every time Larry phones him and asks him if he is in his 'office'. If only all offices could be like Derek's workplace. It only has three sides and looks out over lush green bushy hills up which the breeze sweeps, fresh and sweet and unpolluted.

Not long after the mower's mechanical hiccough, Malcolm told Larry that our tractor had problems too. Malcolm has become Larry's tractor guru. So we called Derek for a home visit and this time Derek's old four-wheel drive clattered down our driveway and pulled up by the machine shed where the 'patient' was parked. He climbed out leaving the front door open and went into the shed to look at the tractor. I went to greet him and there was Hobo in his travelling cage in the front seat. I went over to say hello but he got in before me: 'G'day,' he yelled, greeting me with considerable head-bobbing as if he had been driven over especially to see me. He looked so happy to be chatting with me I momentarily felt guilty leaving him there to get back to my chores.

To console himself after all his mechanical catastrophes Larry took himself into town and bought a pair of his-and-hers cordless drills. Larry is nothing if not romantic! His drill is a big mother of a thing that could dismantle the Harbour Bridge, while mine is a very feminine little number that is capable of mending the tiny screws on the hinges of my sewing box!

Gradually we are acquiring all the necessary tools for farm work and even more gradually Larry is becoming proficient in some basic handyman skills. It is so easy in the city to get a tradesman to come and do things, even minor things around the house. In the future, we are increasingly going to have to do our own basic mending and fixing as replacement parts become more expensive, especially if they are imported. When the push motor-mower also broke down Larry wheeled it into the shed and fiddled and tinkered until miraculously it started with a full-throated roar. He came back into the house with a look on his face akin to a man who had just delivered his own baby!

Larry had always been so busy with his IT work that picking up a phone and calling in someone else to do the little jobs needed at home was the obvious thing to do. Now, a new dimension has been added to his work. The physical exertion and constant exercise every day have started changing him from a pot-bellied, middle-aged desk-jockey into a bronzed, slim and fit person. His daytime activity incorporates both physical and intellectual stimulation – he is actively applying permaculture theories, putting into practice the things he's been reading about, and solving problems on a continual basis – but he is also using his body and he loves it.

From my working days I remembered all the sweaty executives who used to don shorts and a singlet and go running through the city at lunchtime, sucking in lungs full of carbon monoxide fumes from the passing traffic. I wondered if that was their way of adding that basic physical dimension to their day. It feels so clear to me now that sitting in an office all day is not what we are actually cut out to do. Larry and I did it for thirty years but now we just walk out our front door and step off the veranda into the sun and the fresh air and we are at work. It feels so good – surely this much fun is illegal!

The change from city to country is at times invigorating and exciting and at other times still frightening, but we are changing, gradually, in many ways – mostly in the ways we had talked about and planned for.

What we hadn't planned for was a sort of natural emergence of specific old-fashioned gender roles. It hasn't been a conscious thing. It just seemed to happen. I have been down the feminist road in my life. Not that I burned my bra, braided my armpits and marched in the streets with my head shaved and my arms linked with my sisters. When all that was happening I was raising a family alone and running my own company. I had been a 'suit' in corporate life. I had smashed through a few glass ceilings but not for the thrill of proving anything or making a stand for the women's movement. I just had to put food on the table. I never had the luxury of riding on the 'power-trip bus' because by the time I was thirty I had no husband and three kids to feed, and I was in full survival mode.

When Larry and I married everything was pretty equal because we were doing the same corporate thing and the same parenting thing. But here on the farm, it's different. Larry automatically does the heavy toting and carrying and the driving of machines and all the dirty stuff. He revels in it. It's brought out a natural kind of 'man thing' that was missing in his corporate life. Where he was the consummate professional before, comfortable in his white shirt and tie, his clean-shaven face and short executive haircut, here there are traits that are developing slowly that set him apart from that smooth city professional, and are roughening up his edges a little. It is very attractive, very 'natural', I guess. His grey hair is now long and curly and his white beard is in stark contrast to his nut-brown Polynesian skin. His preferred footwear is his tough pair of work boots. Because they can't be worn inside, he will come to the door and call me for whatever he needs. And, like the 'little woman of the house' I happily go and get what he needs, in favour of having muddy boots in the house or holding up his work by making him take them off and put them on again. Similarly, although I automatically offer callers a cup of tea, when the caller is a mate of his, Larry offers a beer which is something that we didn't always do in Sydney. He never leaves the house without his hat which is a floppy old cloth thing that sits on his head at any angle it lands. Sometimes the brim is over his eyes, sometimes it is tilted at a ridiculous angle like a cock's comb. It seems to have a life of its own. No farmer leaves the house without a hat.

I am happy with the cooking and baking, and cleaning the house. I love snipping about in the vegetable garden and planning meals and planting seeds and raising seedlings in big black trays. It may be our ages, or it may be that the tasks we have automatically gravitated to are more natural to us. Mine is more nurturing and nest-building while his is more outdoorsy and rough.

Larry's tractor skill has been developing well. Our neighbour Malcolm gave him his first big tractor lesson which didn't last all that long but left a circle in the big paddock that we called our UFO crop circle.

Malcolm's wife Sandra explained to me the intricacies of driving a tractor and the dangers it presents. Sandra and I were sitting on the veranda watching Larry having a lesson on the tractor with Malcolm walking beside him. They seemed to be going at a snail's pace and I was pleased to see that. Sandra told me how easy it is to have hideous accidents with a tractor. Even though she was born and brought up in the country, Malcolm has never let her drive their tractor because it is so dangerous.

Malcolm is an excellent instructor and insisted that Larry drive in first gear only and very slowly until he develops some skill and confidence. Tractors have large tyres and a lot of grunt, and can flip themselves or tip over without a lot of encouragement. Because they are usually dragging some hideously lethal piece of kit behind them, it is not surprising that there are a lot of accidents and deaths among the farming community. Farming is a dangerous pastime. Whenever Larry is on the tractor, I feel a sense of dread and stand watching him painstakingly circle the paddock as he slashes the long grass to make mulch for our gardens.

With a little time and practice, Larry's burgeoning tractor expertise means that he is able to slash the paddocks himself without Malcolm's watchful eye. It is not our intention to do this forever. Slashing the paddocks costs a great deal of money in fuel now. In the future it will be too expensive. We will be in the same situation as many farmers who won't be able to afford to run their machines. But on our farm, we don't need vast grazing pasture. We are gradually planting hundreds of trees thickly and covering the grass in between with cardboard and thick mulch to kill it. Ultimately the grass will be gone just as in a natural forest. We will encourage native grasses or ground cover elsewhere, and mowing will be limited to a few areas only – in fact, we'll be using a scythe, not a mower.

We went to a recycling place near here and managed to find an old grass scythe which Pete is restoring for us. As each section is planted we refer to it as a no-mow zone. And along our boundary fences with Lindy on one side and Malcolm and Sandra on the other we will be mulching heavily too. This means that our neighbours will no longer have to use herbicides along those fences, as no grass will grow there either. That is a saving for them, and it means no poisons will be used on our land.

The creation of the no-mow zones is a deliberate plan. The insidious price creep of oil and oil derivatives is happening already. Larry went in to town to buy some cans of oil-based paint for the fences around the house, and the guy in the store asked him if he wanted to stock up. Larry asked him why and he said, 'Well, you reckon this can is expensive. I've got two more price rises coming in the next two months. Anything with oil and anything that has to be transported is going up, mate, going through the roof.' Larry didn't have to ask why.

Unlike the oil crises of the 1970s and 1980s when prices were high, the current increases are not going to go back down again. They will just get higher. These high prices are the beginning of the effects of Peak Oil.

The preceding forty days of preparations in the house had built to a crescendo with my ever-lengthening to-do lists prior to the arrival of everyone for the Christmas–New Year break. First to arrive were Josh and Tomoko and baby Jasper, then Missy from Melbourne and then Katie and Michael. The frenzy of activity before they arrived morphed into a frenzy of food consumption and laughter.

The day they all arrived it was 40 degrees and they piled out of their cars and headed straight into the pool. It was magic to again have a house full of people and chaos, voices in every room, things strewn everywhere. Josh had brought his fishing gear and his huge kite as well as all the paraphernalia needed for a new baby. The house passed its 'road test' with so many people in terms of accommodation. Everyone was comfortable and there was enough room both inside and out so that we didn't feel like we were in each other's space.

Josh left early each morning and drove to the beach and brought back dozens of whiting which he battered and fried or barbecued. He had brought all the vegetables that were ripe from his own vegetable garden and so the kitchen took on the look of a greengrocer's store. There were so many green tomatoes I looked up some recipes and found one for green tomato relish. Josh made a huge pot of it and bottled enough so that we were able to give it away to whoever dropped by. It thrilled me to be in a position to be able to give away things that we had made, as so many people had given homegrown or homemade things to us.

The different dynamics of our kids is like a study in the diversity of human nature. During that fleeting and precious time with the family, in the heat of those lazy summer days, I watched them all – one absorbed in a jigsaw puzzle, one snoozing on the veranda, a couple swimming, someone cooking or flying a kite. I wondered at what point they would ultimately make the decision to leave the city. I fervently hoped that they would join us on the farm. But at the same time, deep in my heart, my strongest wish was that they would never have to make that decision. Their lives were so full and interesting and promising, the thought that all of that may have to change brought back the fear and the fury and frustration I had felt when I first learned about Peak Oil.

What I wanted more than anything in the world was somehow for our fears for the future to be proved wrong or wiped away. I wanted there to be no problem with oil, no recession or depression on the horizon. I would have serious discussions with God about it. I told God that I would be totally contented living on the farm and doing all the things we set out to do just as a pleasant retirement for Larry and me, if only there wasn't the threat of a looming catastrophe. One of Rick's friends calls it the 'Principle of Anyway', which is doing things in preparation for Peak Oil which feel good to do anyway even if it doesn't get to that point.

God and I had many discussions over the years. Years ago, when I was a working single parent of three young children, I had accused Him of using me as a sort of crash test dummy to find out how much stress the modern woman could take. I said I had come through all that for Him and I would cope with whatever came, but please, let it only affect me and not my kids. The trouble with chats with God is that sometimes He is in a talkative mood and sometimes He just isn't.

The much-anticipated arrival of Geoff Lawton and his beautiful wife Nadia was supposed to occur in the first week of January but he called and said they would be arriving early. They turned up when all the family was here so we had a very full house.

I had talked incessantly to Larry about Geoff's permaculture knowledge since coming home from the Melbourne course. I was in such a state of excitement about Geoff and Nadia arriving that I felt like we were being visited by the Pope and the Queen. Some weeks earlier, in anticipation of their arrival, we had written out our objectives for their visit and also a page of items we wanted to achieve on the farm. Geoff and Nadia read through the lists and also examined the contour map we had obtained of the property. We talked a bit about our ideas and plans for creating self-sufficiency and then, armed with a pickaxe and the map, we all set off to walk the property with him.

Geoff, a tall, gangly guy with dishevelled hair and a strong English accent, strode out purposefully with his long legs and all the rest of us scurried behind like a gaggle of goslings off on our first trip to the pond. He would stop suddenly and dig here and there, with all of us standing about peering into his divots with studied concentration as if he were a mother bird intent on finding something juicy to feed us all. Then off he would go again, flinging snippets of fascinating observations back at us about this tree or that gully or a weed. Occasionally he would stop and taste the soil. I didn't fancy doing that but was content with his explanation of it either being sweet or sour which, I learned later, meant acid or alkaline. I decided I would just trust him on that one.

We loped about the big paddock and down to the dam and then into the forest at the river end of the property. It was the first time I had actually been into the forest. A few steps past the tree line and the farm disappeared and the green canopy of the tall trees and dense vegetation closed in around us. I was spellbound. The soil was soft and springy and black and covered in small-leafed native ground cover and hundreds of years of decomposed leaf litter and silt from when the river had flooded. It was quiet and cool and dark. On our way to the river we crossed the first of several brackish billabongs that teemed with tiny aquatic creatures and insects and moistened the air. Maybe this is where the platypus lived.

It was hard for me to realise that we actually owned a real rainforest. I couldn't follow the others to the river – my back would rebel if I tried to climb over all the fallen trees on the way – so I decided to wait. Larry promised me he would clear the fallen trees from the path so I could walk further and see the river and our island as soon as he had a chance. When the others left I just stood there, looking about at the cathedral-like green majesty of the place. Beautiful is a pathetic descriptor for that place. Magical is better.

We knew that other farmers along the river had, over time, removed all the rampant privet and camphor laurel trees that crowd out the native vegetation, and I could see that our area was in desperate need of the same sort of clearing. It's a long and arduous process but I envisioned a time when all the strangling weeds were gone and we could walk easily to our river and enjoy the natural beauty of the place.

Too soon Geoff and the rest of the family were back and we all marched single-file out of the forest and back up the property to the veranda again for another conference. Geoff attacked our contour map with coloured pencils and drew dams and duck ponds and swale lines on contour, water tanks, polypipe lines for irrigation, driving tracks and planting corridors for food forests. When he had finished we had a classically designed permaculture site plan, one that in time will actually mimic the random living chaos of the rainforest but which would provide abundance in fruit and vegetables and natural beauty. Geoff told us we had to plant eight support trees for each fruit tree we choose, and where there is nothing growing but grass in certain places we were to pack in the trees. We can always take trees out if there are too many in one spot, but once a forest is planted, new seedlings may not get enough light to thrive.

We wrote lists and notes and questioned Geoff about everything we had thought of before his visit and he presented us with huge amounts of information. We realised we had so much to consider and so many alternatives. He gave us lists of trees to plant, and things to do. After all the telling and asking and lecturing, the day culminated in a big, noisy dinner. He and Nadia stayed the night and finished up the consultation in the morning, before climbing into their battered little red car, promising to come back whenever they could. A week or so passed and a package arrived from them. They had sent seeds and cuttings for us to plant to get us started.

We felt as though Eden Forest was officially underway. Geoff and Nadia's visit left us with a mountain of work to do but it was what we had been waiting for since we arrived.

Chapter Twelve

Geoff's plan for the farm involved major earthworks. On the plans he had drawn up he had indicated where we were to dig a dam, a pond and two long swales. Swales are level ditches cut on contour which capture water and hold it instead of it running off down to the river. The captured water slowly sinks into the soil and the water is retained on the property much longer. Water falling on the property without the swales would take about twenty minutes to run from the top of the property to the river. With the swales, that same water would take two years to reach the river. All this was designed to follow Bill Mollison's principle of 'putting water to its duties'.

We showed our new local friends the plans and they all insisted we shouldn't embark on any earthworks before the rainy season was over: the heavy rains would wash our topsoil into the river and the farm would be ruined. When we tried to explain that the proposed swales and dams would actually slow down the flow of water on the property, our friends said that we had no idea how devastating and how heavy the rains are. Once we see them for the first time, they said, we will be glad we waited till after the rainy season before we disturbed the soil. This advice placed us in a dilemma. Should we listen to the local farmers who knew the area and the weather and the land, or do we listen to the permaculture expert? The earthworks were going to be extremely expensive, involving hiring heavy earthmoving equipment, skilled workers and trucks. If what the knowledgeable locals said was right we would not only have wasted a lot of money, but we would also have to truck in tons and tons of topsoil if we lost what we had. We couldn't afford to do that. We didn't know what to do. Our enthusiasm was taking a beating and our credibility as permaculture farmers was on the line.

We consulted Harry, a local dam builder. He came and listened to what we wanted to do and shook his head. 'Y' can't do that now. Y' can't do it till after the rains. If y' do, I'll be seein' ya float past my place on the river.' His grim words made us even more depressed.

After he left, Larry and I sat on the veranda together with hot cups of tea and worried about what we should do. Larry said, 'Should we leave the earthworks till after the rains like everyone is telling us or do we risk it all and trust that Geoff's permaculture experience is right?'

'I don't know. I feel totally torn. The locals know this area better than Geoff. On the other hand, Geoff has consulted all over the world, in places he has never been before. Surely that says something.'

Larry sat silently for a long while and I was hoping that he would be the one to make the final decision. I didn't want to make it because so much was riding on it. He said, 'I'm not a good risk-taker, what about you?'

'You know I'm a risk-taker, but this one feels too great. Then again, if we really believe in the principles of permaculture, we just have to blindly trust that it's the right thing to do otherwise we can't honestly say we believe in it totally. What does that do to our credibility and our commitment to this process? I feel like our belief in permaculture has backed us into a corner.' I looked out over the pristine grassed paddocks of our property. This decision was major and I had so little expertise to fall back on. Finally I turned to Larry and said, 'I think we have to go against the locals and stick to what we believe.' Larry agreed with me. As I said the words, I felt total terror. We would be risking the success of the farm. We would be risking a lot of money. We were going ahead with the earthworks at the riskiest time of the year.

We called Harry and told him we were going to go ahead. He tried to dissuade us again but we had made the decision and we were going to stick to it. He couldn't give us a definite start date because of the unpredictability of the weather but scheduled it tentatively for the end of the following week.

A day later I woke at 3 am to the heavy thrumming of torrential rain on the tin roof. For it to wake me without my hearing aids gives some indication of the level of the noise. When the first light of dawn came we stepped onto the veranda to see what was happening. Because we are situated in a valley, we can see the rain coming up the valley like a thick grey curtain. As it moves towards us it first obliterates the horizon, Mt Coramba disappears completely, then the paddocks at its base, then the trees dotted along the valley, then Malcolm and Sandra's house and then it hits us preceded by a strong wind. It is a magnificent sight! Larry went out to check the water movement across the paddocks. I checked the internet and read the flood warning and tried to call some friends but the phone line was out. The mobiles were not hanging on their usual hooks. I started to panic. I suddenly realised that if Larry fell now, or was hit by the lightning, I would be isolated and unable to call anyone for help.

The rains kept falling. Sheets of heavy driving rain pounded down on us, unremitting in intensity. The sound on the tin roof made hearing each other difficult and the house suddenly felt like a stilt house built over a pond. The level land on which the house had been built was becoming a lake. We put on wet-weather gear and went out in it so that Larry could show me the sheets of run-off that were coming from the north hill and racing like a raging river down the hill, taking everything with it on its way, even rocks. We understood our friends' concern about losing all our topsoil. The power of the rainwater was something I had never seen before. We trudged about in ankle-deep water, with rain pouring down our faces.

Back at the house, when the phone line restored itself, I called friends to make sure that they were alright. Bill and Diane were already flooded in. Their two causeways were under water but Bill said they had enough beer and that was all that mattered. Alan said he and Denise had just gone down to the river and it had a little way to go before it broke the bank. He said they were fine and their beautiful pecan trees were still standing but 'there's an old bugger with a long white beard in the next paddock building what looks like a bloody huge wooden boat!' Denise came on the line and advised us to stock up on milk and bread in case the local shop ran out of supplies and couldn't get restocked if the roads went under water. Jim and Connie called to say they had spent the day trying to dry out the guest house for their kids who were arriving in a few hours. All the carpets were ruined but their farm was fine and so were they.

Larry jumped into the truck and zoomed off to Coramba to see how high the river had risen at the bridge and to buy bread and milk. When he got home he said the river was running hard but not flooding yet. He walked down to survey our rainforest. The first billabong which had been a brackish pond when he last went in was now a fast-flowing creek and the crossing to the island was under water.

Lindy next door was having her own drama. Her entire herd of cows, including calves and her prized Brahman bull, were all on the river flats at the bottom of her property. They were cut off by the rising waters of the Orara River and couldn't get back to a safe paddock closer to the house. Lindy tied a rope around her waist and tied the other end to a tree and endeavoured to cross the torrent to encourage the lead cow across but it was too deep. The water was up to her chest. She feared she would lose her entire herd and there was nothing that she could do to save them.

I could see Malcolm and two buddies sloshing about in his lower paddock and I called the house to see if they needed help. His daughter Carlie said they were alright, just mending a fence that had been washed away.

I'm glad we don't have cows. When our vegetables are growing in the garden at least they won't escape like cows can. And a dead lettuce is a lot less expensive than a dead cow. Malcolm's cows are vocal ladies in this torrential downpour. They sound like they were the last to join the school band and the only instruments left for them were tubas. They can only play one mournful note and even that isn't very good.

We waited for the next flood warning to be issued. We both felt a sort of perverse thrill in all this. It was serious and if it kept up it could even be dangerous. In Sydney nothing had ever happened to make me feel so aware of my mortality, so 'alive', and aware of the world around me. In Sydney we were Fox News and CNN addicts watching the world unfold every day from our armchairs. We were living our lives vicariously

whereas here in the country we were living precariously …
and it was strangely exhilarating.

As quickly as they came, the rains left that day. Lindy's herd
of cows were eventually able to cross to a higher paddock and
none were lost. Our land was covered in thick, deep sucking
mud. The heat of the summer sun dried it quickly, leaving
solid casts of our footprints wherever we had walked during
the deluge.

On the day scheduled for the earthworks we were very
nervous and unsure that we had made the right decision. At
the same time, like two kids who were doing something our
parents would disapprove of, we felt a bit brazen.

Harry arrived early with his huge earthmover on an
enormous trailer which he parked out front of our place. Our
front gate is set back from the road as there is a big bus-turning
bay right where three farm entrances converge. We could see
Harry had parked his trailer right in the bus-turning bay.
Larry rushed out and said, 'Harry, I don't know about you
parking your trailer there. I don't think the school bus driver
would be very happy about that.'

Harry tipped his hat to the back of his head and grinned
a watery-eyed grin. 'I don't think he's gonna mind one
little bit.'

Sometimes these country folk can seem a bit too relaxed.
Larry persisted, asking how he could be so sure about that.

Eventually Harry cracked, and said, ''Cause I'm the bus
driver!'

Harry had told us during our initial meeting that every farm
needed a wide entrance for large equipment and ours wasn't
wide enough. It needed to be around four metres wide. We
had arranged for him to break through the tree line and make
a new entrance. I stood some distance from the tree line with
my camera ready to shoot him coming through. The thickness

of the trees meant that I couldn't see him at all on the other side and then the trees made loud cracking sounds and the branches swished and snapped and they just fell away like matchsticks as the big yellow mechanical monster came pushing through with Harry caged-up safely inside the cabin.

Having crashed his way onto the property, Harry rumbled his way down the slope towards his first task, building the dam. The skill with which he manoeuvred those tons and tons of machinery astounded us. He could have been driving a little sedan. As the hole in the ground got bigger and bigger Harry and his big yellow earthmover crawled in and out of it like a gecko climbing up a wall.

Then the dam was finished. I wondered how long it would take to fill such a yawning great hole. It was a massive empty clay scar in the earth, and the paddock grass was all scarred with the marks of the heavy machinery. It all looked rather ghastly. As soon as the machinery left, Larry went out and scattered cow pea seeds all over the dam as Geoff had instructed him to do. He covered the cow pea with a light sprinkling of mulch. Geoff had said that the cow pea would provide quick-growing ground cover and would also help to hold the disturbed soil in place.

To build the swales and the pond, we needed other, smaller, pieces of equipment and another operator. Karl's skill matched Harry's in manoeuvring his heavy gear. To dig the swales on contour was a precision job requiring a laser level to ensure that the swales were dead flat. Both Karl and Harry were very sceptical about these swales. They thought we were quite mad for wanting them and were convinced that we would regret our decision when the next rains came. One swale came off the end of the dam as a sort of spillway. The other one was dug at the end of a long drainage ditch that first entered the new little pond at one end, came out at the other end of the pond and continued down the hill to meet the swale further down. This bottom swale would hold water on contour, taking out all the force it had gathered racing downhill. Well, we hoped that is what would happen. We were yet to find out when the next rains came.

And the rains did come a few days later. In fact, so much fell that the dam filled within forty-eight hours. Over a quarter of a million litres of water collected in our new dam. We were astounded. And then the rain kept falling and falling and falling. We were living on an island again, surrounded with mud. Early in the morning, during a break in the rain, we put on our big Wellington boots and walked out to see if there was any damage. We were anxious to see if the dire predictions of all our friends and the earthmovers were right. Had we lost all our topsoil? Were we effectively ruined? Was our farm now just part of the silt rushing along in the Orara River?

Well, the dam was still there. The pond was still there. The drainage ditch leading to the bottom swale was a fierce torrent, with water shooting into the air as it hit the rocks we had placed along its path. As the water raced down the ditch it hit the bottom swale, spread out along its length and just sat there, gently spilling off the end on its overflow path to the little old dam at the end of the property and on to the river. The concept of the swale was being demonstrated to us graphically. It had worked!

We walked towards the dam and behind the high wall that Harry had built to hold all those thousands and thousands of litres. As we approached the centre of the wall we could hear water – tumbling, rushing water. To our horror, water was angrily cascading down from one spot at the top of the dam, eating away at the bank. We raced back to the house, slipping and sliding in the slick mud and rushed for the phone. We called Geoff to ask him what we should do. The dam was breaking! Every second counted. We were going to lose the dam. He told us to stuff straw bales into the breach and keep stuffing them in until the water stopped.

The rain was falling again and we ran outside, loaded up a barrow with the rotting straw bales we had been saving for mulch, and while Larry pushed and shoved the barrow through the slick heavy mud, I balanced the bales until we got to the breach. So much water had fallen through the break at the top of the dam that the ground at the base was saturated. Our boots were sucked into the mud over our ankles. We fell into it over and over and slipped against the dam side but we didn't care.

Armload by armload, Larry started from ground level and pushed the bales into the earth, gradually building a wall of bales leading to the top. As we emptied each barrow, our fear was growing. The water was still tearing out the soil in the top of the wall. I was panting and coughing and wheezing with asthma and aching in every part of my body. We were both covered in sticky mud. My heart was racing but there was no time to stop for a rest. If the wall broke while we were underneath it, I imagined us being swept away. Neither of us knew if we were packing it correctly, but Geoff had said to just keep packing until the water stopped.

The rain was still falling, making it hard to see and walk and even breathe. When we ran out of old bales, Larry jumped into the truck and screeched off down the road to a neighbour who was selling straw bales. He came back with the truck and trailer piled high with forty bales. Suddenly, down the driveway came two dark-garbed figures. It was Malcolm and Sandra. Sandra had on a full-length Driza-Bone raincoat and a broad-brimmed, plastic-covered hat. Malcolm had on a shorter coat and his usual short shorts. He was pushing a barrow twice the size of ours. They must have seen our struggle from their house and had come to help plug the dam. Their arrival immediately lowered my blood pressure. I felt suddenly as if the cavalry had arrived and we were saved.

Together the four of us huffed and puffed our way to and from the wall with the straw bales until the men had built the bales up to the top and the water finally was being held back. For now, the panic was over. Wearily we all sloshed up onto the veranda and had a beer. Sandra and Malcolm's easy chatter and their tough confidence were like salves to our concerns. Their 'oh well, shit happens, get on with it' attitude was something that we would learn as our country experience grew. I knew that it was an attitude that would save us time and again in the future.

As we looked out across the dam, and the long swale, we realised that in spite of the breach in the wall, the soil had not been lost in the deluge. The water falling and running onto the property was doing exactly as Geoff had predicted it would. The swales were holding the water and the soil was not being swept into the river.

Early the following day we heard footsteps on the veranda and it was Harry the dam builder. He had come to see how his dam was holding up. He muttered and blustered and limped his way over the dam wall surveying the damage and the way we had patched it with straw bales. He blamed the level of the swale as the problem, while we felt that the dam wall shouldn't have been built against our lone gum tree. But whatever the reason, the dam was saved and the farm was safe from the deluge of the rainy season. Our faith in Geoff's permaculture knowledge was intact and our commitment to its principles was now rock solid.

We will ultimately have to remove the tree which is so sad because it is the home and meeting place of such a large and diverse number of birds. When the rainy season is over we will dig the swale deeper and use the clay from that to fix the dam wall. This will entail unplugging all the straw bales and plugging it up with clay and growing grasses over it to give it strength.

Within days, the cow peas were sprouting all over the areas that had been scarred by the earthworks. As the earth healed itself, I pondered on the incredible mystery of nature. All around us there are literally trillions upon trillions of life forms doing their work silently, deliberately, and we are simply a part of that incredible web of life.

We believe we are the most intelligent, most important form of life on earth, but we can only believe that when we are unaware of the totality and absoluteness of the power of nature. It seems that wherever man goes in the world, wherever we go on our little farm, following on from us and repairing our damage are all the other forms of life we don't see. Where we dig the soil, immediately something rushes in and grows over the gap. The awareness of it was a humbling experience. As Rick Embleton says in his book, 'we are not the gods we wish to be'.

Just as our skin heals a scar without our conscious choice, so too does the earth heal, and when the damage we do is too great, much dies and the delicate and deliberate chain of life is broken. I remembered Bill Mollison describing the damage we do to the earth.

> Agriculture is one of the greatest contributors to the destruction of our environment. Forty percent of the world's soil and water have been polluted by farming. The great challenge for sustainable agriculture is to produce the food and fibre needed, while maintaining fertile soils and clean water, and enhancing the health of ecosystems.

The rains receded, the earth was healing and the work we had done was changing the nature of our farm; changing and improving it and returning it to the way it should have always been. It would take the new dam about a year to stabilise and settle and for grasses to grow on the banks.

Our first visitor to the dam was a little black darter. I chose to believe it was a female, because its actions were so graceful. Ducking and swimming under the water, she would feed in the silver shimmer of the early morning sun, and then eventually she would emerge elegantly onto the high side of the dam wall. She would then sit quietly in among the cow pea, craning her neck and looking in all directions to make sure she was safe. Eventually she would hold out her wings for the sun to dry her feathers. She came every day and gave us silent moments of joy as we watched her.

Eventually she was joined by a very smartly dressed grey heron who wore a snowy-white mask. The heron, balancing on impossibly thin stick-like legs, would walk slowly and purposefully along the water's edge. She would stare into the water, not moving, as if she were a sculpture. When an appetiser would swim within striking distance she would suddenly dart her head down and snap it up. How these edible delights got into our new dam we had no idea. Before the big rains came, the dam was a clay hole in the ground that got filled with rain. It's still a mystery to us, but they are there: a teeming city of little creatures that delight the birds who now come regularly for their dinner.

The dam will serve several purposes. It will be a valuable source of water for irrigation and we also intend stocking it with fish as a protein source. In order to actually breed fish in the dam we have to learn about aquaculture, but that is a long way down the 'to do' list. The list is impossibly long, but the learning can't stop. We need to gather as much knowledge as we can.

One of the most important things we can do during this first year is just observing how the seasons affect each part of the property. This gives us the understanding of what we have to do to take advantage of our location and of the weather.

Our farm is in the lee of Mt Coramba and we can sit on our veranda and watch the rain falling on the mountain and slowly making its way down our side and up our valley. Often we watch it start to rain only to see it stop at the mountain. One morning before the dam was filled, Larry and I were sitting having our morning tea watching the mountain disappear and reappear shrouded in a curtain of grey rain. I thought it was coming and then it stopped and then the mountain disappeared again. I was exasperated and said to Larry, 'Those lucky mountain people! Now they are building a bloody ark and we are sitting here *parched*! We will have to fill the dam with bottled water at this rate!'

Watching and learning about the weather has become a daily event. We notice when the ants are climbing up rather than walking along the ground. We notice when the wind changes, when it is cloudy, and look in the direction the wind is coming from to see how low the clouds are in the valley. We know so little but we are lucky that at the very least we are aware of what we don't know, which gives us the opportunity to learn and fill in the gaps. I am assured by people with more experience that in time I will learn to smell the coming changes of the weather. I can see myself as a craggy toothless old grey-haired hag sitting in my rocking chair on the veranda, corncob pipe in my mouth, watching the grandchildren in the yard and muttering to myself, 'Yup! The rains are a-comin'.'

Now that the dam and pond and swales have been dug, and water management on the property is almost complete, our next task is to plant trees. The objective is to make Eden Forest into a 'food forest', but we can't just go out into the paddock and plant whatever we fancy. We first made a list of all the fruit we have always eaten, and scoured fruit-growing books and catalogues for other ideas. Our area is prone to frost and so some of our preferences are going to have to be protected from that as they are frost-sensitive. Some of course we won't be able to grow at all. To create a microclimate suitable for certain fruits, we will need to heavily plant fast-growing legume trees to act as 'nurse' trees for our fruit, acting as a weather barrier and protection for them.

We've chosen a north-facing hill to start with, and have planned out a series of three rows of wide arcs one behind the other. On the line of the arcs we will plant eight different nurse trees and in the middle of each arc, once the nurse trees grow, we will plant the fruit trees. The planting was going to be exciting.

I ordered the first of the hundreds of trees we would need and the first fifty-two little black forestry tubes arrived in a big box ready for us to begin the planting of our forest. I had ordered a variety of different Australian natives – acacias, callistemon, melaleucas, cassias, mutton-woods and casuarinas. With my work boots on and some clothes that even the most polite person would not say were flattering, I headed out with my trowel and pick and all the new little trees.

It was while I was kneeling in the soft damp earth that I realised that I had quite a severe disability. I realised that I am extremely entomologically challenged! Beside my knee, I noticed a very neat round hole in the ground with its occupant at the entrance observing my gardening. We looked at each other for a moment and it occurred to me that this little creature probably doesn't have spaghetti bolognaise at least once a week and doesn't fret if it misses an episode of *The Bold and the Beautiful*. We were aliens on the same patch of dirt. While I could have stomped on it with my steel-capped, tractor-tyre-soled boot if I were quick enough, equally it could have darted out of its neat round funnel-shaped hole and injected me with a fatal drop of poison. We stared, neither moving for some seconds and then I made an executive decision. I stomped on it. I then stomped closed all the holes I could see and there seemed to be a large number of them. I really don't know whether that creature was a venomous funnel-web spider but I acknowledged that yet another great yawning gap in my knowledge base had just opened up. I am currently giving myself about a C-minus average in flora but I am definitely a straight F student in the six- and eight-leg category of the arachnid and associated insect department. It's a bit rough when you are staring down the wrong side of fifty-six and you know you have at least a forty-year learning curve to hurdle.

The garden I was working in was very weedy and overgrown. I was glad of my permaculture lessons about soils because it meant that I knew I didn't have to dig it all up and turn the soil. I pulled or just cut down the weeds and laid them back on the ground and sprinkled blood-and-bone and chicken poop and sheep poop everywhere. Then I covered the whole garden with thick sheets of newspaper and watered it all. Where I planted the baby trees I left a gap between the layers of paper, but not much, just enough for the trees. Over the paper I spread heaped piles of mulch that Larry had slashed from the paddocks.

Larry tackled the north hill which was heavily grassed. He used the same method but instead of newspaper he covered the whole area with sheets of cardboard before mulching. The north hill is going to be our citrus orchard. My friend Connie has well-established fruit trees and when her orange trees are heavily laden with fruit she goes into orange cake production or jam and preserve making. When I told her how I envied her skill she told me she had been brought up to do these things. When she was little, her family in Melbourne routinely laid up the excess produce from their land simply because that is what people did in the days before refrigerators and mega-supermarkets.

Connie has about a fifty-year head start on me in the skills department. I had just got used to making a loaf of bread whereas whenever Connie is going to visit someone she can scan her larder for chutneys and pickles, jams and homemade goodies from her vast garden which she can give to friends. Regularly in my emails a recipe will pop up that she has sent me. Similarly I receive recipes or tips from Sandra next door.

This refreshing kind of sharing of information, which is just 'the way we do things' among my friends and neighbours here, will have to become the way for all of us in the future. Becoming self-sufficient doesn't mean high-tailing it out to the bush and living in a cave or in an isolated homestead. In the future the only true route to survivability in a chaotic post-peak world will have to be community, working together on major projects, sharing what each other can grow or create or do.

Last time Connie was here at the Forest I gave her some Delicata squash I had picked from our new little vegetable garden. I had grown them from heirloom seeds and made delicious soups with them. Now she can grow them too simply by saving the seeds and planting them next season. I also printed out the Delicata soup recipe I had used.

Saving seeds of pure untouched varieties is a hot topic right now. Monsanto, the world's largest seed and agricultural company, pledged not to commercialise their 'terminator technology' back in 1990, but have not ruled out developing or using the so-called suicide seeds at some point. What terminator technology does is genetically switch off a plant's ability to germinate a second time. In other words, a farmer buys seed to produce a crop but he is unable to harvest the seed from that crop to use the following year. He is forced to buy the seed again. In effect, this eliminates forever the ability of millions upon millions of people from being able to gather their own seeds to grow their own food. From the corporate stance it is just great for profits. It forces people to buy instead of care for themselves. What do farmers with no money do to buy new seed? We were glad that we had become aware of the seed-savers groups, with people who actually understood that there was more to life than making money, that eating was a pretty good thing too!

When we were invited to dinner at the local pub to meet a new couple, Roz and Paul, who live down the road from us, they greeted us warmly and Roz handed me a little plastic bag as a greeting gift. On the bag were the handwritten words 'purple climbing beans'. It was a gift that meant more to me than if she had presented me with a nugget of gold or some fancy gift-wrapped store-bought thing. It said more about her as a woman than if she had sat and told me her deepest philosophies of life. She gave me what would become next year's crop of non-genetically engineered beans.

Each time we seem to be getting on top of things a new phase begins. Interlaced in our daily activities is the constant feed of Peak Oil news which is now quite prolific on the internet, and is also now popping up more and more in the press and other mainstream media. It keeps us on track and focused and gives purpose to all the things we want to achieve.

Our next task was to build a fence around the house to keep the dogs in and our future chickens, ducks, geese and possibly goats out. Larry had already dismantled all the horse fencing on the property, saving all the bolts and screws to recycle when the fencing was reassembled around the house. When the time came, Pete offered to help Larry do the fence, and Nili and

Pete arrived for a fencing day. Pete had brought a post-hole auger to dig the holes. I had to sheepishly admit that until that moment I had not only never seen an auger, I didn't know such a thing existed. Nili took up an overseer position on the veranda, with her intricate and complicated knitting on her lap, watching Pete and Larry 'aug' (clearly if the item being used is an auger, then one must 'aug' with it!).

The auger is an enormous metal corkscrew-looking tool that digs holes in the ground. It starts with a pull rope like a two-stroke mower and the corkscrew screws into the ground; when it's pulled out, the post-hole is 'auged'. Larry then got a huge double-handled thing that looked to me like a giant's salad server. With it he pinched up the loose soil in the hole and then they moved on to the next spot.

I was intent on finishing my tree planting and Nili gave up her knitting to help me. On their sheep and cattle station they had planted thousands of trees and I think that after they sold their property and retired to Coffs Harbour, she believed she would never have to bother with such arduous tasks again. But as the summer heat blanketed us, we pressed on with the planting for much of the day, while the men toiled away at the fencing. It felt good to have someone to share the tasks with, and working with Nili and Pete is just plain fun. I realised during that planting that it had been a long time since I had shared such plain and simple fun with someone else.

To keep up our planting work, we needed wooden stakes for various parts of the garden. Larry bought 500 tomato stakes from a colourful chap living tucked away in the bush to the north of us. When Larry went to collect them he met a craggy old fellow who had been working at his mill seemingly forever. This old fellow held fast to the world he has always known.

'Don't give me this metric stuff,' he grumbled when Larry asked for his order. 'Them fellas who use that metric stuff are out to rip a fella off! Y' know what a man's talking about when he says "2000 board foot o' timber". Y' can understand that. Y' *sees* that in y'mind. Know what I mean young fella? But this metric stuff ... bad news ... just a rip-off. Now young fella, what was you wantin'? A bundle of three-foot tomata stakes was it? Inch-be-inch?'

Larry nodded seriously to him and repeated, 'Yeah, inch-be-inch thanks mate'. He was still smiling when he drove in the gate with his 'inch-be-inch tomata stakes'.

Finding the right things we need is an ongoing issue and we know that it will be a growing problem as resources deplete or the cost of fuel makes driving long distances to collect things unviable. Larry had spoken some while ago to a fellow he had met casually about our need for lots of trees. Next thing we know a white truck comes rumbling down our drive. It was the fellow Larry had met. He jumped out of his truck, plonked on a hat with a brim wide enough to shade people walking either side of him and, with a grin from ear to shining ear, he announced that he had brought us a box of trees from his property. 'Dorothy,' I said to myself, 'this is *definitely* not Kansas!' They are little trees at the moment but some are Moreton Bay figs and other fig varieties, so we expect some of them to grow to enormous sizes eventually. We subsequently found out that native figs tend to lure millions of pooping screaming bats! But his gift was very welcome. After a short chat about the trees he retreated to his truck, still grinning his broad grin. He then adroitly manoeuvred his monstrous hat into the vehicle and rattled away. We looked at the box of trees and were quite overcome by his generosity.

Our tree planting program has resulted in nearly 400 trees in the ground so far. Thousands more are needed before Eden Forest is a forest. The task ahead of us is huge. Just the decision-making process is daunting. Where do we put the olive grove?

Where should the woodlot go so that we have wood to chop for the wood stove we don't have yet? If it is too close to the house it would constitute a fire hazard, if it is too far from the house it would constitute a problem in getting the logs to the house for use. Where should the apples go and the plums and peaches and grapes, the oak trees and the neem trees and the tea and coffee trees? Our heads are whirling with all these decisions. When our blueberry trees were ordered, a note came from the nursery to say that when they are planted, we have to knock off the flowers for the first two years to allow the trees to concentrate their energies on just growing and establishing. It brought home to us just how much time it takes to grow things to eat. Macadamia nut trees, for example, can take up to eleven years to reach full production. We feel lucky that we have this time while life is still reasonably stable.

Chapter Thirteen

While we are establishing the food forest and the vegetable gardens and focusing so heavily on achieving self-sufficiency, one of the most vital but most pleasant elements of our move to the country has been meeting the people among whom we live. Being accepted by a community and establishing ourselves and our place here is as important to us as making the farm successful.

We will all need each other in the years ahead. We will need strong community ties, strong bonds with people in our area. In our planting plans, we have estimated yield from our gardens to ensure surplus for sharing, bartering, trading and selling. We want to be a source of good healthy natural food for us and our family and for the people who live around us.

I don't know if we were just lucky to have found ourselves among such genuinely wonderful people or if it is like this all over the country. Our social life is busier now than it ever was in the city. We had Jim and Connie and Alan and Denise over for afternoon tea one Sunday. Jim and Connie brought some fresh-picked squash the size of butternut pumpkin from their vegetable garden, and Alan and Denise brought two potted Nelly Kelly passionfruit vines, a jar of homemade passionfruit jam and a tomato plant. We sat on the veranda and ate and drank and laughed and they talked about their farms and all the funny things that happen, and gave us, as usual, a tremendous amount of advice and guidance. We were like kids being read to, soaking up all their stories.

They are good people, ordinary, pleasant and unassuming. They don't wear designer clothes, or drive expensive cars. The women don't have manicured nails or freshly coiffed hair or wear make-up. They dress for the weather and their hands are hands that work hard. Most of them have come from the big cities to make their lives here, leaving their kids as we have done, hoping to create something special out of their properties. They may not have come to the country to ready themselves for the downside of Peak Oil as we have done; they have made the change for a variety of reasons, whether for lifestyle, for financial reasons, or just for a change. They are in some cases older than us, but still they have made the break from the city and made it work.

Our lifestyle choice was made while the choice was ours to make and not imposed on us by a dangerously uncertain future. Our sense of purpose and rightness about being here is bolstered by the friends around us, although we are the only ones following the permaculture principles. Some are farming organically, while others are using the old methods, with lots of chemical and artificial inputs. The main thing about them all is that they love where they live, love the way of life here, the natural beauty. And they are passionate about preserving the lifestyle in this little valley.

Jim and Connie told us all about their bull escaping to go for a swim in the river. He took a fancy to the neighbour's comely cows and regularly escaped to meet them for clandestine trysts. This particular bull knew no shame and was happy to smash through electrified barbed-wire fences to satisfy his lusty ways. Ultimately they had to sell him but not before he successfully damaged the truck and then smashed up the sales yards where he was taken. Their bull's sexual proclivities cost them dearly.

Living on the land puts you squarely in the face of life and death. After a farmer has been telling you about his cow's lovely disposition, her cute anthropomorphic antics and how as a calf she would seek out his company for a rub on the head, one's corned beef sandwich suddenly takes on a personality all its own which renders lunch a little less appealing. I have a long way to go before I am able to view velvety calves and plucky little steely-eyed chickens as merely objects of nutrition.

Sandra arrived on the veranda one afternoon with an armful of fresh-picked flowers from her garden. She sat with me for a while having a glass of iced water and chatted about her upcoming weekend of deer hunting. She's an experienced shooter and although she doesn't like the taste of deer, she has no qualms about shooting one to be eaten by the other people in her shooting party. To her, the death of animals is just part of country life.

While Sandra was away camping and shooting deer, she had asked us to mind her chickens. Each morning we would take a basket into our garden and pick a load of greens to take to the chickens as an extra treat. On the first morning, when we approached the chook pen to feed them, all Sandra's 'girls' muttered and clucked and gathered at the fence to see who these strangers were who were approaching them.

I opened the gate to their enclosure which is covered by an old passionfruit vine heavy with fruit and the hens looked most concerned. Some retreated into their roost while the others backed up a little to get a better look at me. When I emptied my basket on the ground and they saw that we had come bearing luscious gifts, all tentativeness and decorum disappeared and they all began pecking and squabbling and feasting. A few of the leaves I had gathered had grubs on them so I knew a couple of the hens were in for a real surprise.

I went into the roost where they sleep and lay their eggs. Sandra uses old mower grass-catchers for nest boxes and fills them with shredded paper. One hen was still in her grass-catcher nest, content to sit snuggled in the paper shreddings. In the other catchers were six eggs which I gathered and put in my basket. I found the feed bin and topped up their hanging feeder and then went out to see that the greens party was still very much in full swing.

The next morning when the hens saw Larry and me approaching we were greeted with much excitement and loud clucks as I again emptied their treats onto the dirt. This time there was no holding back, and all of them set upon their feast with contented grorrrrrrks and clucks. No one had thought to lay me any eggs however so we left empty-handed. Our last visit was the same: hysterical joy at seeing us arrive with the basket of greens and then studious dissection of the meal. Three eggs lay unattended in the grass-catchers.

Every time I spend time with Sandra she shares her stories, her wisdom and her vast knowledge with consummate ease. She is a constant source of interest and pleasure. To someone as new to country life as me, listening to Sandra talking about purposefully going out into the countryside to shoot deer for food and sport presented a picture which I couldn't easily reconcile with her natural refinement and femininity. She works in town in a fashion boutique. She would look right at home in any of Sydney's up-market coffee shops. But she hates city life, and she couldn't live without her chickens and wide open spaces. From her lounge room she looks out over acres and acres of green pastures dotted with trees and dams covered with blue water lilies. It is tranquil and lush and beautiful. It's people just like Malcolm and Sandra who will ultimately be the saving grace for many of us. We all need people of the land who are willing, even keen, to share their knowledge, to teach and help people like Larry and me learn how to work a farm. Their willingness to give of their time and their expertise freely is vital for our success here.

Another person here who has done a great deal for the local community is the actor Russell Crowe. He established Heart Start, a first aid service for the Nana Glen area, where the closest ambulance is twenty-five kilometres away in Coffs Harbour. If there is an emergency you first call 000 to summon an ambulance from town, then you dial the Heart Start number and locals who have been trained in first aid will immediately come to your farm and attend to you while waiting for the ambulance to arrive.

It is services like Heart Start that make our valley special. In the years ahead this kind of service will have to be developed across the country to meet the needs of small communities struggling to support each other. The establishment of bioregionalism is not an overnight thing. It takes time to develop and for people to become part of such a community.

Bioregionalism is just another word for centring your activities and livelihood wholly within the area in which you live. It means knowing about the area, its ecology and topography, animals, plants, soils, and human community, as well as the produce and activities that are part of it.

Living in a bioregional manner means eating only locally grown food. This means eating according to the growing season for fresh food, and relying on the food that you have frozen, canned or dried when not in season. Eating in this way eliminates the cost of trucking in food and is more healthy and natural. In a vibrant bioregion with a cohesive community, you shop at locally owned stores and use the products and services that are close to home. The preference is also to support local trades and services, and banking and financial institutions that are locally owned and which invest in the area. You get to know the people around you, and purposefully take the time to care for and about them, socialise with them, and help them when necessary. And you share with them.

I showed Sandra my new heirloom vegetable catalogue and she marked off the things she would like me to grow that I can share with her. I also showed the catalogue to our other neighbour Lindy so she could also choose what she wanted me to grow. I sent away for all the seeds and when they came I filled tray after tray with a selection of the precious seed and then set about designing the area where I intended to plant them.

Beside the house is a path that leads to the veranda and the front door and beside that path was a twelve-by-five metre rectangle of lawn. It was just useless lawn that would need constant mowing to keep it neat. I chose that spot for my first experimental vegetable patch.

The garden was not going to be straight beds with neat vegetables all lined up like soldiers on parade. I designed a meandering pathway from one short side to the other so that there was an entrance to the garden at each end, and I drew another entrance midway down the long side nearest the path. The actual planting beds were all one metre wide so that whichever side of a planting bed I want to work on, I can reach it comfortably in a half a metre without effort.

The idea was not to make it a traditional 'vegie patch'. Instead I wanted an attractive and interesting display beside the entrance path to the house. This would eliminate the need to ever mow there again and would require no back-breaking maintenance. The planting area is more than adequate to yield over 300 kilos of pesticide-free, heirloom vegetables in one year!

This garden would not only be interesting to wander through, and very pretty to look at, but would also be packed full of edible things right at my doorstep. The addition of a profusion of flowers was purposeful. The flowers serve to mask either the shape or smell of the vegetables growing there as much as possible which confuses or deters pests.

Larry lay cardboard down in a rough U-shape on all the pegged-out pathways and then filled the U with crusher dust to make the paths. The garden beds were built directly on top of the grass. By covering the grass with cardboard and then placing soil on top, there was no need for digging. The grass dies and its nutrient returns to the soil. The soil was originally planted with cow pea and a cocktail of chook poop, sheep poop and blood-and-bone and a seven- or eight-centimetre layer of mulch. The seedlings that went in first were soon taken over by the cow pea and I had to go out there with a pair of scissors and 'chop and drop' the cow pea around the emerging vegetables so that I could find them. I felt like a giant doing a harvest. I was down on my hands and knees snipping the green stuff and laying it on the ground. It's called 'green manure'. The result of the cow pea and the poop cocktail and the mulch is soil that almost stands up and drags growing things up to the sky! It's absolutely magic. Liberal helpings of poop and a thick coat of mulch is definitely manna from heaven for the garden.

I found some purple stuff growing during my chop and drop with the scissors and looked it up and found that it is purple basil called dark opal basil. It's magnificent! It not only smells delicious, it has purple leaves and then pink flowers and would look good as a pot plant. I next have to find out how to dry the leaves so I have a good supply of dried basil. It's really fun having a vegetable garden so chock full of things.

The seedlings all came up within a week from being planted. When I was giving them an early morning watering I realised I may have overdone the germination of baby beetroot plants. I had planted two different varieties – Chioggia, which is coloured with red and white concentric circles, and Round Red, the usual blood red variety. It struck me that I have never eaten beetroot deliberately in my entire life. I went to the computer and found so much on beetroot that I'll be able to use them for just about everything from painting the Harbour Bridge to knitting a baby's layette! I saved beetroot recipes from all over the world. It's one thing to grow stuff, but when it has grown, one has to actually *do* something with it.

It's interesting that everything we eat out of the garden – mint, lettuce, basil, tomatoes – whatever I choose – seems to have a stronger taste than what I have always bought in the shops. It must be the animal poop and the minerals liberally supplied by a vast complex of soil organisms invisibly working away out there.

When I make a salad for dinner, I leave it until the last moment and then, with the salad bowl in hand and a pair of scissors, I wander about snipping fresh greens, nasturtium flowers and leaves, and whatever else takes my fancy. A quick wash to ensure there are no bugs is all that is needed then, and it is so fresh it's as if it is still alive. It makes me feel terribly 'Mother Earth'.

The bounty of our vegetable garden made me think again about how vulnerable we were in the city and how totally dependent we were on farmers, on big business, on trucking companies and governments to provide our food. Beginning to grow our own food leaves us with a sweet after-taste of freedom from that dependence. It not only serves the purpose of nutrition, it is just plain interesting to see how different things taste, what their flowers look like and smell like, how long they last, and how things grow. I didn't know for example, that zucchini literally grow over night. I pick what is there for dinner and next day there is another one almost ready to be picked.

It is also precipitating a change in our attitude about the food we buy. Naturally we are not yet able to grow everything we need on a daily basis which means we still have to buy food. But after tasting heirloom vegetables straight from the garden that have not been genetically modified or bred specifically for durability in transport or picked green and artificially ripened, the fruits and vegetables on sale in supermarkets where I used to shop are noticeably lacking in flavour or pungency. Our preference now is to seek out locally grown organic food wherever we can. I feel a degree of anxiousness to get things growing and dispense with the need to buy anything.

Larry made his fortnightly trip to a fruit shop near the coast and came back with our fruit, as well as some local homemade jams and an unlabelled bottle of wine that the fruit man makes from his own grapes. It all gets very personal in the country. It is wonderful to know by name the people who are producing the food that we eat. We are hoping that when we have excess produce we will be able to sell to the fruit man or our neighbours. Larry also brought back a big supply of bicarbonate of soda and six large bottles of vinegar for me to continue to make our own cleaning products. For a bit of a change I throw in a bit of ylang-ylang oil or lemon juice depending on my mood. The place smells divine after I have cleaned.

Now that the kitchen vegetable garden is established, we have plans for larger gardens near the future chicken house and greenhouse. I can't wait to be able to have chickens and our own eggs. Bill, our plumber, told us about five hens and two ducks that his offsider Gary was looking to find a home for. Bill also knew of two geese that were looking for new digs. At first we were thrown into a frenzy of activity, planning their accommodation. This involved designing something that would be fox-proof and snake-proof and able to be easily and thoroughly cleaned.

Later we learned more about the proposed geese and suddenly they weren't as attractive to us. They were a mating pair but they were brother and sister and apparently not altogether friendly. Mind you if I had to be married to my brother or Larry had to be married to his sister we wouldn't be too friendly either. We decided against this pair as we could imagine after a few generations we would be breeding geese with crossed eyes and three beaks! We will procure our geese, in a more relaxed manner, from a better source when we have the accommodation issues sorted.

Subsequently Gary decided to keep his hens and ducks, so the urgent push to build a chook house has passed. In retrospect we are glad because we wanted to be able to introduce our new hens to well-established gardens that were specifically planted with their ideal diet. We don't want to have to buy in chook food for them.

Feeding animals without buying in food is an issue with dogs. Maurice and Becky have led rather privileged lives, eating a mixture of fresh chicken wings and necks, lamb shanks and tinned and dry food. For that to continue we would need to be constantly slaughtering chickens. Instead, I wanted to move them over to eating our leftovers where it was possible.

One night I gave them some of the stew I had made with beef, vegetables and lentils and barley. They lapped it up eagerly and then Becky backed up from her plate, looked sheepishly at me and vomited most unceremoniously. She then spent the rest of the night creating such powerful gas that had George Bush learned of this incredible renewable resource emanating from my dog, I was sure he would be laying plans to invade the Forest in order to commandeer Becky's bowels! I wondered if I should make her some chicken soup. All my life I had held a strong belief in the power of chicken soup to cure everything from dandruff to hang-nail but I resisted the urge to dose her up with my mother's magic chicken soup recipe. It made me wonder what sort of soup I should give sick chickens!

Sandra had told me about her egg-laying chickens not being good for roasting because they were too scrawny. Specific breeds that are more heavily muscled are better as table birds. She said that egg-laying birds do make excellent chicken soup though. I said, "Well if they make good chicken soup, I wonder if I can teach them to make other things for us as well!" She laughed at my lunacy.

In our efforts to become self-sufficient, and with all the learning of new things that it entails, the fact is that self-sufficiency isn't some new-age, alternate, drop-out activity. It's going 'forward to the past'. It's just a return to the way life was before industrialisation, before globalisation. It's how our grandparents and great-grandparents lived. It's giving away the dependencies we have on all the faceless multinational organisations that take our money so that they can provide us with the goods they produce. Self-sufficiency means taking back that responsibility for ourselves and our families and learning to live more simply with more self-reliance. Far from being scary in the light of a post–Peak Oil world, it has an element of liberation about it. I remember back to the time when I began learning about Peak Oil and the terrible fear that I felt. What's changed, I think, is that while our city life was governed by the whim of marketing executives, fashionistas, manufacturers and importers, in our farm life we are masters of our own realm. It is a very powerful feeling to be heading towards becoming independent from all that control.

There is another element to it too, a softer element. Larry was visiting Jim and Connie to discuss some aspect of our farm work for which we needed their guidance and advice, and Connie realised that we were tackling some major work and were very busy. Before Larry left, she handed him a bag in which she had put a freshly made quiche, a jar of Davidson plum jam, a little Davidson plum tree she had grown from seed, a Cavendish pumpkin that looked like an elf ought to make a fine block of apartments out of it and a book on how to use a chainsaw without becoming a double amputee! We were overwhelmed with her generosity. We ate the quiche for dinner and it was especially delicious knowing that Connie's chooks laid the eggs and every vegetable in the dish came from her garden. Living among people who share the joy of growing their own food, and who understand the process and effort it takes brings such a soft, comforting element into our lives. It is returning to the feeling of community where everyone knew everyone else's names and everyone contributed to the prosperity and security of the community. That too is powerful.

In taking on all the experimenting and learning and reading about all the things we have to understand, it occurred to me that in my city life I became complacent about learning new things. I had everything under control and I was comfortable in that control. I guess that the desire to learn new things, to push myself and my boundaries and take risks just lost a spot in the line-up of my day. Here on the farm I am constantly learning and challenged and I can see that on my death-bed I am going to be saying 'bloody hell – there was so much more I wanted to learn!'

The power of being master of our own realm is changing the way we view the work we do. Coming from the structure and stricture of corporate life, what we do now each day is just for us and our family. The person doing our performance appraisal is Mother Nature, not some corporate giant or a bunch of faceless shareholders. The efforts we put in are for our future only. And if we want to goof off for a day then we goof off. We are the masters of this ship and that is an incredible feeling.

Our freedom to do as we please and to work as hard or as little as we choose has had some interesting outcomes. I had been working in the house one day with Kenny Rogers love songs belting out on the CD player at a decibel level that would have brought the police if we were still in the city. Larry came in from the paddocks and the music playing led to a spontaneous outbreak of dancing at two o'clock in the afternoon. We were just two happy middle-aged people dancing crazily together precisely because no one was watching. And then, when the music finished we wordlessly separated and went back to our respective chores as if we had just had an important meeting about flood damage. I had a tiny smirk on my face and a warm happy glow in my belly for hours afterwards.

Farm life and the freedom it gives us have brought some unexpected changes to our way of living. We no longer wear watches and there is just no such thing as a 'weekend'. For that matter there is no such thing as a weekday. There are just days and nights. The work keeps on and has to be done in its time or in its season. And time is different for us now, too. The days are not divided into morning, lunch, afternoon and evening like they were in the city. Time is now defined in terms of 'light enough to do this, too dark to do that'. One's planning and work are totally dependent on the living natural world, not the man-made, clock-driven world. Of course to people used to living on the land I must be stating the bleeding obvious but to us, still basically city people, this is like another planet, the rules of which we are still learning.

Our relationship as a couple has changed dramatically. We play more, laugh more, and talk more; we touch more. We may work feverishly at independent tasks or work together when necessary. We may not see each other from dawn to dusk or we may sneak off to the bedroom mid-morning and not emerge till the afternoon. A mid-week day may be designated as a day off if one of us doesn't have the energy to apply to a task. The freedom to be spontaneous is quite exhilarating.

While the establishment of a farm using permaculture methods is very labour-intensive in the beginning, once it is established correctly there isn't a lot of ongoing work to do. It's Bill Mollison's principle of working with nature instead of against it. At this early stage, though, we have to depend on machinery like our tractor and ride-on mower to slash grass to make mulch to cover the ground. Ultimately the grass we currently have to keep slashing or mowing will be replaced by thick forests and we envisage a day in the future when the tractor will be idle forever both because we will have no use for it, and also because eventually petrol to drive it will be too expensive. When that day comes, we hope our food forest will be lush and productive and a joy to walk around in, collecting our daily food.

With the onset of winter, the mornings and evenings are cold, and when the wind rushes up the valley it bites clear to the bone. On the first really cold day of winter I wanted to start a fire in the slow-combustion wood heater that sits at one corner of the kitchen. It's a squat black metal box with two glass doors. I looked at the levers and knobs and their uses were a complete mystery to me. I figured it can't be all that hard. Programming a VCR for people our age is hard! I screwed up paper and put in the wood and lit it. The paper burned beautifully, leaving the wood almost unscathed. After a few more attempts I got a good blaze going, or what I thought was good, but the glass doors blackened and I couldn't see if it was burning properly. I opened the doors to see how it was going and thick smoke billowed out and filled the kitchen. Directly over my head the smoke detector attached to the ceiling remained silent. I was furious. That smoke detector is so sensitive, if I have a menopausal hot flash while doing the washing up that darned alarm goes off, but when I light a fire directly under it and smoke billows up to obliterate it from sight it just hangs there.

I looked at the wood stove and decided that I had to make friends with this thing or we would do battle all winter. I started again, but this time I put in more kindling and more paper, and then waggled a few levers and knobs and hoped for the best. In a few minutes it was happily pumping out heat, and flames were licking around the bigger logs. A few hours later the whole house was cosy and felt safe and soft and welcoming.

We have become very 'energy aware' and that awareness has changed our habits substantially. When we are cold we can no longer just turn on a heater or flick on the air conditioner when we are hot. Our first response to feeling cold is to put on more clothes, have a hot drink, or climb into bed with a good book if it is too wet or inclement to work outside. I even think twice before lighting the fire, 'is it really necessary right now or can I delay it?' Often I do delay it because every fire I build uses more wood which means Larry has to chop more, and carry more and stack more. And if that wood has been cut green it needs to cure and dry before you can even use it. The fire isn't just a pleasant aesthetic feature of the house in winter. It's a necessity that requires effort. When the temperature is low for a prolonged period, I light the fire from the logs and kindling that Larry chops and brings from the shed and piles into a box on the veranda. He does it once each evening before sunset. I like hearing the heavy 'thurrrump' of the logs being dropped into the box. That sound means night is approaching and we will be warm. It's as comforting as the sound I remembered from our city life, when I would hear his car arriving home after a long day.

It's curious that simple sounds and smells instantly conjure feelings and emotions that affect one's mood without any conscious awareness, but the strongest memories we have are often made from and triggered by smells and sounds. The smell and warmth of the fire, the sound of the wood being delivered onto the veranda, these herald a snug evening with my man. Winter evenings together are different from summer, when we would spend so much more time on the veranda listening to the frogs and the insects, hoping for a cooling breeze. In the soft light of the warm house in winter evenings, somehow we are closer to each other, not physically necessarily, but our isolation in our wooden cocoon seems more absolute and curiously calmer. It pleases me to see Larry stretched out in his recliner either watching TV or reading or snoozing after his day's work. In Sydney he would come home from work, laden with paperwork, eat his dinner and then continue working until bedtime. That would come with exhaustion sometime after midnight when he would finally fall into bed. I always felt that was an unhealthy way to live. There seemed no end to his working day, no disconnection from the company.

The end of the sunlight in the city didn't mean the end of his working day. The element of sunlight and its passage from dawn to dusk was without meaning. Our city life with its schedules and deadlines and mindless use of power masked or muted the effects of the natural circadian rhythms of our bodies.

Here in the country, in the last light of day I see the birds flocking to the trees in which they spend the night. Different insects appear or disappear in the garden and on the veranda. The air changes with the dying light. The approach of night is palpable. When the sun gets low, outside Larry's pace picks up to stow away the tools and to finish up a task. Inside I begin the cooking and prepare for his return to the house. He comes in and may grumble, 'Couldn't finish what I was doing because I ran out of damned light!' He stalks off to the bathroom, has a hot shower and changes into a warm track suit and his slippers. By the time I bring him his dinner, waking him from a light snooze in his chair, in his eyes I see peace. I like that.

Winter was a milestone we had reached. We had been on the farm for six months and we had some solid work to achieve before spring. We had yet to experience the worst of the frosts. So far there have been only light ones that have killed off some of our new trees, but Connie told me that the worst is still to come. Her words reminded me of how I felt in Canada, where the changing of the seasons is so obvious that I experienced them physically. I told her about the end of my first winter in Toronto. Although snow was still thick on the ground, there was a distinct change in the air. Bare branches on the trees in the garden were showing tiny bumps where buds were forming, and icicles hanging off the buildings or branches were beginning to drip. I had an overpowering urge to clean the house. My body was bursting with a new energy and a vitality I hadn't felt during the long frozen Canadian winter.

We were living in an apartment with floor to ceiling double-glazed picture windows that looked out onto beautifully manicured gardens in a huge apartment complex. I filled a bucket with hot water and grabbed a sponge with the intention of cleaning the windows so I could enjoy the sight of the fast-approaching spring days. I flung open the curtains and the big heavy sliding doors and stepped outside into the crisp brilliantly blue day. I plunged the sponge into the bucket and took a wide swipe at the window and at the top of the arc the sponge suddenly stopped. It had frozen to the glass! It stayed there frozen solid for another month as a symbol of 'that mad Australian woman whose spring fever sprung too early!'

When we first moved out of the city, we did it because of our understanding of the coming oil crisis. We didn't know for sure if we were actually crazy or if we were way ahead of our time, or if we were wise to go when we did. Now that we've had six months here, we feel very grateful that we'd been able to leave. At one point Missy called from Melbourne. As a case worker in a family crisis centre she isn't earning a huge salary and she told me she is really feeling the bite of the increased costs of fuel and food. And with the increased costs, TV news had begun covering the problems ordinary people are encountering as the inevitable price creep starts to hurt in a real way.

It still angers us greatly that the media continues to treat stories about oil price increases as some form of anomalous and insidious construct of the oil companies alone or just the usual market fluctuations. No mention is made of the real reasons for the peaks and troughs of the oil prices and there are no warnings of what is to come. No one is being told what to prepare for. We know we did the right thing. There is no question in our minds about how hard it is going to be but we are happy that we are able to take more responsibility for our own existence and well-being. In a way we have given ourselves the advantage of being able to make mistakes and learn how to do things before it is an absolute necessity. I've never felt the passing of time more keenly, with the knowledge of all I need to learn.

We can actually see some of the social issues resulting from the effects of the end of cheap oil playing out now in people's lives, although not necessarily due to oil prices. Australia has adopted new workplace agreements that workers are grumbling about. People are losing their jobs. Wages are going down and work hours are getting longer as prices rise. While we have deliberately set ourselves the task of changing our lifestyle to resemble that of our grandparents in the 1920s before the advent of cheap oil, city workers are finding themselves slipping into workplace agreements that resemble the dawn of the industrial revolution in the 1870s, the time of sweatshops with minimum wages. The eight-hour day, hard won at the beginning of the twentieth century, was being eroded and people were now working longer and harder for less.

Denial is a powerful cloak for the truth but ignorance has no excuse. All the facts about Peak Oil are out there, easily accessible on the internet and in bookshops for anyone to learn about in the same way as we did. Now, though, there is a lot more evidence, a lot more articles and books and websites to read than when we first began. A lot more people are becoming aware of the issue and making changes in their lives.

Chapter Fourteen

Winter nights with all the curtains closed and the wood fire glowing warmly in the corner of the kitchen made the house look like a Norman Rockwell painting. We were contented and happy alone together. I would wake at dawn and rush outside to see if there was a frost and on the mornings that there was, the paddock was white in exposed places. I would wander about the garden to see what had succumbed to the frost and note what was surviving. All my lovely nasturtiums didn't like the frost and in the process of thawing they died and stank. I pulled them all out thinking I would have to buy more seed in spring but I was wrong. Soon after the last frost, baby nasturtiums began to emerge and in what seemed like no time I was randomly pulling them out again because they grew so profusely they were smothering everything. It was interesting to notice that the yellow- and orange-flowered ones fared better than the red-flowered ones, but I don't know why.

262 Choosing Eden

Larry and I signed up for an organic farming course together as we felt we could benefit from formal education in farming. Organic farming is, in principle, a method of farming that requires no use of chemicals. It is natural farming.

The course was only one day a week and it proved to be not only incredibly valuable but real fun too. We found ourselves competing against each other for the best marks in our assignments. Mine were written in a sort of conversational style while Larry's sounded like a professorial paper. I was quite daunted by that, feeling like I sounded like a kid writing 'What I did on my holidays' where he sounded so scholarly, but there were times when I got better marks than he did so that lessened my feeling of intellectual inferiority somewhat.

One assignment I was dreading but which turned out to really rivet us was one on the identification of weeds. Weeds! I thought I knew about weeds – you see one and you pull it out. How could I write a whole assignment on stupid old weeds?

We each had to choose thirty weeds and write about them so we would recognise them and know how to deal with them. To the list of questions to be answered, I added two of my own – uses, and interesting facts. I felt if I was going to really understand weeds, I should know more than just their names and how they grow and how to deal with them. The uses and interesting facts part of our assignments proved to be the most fascinating. I remembered Bill Mollison's statement about weeds in my permaculture class. Bill said, 'Observe your weeds. Stop hating things. Walk your land without prejudice. Imitate weeds but do a better job!'

It wasn't until I began studying weeds that I really understood what he meant. A weed, unlike what I had always known as a 'pest', is just a plant growing where you don't want it to grow, or a plant whose benefits you don't yet fully understand.

Researching the sixty weeds we chose between us taught us that growing all over the place were weeds that could either be used as food, medicines, soil improvers, indicators of soil types and more importantly soil condition, pest repellents, or useful for making things. The list of uses went on and on and opened another door to a body of fascinating knowledge we intended to follow up.

The course involved often trekking down to a large vegetable garden on the campus grounds that was used to demonstrate the organic methods. The gardens were profuse and robust with a huge array of healthy vegetables. Everyone would return to class red-faced and sweaty from the efforts they had put in. Muddy boots were lined up outside the room and the afternoon session of lessons would begin again.

Our classmates in that first semester were a committed and likeable bunch. They were young and old, with or without properties of their own, but all like-minded people who wanted a better life on the land, to be masters of their own destiny in a toxin-free environment. The sharing of knowledge and ideas, heirloom seeds and endless anecdotes were as wonderful as what we were learning from our fantastic tutor.

We would come home from class with new enthusiasm and new information each week that would fuel long conversations and hours of extra reading. We also began a new vegetable garden on the farm where I could experiment with different methods and different seeds.

When I planted my zucchini seeds in our new big vegetable patch they came up very easily, their big green leaves looking verdant and robust. The soil was very fertile and the zucchini plants flourished. I didn't take much notice of what was under the low canopy of their leaves until one day when I thought maybe there would be something delicious to add to the dinner menu. I did know that zucchini grow quickly, I just didn't know what would happen if they were left to their own devices for an extended period of time.

I trudged down to the garden in my heavy brown work boots, carrying my gathering basket. First I searched through the tall cornstalks and picked some cobs and then searched the cornstalks for the bean vines growing up them and picked some beans, just enough for one meal. I also found some mini cucumbers that I thought I would have a try at pickling. When I came to the zucchini section I bent down to peer under those huge hairy green leaves. I found some nice young little zucchini still wearing their gaudy yellow flower-petal skirts at one end like wild Latin American dancers. I picked those and popped them in my basket and kept searching. Suddenly I saw what looked like the green trunk of a tree lying under the leaves. It was quite hard to keep all the leaves back but I pushed further in and found that quietly, under its green canopy, one zucchini had grown to the size of my lower leg! Getting it out of there took some grunting and pulling but it reluctantly left its hiding place and I rested it in my gathering basket. It wasn't a zucchini as I had always known them to be. It was a *great mother of a zucchini* with muscles and attitude! We looked at each other for a few moments and I said to it, 'See what happens when you lie around doing nothing but eat? You end up looking like *me*!' I found two of its sisters and when I lugged them back to the house the three of them weighed a total of almost seven kilos. They were big enough to stuff with whole chickens or a newly born lamb!

Our patches of strawberries were spreading and it is now one of our treats as we walk past to reach down and ruffle around the leaves for the latest ripe berries. They are ridiculously sweet. I have decided to dedicate a special area just for strawberries so that we will have enough for making jams and preserves and for serving for dessert instead of just the odd morsel as we pass back and forth.

I had planted two different types of corn. In the kitchen garden by the house I planted heirloom Bloody Butcher or Vampire corn. I was very curious to see what it would produce. In the bigger vegetable garden near the shed I planted sweet corn. The Bloody Butcher variety grew to be about two and a half to four metres tall and the cobs when young were reasonable-tasting, creamy pink in colour and a bit floury in texture. The sweet corn looked the same as the corn I had always bought in the supermarket but was much sweeter. I let some of the Bloody Butcher corn mature more and the kernels became dark red. They are a form of maize which traditionally was used for making flour. I decided that for the next season I will plant more so that I can try making the flour. The other new thing I am experimenting with is amaranth. Its grains contain more protein than any other form of grain.

I harvested a huge amount of mint and when I made my first batch of mint jelly I was so proud of myself I strutted around as if I were Jamie Oliver. It was delicious and embarrassingly easy to make. The recipe called for Granny Smith apples and rather than throwing the peels and cores into the compost box I keep in the kitchen for scraps, I eyed the seeds and thought I would stick them in a pot and see what happened. Magic happened! The Granny Smith apple seeds sprouted and now we have baby apple trees proudly standing in their seedling tray waiting to be big enough to grow into trees to feed my family.

Keeping seeds became a habit. We did a favour for a friend and she repaid us with a bag of loquats from her tree. We ate the sweet fruit and I saved the seeds and put each one in a seed tray with fifty sections in it. Now we have fifty baby loquat trees to plant out. It's that easy! We only have to find a way of combating the fruit fly they attract.

One day Larry and I were sitting on the veranda and I was eating an apple. It was red and juicy and when I had finished it I absent-mindedly threw the core out into the garden where it landed in the grass by the fence. Larry was horrified. 'Why didn't you throw it over the fence?' he asked me indignantly. 'If it's on this side of the fence that is where I mow.'

'This year I intend removing all the grass from around the house,' I said to him. 'What do we need grass for? We need paths but we don't need grass.'

Larry was smiling. 'Where's the permaculture design science in that?'

'It's called "the design science of how far I can chuck an apple core!"'

I hope it grows right where I threw it to remind us of the laugh we shared.

The scary part of seed saving is that if big international companies have their way, the food we all buy in the future will have been grown from terminator seeds which don't reproduce. The pressure on me to become successful in saving all kinds of seeds is very strong. I have a long way to go before I know enough, and am skilled enough to reproduce our food season after season and in enough quantity and quality to be beneficial and true to type. It's a real art and I need to master this so that I can pass that knowledge on to other people, and to my children.

The end of our first year was in sight and that meant the family would descend on us again for the holiday period. I was keenly aware that to them it would appear as if we hadn't achieved all that much. So much of the things we'd done in our first year had been intangible. Observing the seasons, becoming part of the community, experimenting with little things, learning to use and fix our machinery, and listening to the people around us. We had learned how to be together twenty-four hours a day, seven days a week, focused and committed on the same task. We had learned how to make do, and to have quick water-saving showers. We had got used to the blackness of night, so unlike night in the city. And we had, more than anything else, acclimatised to our surroundings. We had got used to not having a shiny clean car because of the waste of precious water and we had learned how intrinsically entwined with nature are our lives and our health. Our values had changed dramatically.

A lot of things I learned had happened by accident. For instance, one morning when I was cleaning the kitchen, I first used my bicarb soda and vinegar concoction to scrub down the benches and then sprayed them with a mixture of water and lavender essential oil, as I had been told that the lavender has an antibacterial action. While I was spraying the lavender and water, a fly landed on the windowsill that I had just cleaned and sprayed with the lavender. The fly promptly dropped dead. I stared at it for a moment and wondered if it was just a poor decrepit old fly whose time had come or if it was the lavender. I went on a fly hunt and sprayed each one I found and each time they staggered about for a moment and then died. It was amazing to me. I felt like I was the first to discover fire! Imagine having an insecticide that wasn't toxic and smelled as beautiful as lavender!

As our first anniversary of leaving the city came closer, we felt that there were many things that validated the move we'd made. When Cyclone Larry devastated the banana crops of northern Queensland in March 2006, banana prices skyrocketed to $14 per kilo in the supermarkets – but for us, buying our bananas from a local fruit seller, the price was still $2 per kilo. While the cost of everything was gradually going up, we were eating free vegetables from our garden. While Australian cities and towns had severe water restrictions we had no water problems. Oil prices were going through the roof but we knew that they would fall and rise periodically as the price is so dependent on the US demand. And we knew also that the fluctuations in price had little to do with Peak Oil yet. We are on an oil production plateau where supply and demand dance around each other, responding to the music of mild winters and temperate summers. Only wild unpredictable weather patterns, major heat or cold snaps or political unrest or wars throw the dancers into a frenzy. But, like all dances, eventually the music comes to an end and one partner is going to leave the dance floor.

The issues related to climate change were *finally* being understood and acknowledged by government and business, and there were more news items about the development of biofuels, those fuels made from renewable sources. The problem with making a commitment to producing biofuels as an alternative fuel, Rick told me, is that it is not unlike a heroin addict going on a methadone treatment. Instead of changing our unsustainable ways and our addiction to all the things that are most common in our lives, we cling to the current lifestyle but with a seemingly safer substitute. Some countries around the world are using algae and seaweed to make bio-diesel which would not take good arable land away from food production, but to think that such production could replace oil is folly. An even greater folly is to use arable farming land for fuel instead of food production. There is precious little good quality soil and water supply to grow food as it is.

What we were waiting for with great anticipation was a Senate report on Australia's future oil supply and alternative transport fuels, due to come out in September 2006. We wanted to see how the Australian government – now that they were grudgingly beginning to accept that there was a problem with climate change and fuel supply – would attack the issue.

The full report is available on the internet; however the salient points of the report made us both very sad and very angry. We were sad because from the first time we ever heard about Peak Oil, we desperately wanted to find data that would refute the theory, that would tell us that actually, everything would be okay. Unfortunately the report on fuel only gave us the same bleak and frightening information that the Hirsch Report had delivered to the US Senate eighteen months earlier. The anger we felt was due to the fact that now we knew for certain that our government really did know about Peak Oil and all the dire ramifications it posed for the future of all of us, but still, no political party and no news reports spelled it all out in plain English for the average Australian family.

Simply put, Australia does not have a post-Peak Oil plan and no radical new policies have been formulated to meet the very real dangers head on. We are not being prepared, we are not being given choices, and we are not being educated to how life is going to be for all of us and for future generations. To our minds, that was a cruel and dangerous situation.

The report basically comes to the conclusion that Peak Oil is a certainty, and goes on to say:

> In the Committee's view the possibility of a peak of conventional oil production before 2030, even if it is no more than a possibility, should be a matter of concern. Exactly when it occurs (which is very uncertain) is not the important point. Australia should be planning for it now, as Sweden is doing with its plan to be oil free by 2020.
>
> [...] The 2005 Hirsch report for the US Department of Energy argues that Peak Oil has the potential to cause dramatically higher oil prices and protracted economic hardship, and that this is a problem unlike any yet faced by modern industrial society. It argues that timely, aggressive mitigation initiatives will be needed and that timing this is a classic risk management problem. Prudent risk management requires the planning and implementation of mitigation well

before peaking. Early mitigation will almost certainly be less expensive than delayed mitigation.

Reading the report made us reflect again on our move to the country. We felt that it was unequivocally the best thing we could have done. We knew that the food forest we were endeavouring to create was most definitely going to be the best legacy we could possibly leave our children and grand-children. We would not be alive to see the end results of our work, but the work itself was sufficient for us. We were living close to our food, we had control over our lives and how we lived them, and we were gaining the knowledge that would be so necessary in the future. We were 'unhooking' ourselves from dependence on the dictates of big corporations and government as much as possible, and now that we knew how long it takes to gain that knowledge and apply it, we had no thought of ever going back. Our sights were firmly on the goals we started out with, and our sense of urgency to get things accomplished on the farm was still as strong as ever.

When the family arrived at Christmas time, again I felt complete and content with them all around me. My grandson Jasper had grown and was now a toddler with a wonderful little personality all his own. His constant baby babble and even his crying were music to my ears. And after the holidays we would have another grandchild. My daughter Katie and her husband Michael were booked to fly to China to bring home their adopted daughter, whom they had named Ruby.

Josh learned to drive the tractor and did an incredible job for a first-timer. His fishing expeditions early each morning yielded nothing which was disappointing because the previous Christmas his fish bounty was overwhelming. It wasn't surprising to us, as there had been a lot of news about fish stocks being depleted, only this time it was really touching us personally as we had no fish for the family during that visit.

When everyone left after the new year celebrations, Larry left also to travel to Melbourne to do the same permaculture course that I had done with Bill Mollison and Geoff Lawton. I was alone on the farm for the first time. It was a strange feeling at first, being in our house with just Becky our Jack Russell for company. Our little old Maltese, Maurice, had died at Christmas time. When Larry asked me where I wanted him buried, I had already chosen a spot for him. He always liked to sit in a corner of the garden and watch Lindy's horses and I wanted him buried there. Larry was aghast. The ground I had indicated was hard dry clay and shale but I was adamant that it was his favourite spot and that was where Larry had to dig. It took him hours of hard labour, cutting through the dry earth, and when he was finished he was sweating and exhausted. He lay little Maurice in the hole and said some prayers for him and then we covered him over. A little dog whose life I was privileged to share for fifteen years was gone. I can see his tiny grave from the kitchen window and smile a 'good morning' to him as I make my first cup of morning tea.

After everyone had headed south, I sat on the veranda and stared out into the sunrise thinking of my family so far away. To keep myself busy I started polishing Larry's work boots. The rich smell of the boot polish took my mind back to my early school days. Every week my mother would make my brother and I polish our school shoes until they shone. We would sit on newspaper on the cold cement ramp at the back door, brushing and then rubbing our shoes hard. I think we deliberately got ourselves covered in black polish, teasing or fighting with each other for the tin of polish.

The memories evoked by the smell of the polish and the leather flooded over me. That was such a simple time, so safe and ordinary. Our lives were orderly and protected and predictable. We didn't know fear. Our house often smelled of cakes baking and there was always the sound of jazz music playing either from the record player or from my brilliant father sitting at his piano. My brother and I walked to school, or would be given a silver threepenny coin to catch the bus. We often walked home and when we would pass under the huge Bowen mango trees near our house we would pick some off the ground and carry them home to have for our afternoon tea. My mother would put us both in the bath to eat them because they were so juicy, we would be covered in juice. We would laugh and slip around in the bath slick with heady-smelling mango juice.

I thought of my new granddaughter Ruby, an eighteen-month-old baby girl in a crowded orphanage, completely unaware that her life was about to change forever in just a few days. My daughter and her husband were flying thousands of miles to make her part of our family, part of our world. Myriad thoughts and images tumbled around in my head as I rubbed the work boots and I realised that tears were streaming down my face. What would that world be for her in years to come?

From the poverty of the Chinese countryside where she had been abandoned, she was being brought into the affluence and comfort of Australia. But what would Australia be like in ten years, in twenty years? Would our little farm have mango trees heavy with fruit for her to bite into so that the juice ran down her chin and her arms and onto her little belly? Would climate change and Peak Oil make her want for things? Fear things? Would she have to do without things? As the boots took on a decent shine, I thought of my brother John and my mother and father in our comfortable home in Brisbane. We were the first in our street to get a washing machine, the first to get a television set. We had a housekeeper and we always had plentiful food, good food, always the best of everything. That was more than fifty years ago. Now we were looking at the opposite scenario for the future, where the most basic of things would become too expensive and then too scarce for people to afford.

At the same time as Katie and Michael were flying away to collect Ruby, a very special old friend of mine had emailed me to tell me he was flying off to Bonn at the invitation of the United Nations. He had been in the environmental waste management field in Sydney. I was unaware that he had become an international expert on climate change and now he was going to participate in a series of workshops and meetings on the disastrous results of the global problems created by the effects of our addiction to burning fossil fuels. This series of meetings would probably never have happened a few years ago, but official recognition of the problems ahead felt more frightening than reassuring. Everything was changing. The world I knew as a girl was gone. My brother and mother and father were gone and my own children were now adults with partners and children of their own. What I had always wanted for them – the warmth and comfort and safety, the affluence and ease of my own child-hood – was torn out of my grasp. It was a legacy I could see I would not be able to leave them. All Larry and I had was Eden Forest, our little farm and the task ahead of us to make it self-sufficient loomed so large a new crop of tears flowed down my face.

The boots were as shiny as I could make them. Although worn and creased, they were black again and with the addition of a good rub of dubbin to waterproof them they looked cleaner and softer, ready for another year of hard work. The boots were a year old. Eden Forest was a year old. Everything was ahead of us now.

I walked out into the garden for a breath of fresh air. The tomatoes needed picking to be made into sauce. The chamomile flowers were ready for picking to be made into tea. The mint was ready for harvest to make into jelly and sauce. The cornstalks were drying and soon would be ready to pull out. Bees buzzed about in the fennel and the parsley flowers. Soon the seeds would be ready to gather. There was so much to do. The weeds were getting high. The potato plants were flowering and the strawberries were spreading. The strawberries made me think of Jasper. When he was here at Christmas time, I took his chubby little hand and we walked through the garden together. I let him pick a strawberry and eat it right off the plant. Rivulets of red juice ran down the side of his chubby cheek and it made me laugh.

It was difficult to believe in a way, but our second year was beginning. When Larry returned from Melbourne, he had the same fire in his belly that I had when I'd finished the permaculture course. He saw the farm with new eyes, new insights. Our great expanse of pasture needed to be heavily planted with trees, and he'd come back inspired to get this underway. Apart from fruit trees I wanted to plant a grove of cedar, which had grown in our area in the early days of its settlement.

I told him about a picnic I had been on in Canada with Rick and Gwyneth. They took me to an old cedar forest and we spread out our lunch on the forest floor. The smell of the cedars was intoxicating and relaxing and the leaf-littered ground was as soft and springy as a comfy bed. By the time our cedar grove was that glorious to lie in, I would probably be long dead – but I wanted it for my kids. I also wanted a grove of oak trees for good carpentry wood and for acorns which are edible. As well I wanted to plant a grove of ironbark eucalypts for firewood and of course, an olive grove for oil and food. While we would plant them, it would be Jasper and Ruby and future grandchildren who would benefit from them and I hoped in turn that they would plant the same for their grandchildren, as it had been done in days gone by.

We talked about the plans we had for removing all the lawn around the house and making it into garden with serviceable paths. Those garden beds would be for more vegetables and lots of flowers. I was determined to have my beloved rose garden again, only this one would be more magnificent than my last one in Sydney.

Another of my plans for the new year was to concentrate more on growing herbs. After I finished our organic farming course, I was thinking of enrolling in the School of Natural Therapies to study herbal medicine. I knew that if I achieved that I would be in my sixties but I didn't care, so long as my health held up. I found studying up on weeds and herbs fascinating, and I was becoming quite passionate about this knowledge. Maybe I took after my father – he had gone back to university when he was well into his seventies for a second degree and did very well.

The new year in our little world on the farm is packed full of planned activities and goals to achieve, while outside our perimeter fencing we wonder what the new year will bring for the rest of the world. There isn't a lot of time to prepare for the changes that are going to affect all of us and there is so much we all could be doing to make the transition from a world of abundant cheap oil into the very different post–Peak Oil world – but that would fill another book.

Rick Embleton's loaded question about the veracity of our decision to uproot ourselves in our middle years and become self-sufficient in the country comes back to me occasionally and when it does I know we made the right decision.

He said to me, 'Let me ask you this: knowing that the shit is going to hit the fan at some point, what would you rather do – prepare for it to happen in five years and find out it happens in fifty, or prepare for it to happen in fifty years and find out it happens in five?'

Epilogue

There is a huge volume of freely available information on the internet about Peak Oil. Not studying it thoroughly to gain a full and broad understanding of the dual threats of oil depletion and climate change is foolhardy in the extreme. Trusting in governments and scientists to solve the problems that will affect you is equally foolhardy. If you have children and family that you love, I believe you owe it to them to gather as much knowledge as you can, and do something positive for their future.

In an article called 'The Fragility of Microprocessors', energy journalist Alice Friedemann quotes Pulitzer Prize-winning science writer Dr Jared Diamond on the potential collapse of civilisation in the future. He lists five main factors for a collapse and says the first two, environmental factors and climate change, are already evident. The third is our inability to adapt to changing conditions. He supports the belief that we should have begun to adapt to the decline of energy in the 1970s. The fourth factor relates to terrorist activities targeting key infrastructure. He speculates that Russia, China and Europe should take steps to ensure the US doesn't take the 'lion's share' of remaining oil. The final factor is our dependence on trade between countries. If environmental factors tumble one or some of those trading partners, that collapse can bring down the other trading partners.

Friedemann goes on to suggest that it's unlikely that computers will survive petrocollapse:

> As global shipping, factories and countries have a hard time keeping the lights on, computers will stop being made as supply chains break down. If even one of the dozens of types of single–sourced equipment or pure chemical suppliers goes out of business, the assembly line stops.

The article quotes Andrew Gould, CEO of Schlumberger, the world's leading oil services technology company, who, discussing the potential rate of decline in oil production after Peak Oil, suggested that 'An accurate average decline rate is hard to estimate, but an overall figure of 8 per cent [per annum] is not an unreasonable assumption'.

US President George W. Bush's energy adviser, investment banker, Matt Simmons, is also quoted as saying that an 8 per cent rate of decline is possible, suggesting that it's highly likely that many oil fields' reserves are currently much lower than are publicly reported.

The decline after peak might initially be low, buying a few years' time, but if it does reach 8 per cent per year, world oil extraction would decline by almost half in *eight years*. That is likely to lead to the collapse of civilisation, because there is too little time to adapt.

Recommended reading

Peak Oil is a daunting and difficult subject and the range of reading material is enormous. In 2004, when we first started our 'Peak Oil journey', the challenge was to find information sources that provided solid and comprehensive data, along with concrete advice. I've listed a selection of the best books and websites here for the benefit of readers who might wish to make changes as we have done. It's important to know that the information you have is reliable; that the changes you choose to make are reasonable; and that you're headed in the right direction.

ONLINE RESOURCES

I have been reading many Peak Oil sites for three years now; others have come to prominence in recent times.

In reading about Peak Oil, for some the glass is half full whilst for others the glass is half empty. Sites discussing peak oil can be full of doom and gloom while others see peak oil as a real opportunity to re-engineer our society in to what might be considered to be "positive directions".

These links were last checked in July 2007.

www.aph.gov.au/Senate/committee/rrat_ctte/oil_supply/index.htm
This is the official government site for the Australian Senate report into oil prices and alternative energy sources. It also contains links to submissions and transcripts of discussion that the committee held.

www.abc.net.au/4corners/content/2006/s1682118.htm
This ABC site provides a list of excellent links from a variety of sources. The main themes addressed are background, the body of evidence and transition strategies. Both sides of Peak Oil are discussed with links to many documents and points of view.

www.energybulletin.net
Energy Bulletin is the Peak Oil clearing house and has a wealth of regular information and updates across regions, and the implications for agriculture, society, the economy, transport and so on.

www.postcarbon.org
The Post Carbon Institute is another excellent site with emphasis on transition strategies. It also hosts a series of sub-sites, including Global Public Media, that contain many interviews and references to Peak Oil.

www.theoildrum.com
The Oil Drum is an ongoing Peak Oil discussion forum. Like Energy Bulletin, the Oil Drum features regular contributors who have been involved with Peak Oil discussion over an extended period.

www.peakoil.net
ASPO is the Association for the Study of Peak Oil & Gas. In addition to this peak site, there are sub-sites covering ten OECD countries including Australia and the United States. A most authoritative site on the subject of oil depletion.

www.lifeaftertheoilcrash.net
Life after the oil crash is one of the longer standing Peak Oil discussion sites. While it takes a decided 'end of life as we know it' stance, the site does contain a wealth of background and discussion.

www.wolfatthedoor.org.uk
This site, created by Paul Thompson of Reading in the United Kingdom, provides a straightforward introduction to many of the issues surrounding Peak Oil.

http://oilbeseeingyou.blogspot.com
This is Richard Embleton's blog. I've referred to Rick throughout this book. It is to Rick that Larry and I owe the 'heads-up' on Peak Oil. His blog continues to raise matters of importance in any discussion of Peak Oil.

Books

Deffeyes, Kenneth, *Hubbert's Peak: The Impending World Oil Shortage*, Princeton University Press, 2001

Deffeyes, Kenneth, *Beyond Oil: The View from Hubbert's Peak*, Hill and Wang, 2005

Embleton, Richard, *Oilephant Down: Canada at the End of the Age of Cheap Oil*, PublishAmerica, 2006

Heinberg, Richard, *Power Down: Options and Actions for a Post-Carbon World*, New Society Publishers, 2004

Heinberg, Richard, *The Party's Over: Oil, War and the Fate of Industrial Societies*, New Society Publishers, rev. 2nd ed, 2005

Kunstler, James Howard, *The Long Emergency: Surviving the Converging Catastrophes of the Twenty-First Century*, Atlantic Monthly Press, 2005

Leggett, Jeremy, *Half Gone: Oil, Gas, Hot Air and the Global Energy Crisis*, Portobello Books, 2005

Simmons, Matthew, *Twilight in the Desert: The Coming Saudi Oil Shock and the World Economy*, John Wiley & Sons, 2005